A Primer on Salvation

and Bible Prophecy

by

Larry Alavezos, M.D.

TEACH Services, Inc.
P U B L I S H I N G
www.TEACHServices.com • (800) 367-1844

World rights reserved. This book or any portion thereof may not be copied or reproduced in any form or manner whatever, except as provided by law, without the written permission of the publisher, except by a reviewer who may quote brief passages in a review.

The author assumes full responsibility for the accuracy of all facts and quotations as cited in this book. The opinions expressed in this book are the author's personal views and interpretations, and do not necessarily reflect those of the publisher.

This book is provided with the understanding that the publisher is not engaged in giving spiritual, legal, medical, or other professional advice. If authoritative advice is needed, the reader should seek the counsel of a competent professional.

Copyright © 2011 TEACH Services, Inc.
ISBN-13: 978-1-57258-640-6
Library of Congress Control Number: 2010936973

Published by

Acknowledgments

What a blessing it is to have experienced help from others who have authored books. I never fully realized the difficulties involved in writing a book when I first started this project. After I had typed a rough draft, I recognized my book needed a lot of editing before it could be published. I believe God providentially connected me to Allen Barnes, and his son Jason, who agreed to help me in the editing and printing my first manuscript. I want to thank Allen for his superb job editing my words and still communicating my thoughts. He deserves credit for clarifying many of my ambiguous sentences. My brother, Bud Alavezos, deserves credit for proof reading and making many helpful suggestions too. I tried to be my own publisher, but my efforts were not very productive. Fortunately, I contacted TEACH Services, and their editors reviewed my work, and accepted the responsibility for publishing my book. I gratefully appreciate their services, as I could not do this for myself. Also, I want to thank Kalie Kelch who, to my embarrassment found more editing errors that were present in my manuscript. These included grammatical corrections, sentence restructuring, and punctuation errors. Thank you, TEACH Services! However, if there are any errors in this finished product, I take full accountability, as I have checked the facts and made changes repeatedly.

My understanding of Bible prophecies has been greatly enhanced from monthly publications by Jeff Pippenger, entitled Future News. I have read many theological studies, and some are included in my Bibliography. However, Jeff has a more profound depth of understanding prophecy than many of the theologian's works that I have read. As far as I know, he doesn't speak, nor read Hebrew or Greek, but I still believe he is an instrument of the Lord for our days.

There are many other people who have contributed in some measure to my "Primer." Bruce Nicola, Jr., our church pastor, reviewed a number of chapters of my book before it was edited, and he encouraged me spiritually. He even selected two chapters for me to present to our congregation, which were well received.

It is my desire that this "Primer" be instrumental in bringing glory to God. I hope it reaches out to many precious souls, and helps them have a better understanding of the basic issues of salvation, and the prophecies of the Bible.

–Larry Alavezos M.D.

Contents

Introduction		7
Chapter 1	Justification Alone?	12
Chapter 2	Can We Have Assurance of Salvation?	23
Chapter 3	A Thief in the Night	36
Chapter 4	The Covenants	46
Chapter 5	Jesus and His Sabbath	59
Chapter 6	Modern Bible Versions	71
Chapter 7	History Repeats Itself	85
Chapter 8	Daniel's Prophecies for Today	97
Chapter 9	Jesus in the Book of Revelation	109
Chapter 10	The Churches of Revelation	124
Chapter 11	An Overview of the Seals and the Trumpets	136
Chapter 12	The Three Angels' Messages	157
Chapter 13	Movement of Destiny	174
Chapter 14	The Making of Modern Babylon	190
Conclusion		206
Appendix A	General Principles of Prophetic Interpretation	208
Appendix B	Supplement to Principles of Prophetic Interpretation	224
Appendix C	A Study on Daniel Chapter 8	228
Appendix D	Daniel 8:9-12 Displays Hebrew Parallelism	234
Appendix E	History Repeats Itself - Supplement	235
Appendix F	Sequel to Modern Bible Versions	240
Selected Bibliography		242
Reference Materials		251

Introduction

This book is designed to share with you what I have learned from my studies on salvation and Bible prophecies. Years ago I submitted my name to the local church pastor to give Bible studies, but there was no response. Since I was ordained as one of the elders, it became our responsibility to give the worship hour message every other week while the pastor was performing his duties at another church. Thus, I took this opportunity to give Bible studies on Daniel and Revelation to our congregation. It required some ingenuity on my part to present these studies in sermon formats. Furthermore, I kept my notes, which were fully scripted since I do not give extemporaneous presentations very well.

Then, one day pastor Bruce Nicola Jr., the pastor of the Seventh-day Adventist Church in Lakeport, California, gave me some important advice after reading one of my "sermons." He told me it is more important to reveal the God of prophecy than the details of the prophecy itself. With his advice in mind, I returned to the prophecies in Daniel and Revelation and revised all of them in order to focus more on Jesus. I included many of the different roles that Jesus performs for and in us in order to give us salvation.

In chapter 1, my primary emphasis is to show how and why sanctification is a necessary component of the salvation process. Then, in chapter 2, I clearly indicate the "how to" have assurance of salvation.

Finding the transition from the essentials of salvation to one of the major delusions concerning Jesus' second coming became a challenge, but I felt it was necessary since many Christians do not realize the danger of the "secret rapture" deception. Therefore, chapter 3 demonstrates the fallacy of postponing salvation, thinking we can take advantage of a "second chance" during the "tribulation."

The following two chapters are a complete unit. They are interrelated and should not be disconnected. Everyone who will be saved must be in a covenant relationship with Jesus. Our Lord God and Redeemer is the God of the Everlasting Covenant. Note Genesis 17:7:

"And I will establish my covenant between me and thee and thy seed after thee in their generations for an everlasting covenant, to be a God [Hebrew: Elohim] unto thee, and to thy seed after thee."

The name "Elohim" is plural, representing the Godhead. "Maker" in Isaiah 54:5 is also plural: "For thy Maker is thine husband; the LORD of hosts is his name; thy Redeemer the Holy One of Israel; The God of the whole earth shall he be called."

Yahweh, Elohim, the triune god, implemented the everlasting covenant to Adam and Eve in the Garden of Eden. We find this covenant first mentioned in rudimentary form in Genesis 3:15, but allow me to quote verses 14 and 15: "And the LORD God said unto the serpent, Because thou hast done this, thou art cursed above all cattle, and above every beast of the field; upon thy belly shalt thou go, and dust shalt thou eat all the days of thy life: And I will put enmity between thee and the woman, and between thy seed and her seed; it [Jesus] shall bruise thy head, and thou shalt bruise his heel."

When we are in a saving relationship with Jesus, and He is living in our hearts, then we also have the Father abiding in our hearts as well. John 14:23 says: "Jesus answered and said unto him, If a man love me, he will keep my words: and my Father will love him, and we will come unto him, and make our abode with him."

Jeremiah equates the new covenant with the everlasting covenant in Jeremiah 31:31 compared to Jeremiah 32:40. But today, Christians do not realize that the Sabbath is the signet (seal) of the new covenant. This is why I believe Paul said in Hebrews 4:9 that "there remaineth therefore a rest to the people of God." It is clear that the Sabbath is a "sign" or memorial of Creation and sanctification in Exodus 31:13-17. Thus, the Sabbath is the "sign" that symbolizes the "rest" which we have in Jesus. So then, should we be keeping the Sabbath day holy, as New Testament Christians? I believe the answer is yes, as the Sabbath is a "sanctuary in time." In other words, the Sabbath is "holy time," as indicated in Genesis 2:3. Please read chapters 4 and 5, so that you can make your own informed decision.

With some concerns, I included a chapter on modern Bible versions. As Christians, God holds us accountable to reveal truth to His people. I realize that even though there are many sincere Christians who have full confidence in their modern versions, they will still miss some of the deeper truths of God's Word that have been filtered out of these Bibles. Dear reader, you may not realize how Satan has undermined the fuller, undiluted truth that is found in the King James Version Bible. Please prayerfully read this chapter, and you will recognize that all of the words authored by the Holy Spirit are important. Yes, I believe it is the thoughts that are inspired, and not the words themselves, unless they are quoted words of God; however, when we have translators who take it upon themselves to interpret the thought behind the Hebrew and Greek words used, then we are really receiving the thoughts of the commentators. I pray that you will seriously consider what I am saying. With these thoughts in mind, the remainder of this book will be better understood if you use a King James Version Bible (KJV).

The KJV translators were men of integrity. They used italics for every word translated into English that was not present in the Hebrew or Greek manuscripts that they used. Furthermore, how many true-hearted Christians could possibly believe that God failed in preserving His Holy Scriptures for one thousand years? Can we honestly believe that, during the Dark Ages, God's church in the "wilderness" was forced to use inferior Bibles? Then, alas, some biblical scholars "discovered" older Greek manuscripts, which differed from the "received" text. Now, these higher critics get the credit for finding bits and pieces of the true Scriptures. These scholars are in the business of recovering these "lost" Scriptures. Today we have 27 editions of the Greek New Testament. Consequently, we have had 27 different translations of the New Testament as a foundation for our modern Bibles. It is a fact that when translators change the words, in some cases, it also changes the thought. Read this chapter, and you will be shocked at some of the thoughts that these translators have planted into the Holy Scriptures.

Before launching into the apocalyptic books of Daniel and Revelation, chapter 7 gives us an update on prophecies in general.

How many of us realize that all of the books of the Old Testament contain prophecies? Some of these prophecies are in the form of *types and shadows*, illustrating the invisible realities. Other prophecies prefigure end-time events over and over again, demonstrating the principle that *history repeats itself*. In chapter 7, I am attempting to open our eyes to see the hidden prophecies found in the other Old Testament books, besides Daniel and Revelation. In *Daniel's Prophecies for Today*, I hope everyone recognizes and acknowledges the principle of *repetition* and *enlargement*, in this basic apocalyptic prophecy. I confess that for many years I did not emphasize the role that Jesus played in this book. As mentioned earlier, I corrected this. I only wish that I had done this before when I gave this "sermon" to our church congregation years ago.

Daniel's prophecy is foundational for an understanding of Revelation. We must remember that John was of an Eastern culture and ancestry. If we don't recognize or accept this truth, then we will have problems understanding John's book of Revelation. Hebrew thinking and expressions in their writings were different from those of us who live and were raised in a Western culture. The Hebrew writers used parallelism, which is a literary technique that is not used in our western hemisphere. John used Hebrew parallelism in his first four sections of Revelation. Thus, the seven churches, the seven seals, the seven trumpets, and the Great Controversy sections comprise the first 14 chapters of Revelation. These first four prophecies are essentially parallel. Thereafter, the following three sections progress forward in time, until the final prophecy in chapters 21 and 22, which portrays the restoration of all things into Christ's kingdom, centered around this planet.

I begin my primer on Revelation by giving an overview that is titled "Jesus in the Book of Revelation." This overview is for the purpose of giving everyone the "big picture," before getting into the details of the prophecies themselves. Following this overview, the next two chapters go into some of the details of the seven churches, the seven seals, and the seven trumpets. Since these chapters are just a primer, I won't be going into any of the details in much depth. I hope your interest will be stimulated enough to pursue your own studies into these details. The last three chapters cover a lot of information that will be bet-

Introduction

ter understood if you first read "Principles of Prophetic Interpretation," found in the appendices of this book. I make no apology that these three chapters are coming from the perspective of a Seventh-day Adventist Christian. In my final chapter, "The Making of Modern Babylon (A Do-It-Yourself Religion)," I hope everyone can see the simplicity of our interpretation of these beast-like symbols in Revelation.

Dear reader, please indulge the frequent repetitions that you will discover in my book. Please be patient and understand that I am trying to make each chapter a complete unit for those students of the Bible who are not familiar with the prophecies and their interrelationships. Finally, my bibliography is rather long, but these authors and their works have contributed to my understanding of salvation and Bible prophecies, and I want to give credit where it is due. Please realize, however, that I have not accepted all of their views. Therefore, I take full accountability for what you read in this primer. My prayer is that some dear souls will be led to give their hearts to Jesus. He alone is our salvation. As long as Jesus is abiding in our hearts, we can rest in the assurance of salvation.

May God bless this primer so that it will bring glory and honor to His name.

Sincerely,
Larry R. Alavezos, M.D.

Chapter 1

Justification Alone?
A Summary of Righteousness by Faith

The purpose of this Bible presentation is to refute the popular belief among many Christians that the gospel is about "justification alone." There is a misconception about the role of sanctification in the gospel, or the "good news" of salvation.

Many Christians have been told that sanctification is not part of the "everlasting gospel" but is "good advice" and represents the subjective work of the Holy Spirit. Therefore, they believe sanctification is only a result of salvation and not a part of the saving process.

Many Evangelical ministers teach another "gospel," wherein being "born again"—and that alone—is all that is necessary to be saved. They also believe sanctification can never be fully realized in this life, as long as we live in fallen natures. This belief is a dangerous deception because sanctification is most certainly a necessary component of salvation.

Ellen G. White stated, "Sanctification is not the work of a moment, an hour, a day, but of a lifetime" (*The Acts of the Apostles*, p. 560). This agrees with the New Testament teaching on righteousness by faith. So, the question naturally arises, when do we truly become sanctified? Will it be on our deathbed? The answer may surprise you.

Contrary to popular Evangelical belief, justification and sanctification cannot be separated. In other words, they occur at the same time. We are sanctified when we are converted. Justification is also equivalent to conversion, or being "born again." You may wonder, perhaps, that since sanctification takes a lifetime and conversion occurs at the same time that I am saying we do not become converted until we die. No, I am not proposing that at all. What I am saying is that we are sanctified when we are justified, when we first surrender our hearts to Christ. In order for us to understand this clearly, we need to build a good foundation.

Let's begin with a little story I believe perfectly illustrates what sanctification is all about. There was once a little girl who surrendered her life to Jesus. Whenever Satan knocks on the door of her heart, she says, "As soon as Satan knocks, I ask Jesus, who is with me, to answer the door. Then, when Satan sees Jesus, he says, 'Sorry, I've got the wrong address.'"

Now, what are some of the ingredients of sanctification present in this illustration? First, we find Jesus is inside this little girl's heart. Also, she has "surrendered her life to Jesus." Then, whenever Satan assails her with a temptation, she lets Jesus deal with it. Are you getting the gist of this story? Sanctification is about Jesus living in our hearts. Combining His divinity with our humanity, we receive His enabling grace. Thus, we can live in obedience to the law of God, which is written in our hearts. Furthermore, we even receive Jesus' enabling (empowering) grace to overcome inherent propensities to sin that are ingrained in our sinful nature.

Now, let's consider another crude illustration from Richard Lee's book *Issues of the Heart*. I believe this story illustrates both justification and sanctification. "Suppose a sheep were to fall into a mud puddle, what would it do? Most probably, it would push, strain, and struggle until it got out of the mud. Why? Because, it is not the nature of sheep to want to stay in mud. But, if a pig were to wander into that same mud puddle, it would probably wallow in it for hours. Why? Because, pigs by nature enjoy wallowing in mud."

Now, let's bring these illustrations closer to our own hearts. In the book *Steps to Christ*, page 17, Ellen G. White writes: "But after his [Adam's] sin, he could no longer find joy in holiness [by the way, holiness is one of the definitions of sanctification], and he sought to hide from the presence of God. Such is still the condition of the unrenewed heart. It is not in harmony with God, and finds no joy in communion with Him. The sinner could not be happy in God's presence; he would shrink from the companionship of holy beings. Could he be permitted to enter heaven, it would have no joy for him."

At this time, some discerning person will notice that this passage is primarily discussing Adam's need for justification. Certainly, all of us recognize that when Adam sinned he became unrighteous. In other words, he was unconverted and needed to be converted. He wasn't looking forward in joy for God's companionship. Where does sanctification fit into this picture in God's initiative to restore salvation for Adam, and by extension ourselves, whenever we sin? First, let's read Hebrews 12:14: "Follow peace with all men, and holiness, without which no man shall see the Lord." As already mentioned, holiness is equivalent to sanctification.

After Adam's sin, the Lord had a dialogue with Adam and Eve that is documented in Genesis 3. He even made garments of skin for their clothing. Apparently, Adam and Eve not only had conversions, but they were also restored to holiness, otherwise they could not have survived in God's presence: "For our God is a consuming fire" (Heb. 12:29).

In introducing this chapter, I brought up a little known truth, that justification and sanctification cannot be separated and they occur at the same time. So, let's first hear what Ellen G. White says in *Faith and Works*: "Many commit the error of trying to define minutely the fine points of distinction between justification and sanctification. Into the definitions of these two terms they often bring their own ideas and speculations. Why try to be more minute than is inspiration on the vital question of righteousness by faith? Why try to work out every minute point, as if the salvation of the soul depended upon all having exactly your understanding of this matter? All cannot see in the same line of vision" (p. 14).

Did you notice the words "fine points of distinction between justification and sanctification"? Many Bible scholars severely limit the gospel to forensic justification alone. In other words, they limit this aspect of salvation to just the "objective" historical work in the life, death, and resurrection of Jesus, which is legally imputed to the believer. These same scholars try to eliminate the "subjective" transformation of the believer, which they attribute to the work of the Holy Spirit, as an addition to the gospel. They don't even acknowledge that there is a subjective component involved in justification, which we have already defined as being "born again" or the conversion of the new believer.

Let's read a short passage from *Thoughts from the Mount of Blessing*: "Righteousness is holiness, likeness to God, and 'God is love.' 1 John 4:16.

It is conformity to the law of God, for 'all Thy commandments are righteousness' (Ps. 119:172), and 'love is the fulfilling of the law' (Rom. 13:10). Righteousness is love, and love is the light and the life of God. The righteousness of God is embodied in Christ. We receive righteousness by receiving Him" (Ellen G. White, p. 18).

Therefore, when we are joined to Christ (at justification = conversion) we receive His righteousness. Many theologians believe that when a believer is "in Christ" he or she is justified. And whenever Christ is in the believer he or she is sanctified. However, since righteousness is holiness, we receive Christ's imparted righteousness, which is sanctification, at the same time we receive Him.

Notice Isaiah 54:17, which says, "This is the heritage of the servants of the LORD, and their righteousness is of me, saith the LORD." Another similar verse is Jeremiah 23:6, which I will quote in full: "In his days Judah shall be saved, and Israel shall dwell safely: and this is his name whereby he shall be called, THE LORD OUR RIGHTEOUSNESS." (See also Jeremiah 33:16.)

We cannot divide Christ into parts. The two things—justification and sanctification—are united together in Him; they are inseparable. Jesus has been likened unto the sun, which gives off both heat and light, which are inseparable. In the same way, Christ is unto us both righteousness and sanctification (1 Cor. 1:30). Not only are we fully justified but we are also fully sanctified in Him. Thus, the gift of the righteousness of Christ in justification also involves the gift of His holiness, or sanctification, as well.

We quoted earlier the statement "sanctification is the work of a lifetime," but in the final analysis, we have two aspects of sanctification. First, sanctification is the presence of holiness when we have Jesus living within our hearts. Second, sanctification is also growing in holiness. Let's consider the thief on the cross. In the best-selling book *The Desire of Ages*, Ellen G. White writes, "Hope is mingled with anguish in his voice as the helpless, dying soul casts himself upon a dying Saviour. 'Lord, remember me,' he cries, 'when Thou comest into Thy kingdom.'. . . Many were ready to call Him Lord when He wrought miracles, and after He had risen from the grave; but none acknowledged Him as He hung dying upon the cross save the penitent thief who was saved at the eleventh hour" (pp. 750, 751).

So, what all was involved in the science of salvation for this thief? How was this dying thief saved when he had only one day of life, wherein he became "penitent," i.e., repentant, forgiven, and justified? Somehow he became sanctified (i.e., holy) in his last hours of life.

Justification must be the immediate and the long-term cause of sanctification. In other words, justification is the cause of immediate, present holiness, and continuing holiness is the process of growing in holiness, which is sanctification.

I really appreciate Dr. Erwin R. Gane's insight in *Enlightened by the Spirit*. He writes, "Justification is Christ bestowed upon believers by the Holy Spirit; sanctification is Christ possessed in believers' hearts by the indwelling of the Spirit. Justification causes sanctification" (p. 55).

Even though justification causes sanctification, they still cannot be separated. They are both processes. Therefore, if we have Jesus' presence within us, we are both justified and sanctified.

Now, let's consider the other important ingredients of salvation. In Ephesians 2:8-10, we find the gospel has been encapsulated by Paul. I especially like these verses because they are condensed and to the point. Paul says, "For by grace are ye saved through faith; and that not of yourselves: it is the gift of God: Not of works, lest any man should boast. For we are his workmanship, created in Christ Jesus unto good works, which God hath before ordained that we should walk in them."

There have been many books written on the subject of grace. I don't pretend to know everything about grace, but from that which I do understand, please allow me to generalize what I perceive to be at least five major characteristics and functions of grace.

1. Grace is equivalent to the attributes of God. And, when imparted to us, it produces "fruit of the Spirit" (Gal. 5:22, 23). You may have already noticed that "fruit" is singular in these verses, and the main fruit of the Spirit is love, which is the fountainhead of the other aspects of grace.
2. Grace is manifested in God's unmerited favor toward sinners, i.e., pardoning grace.
3. Grace of Christ gives us the power to live a victorious Christian life, i.e., enabling or empowering grace.

4. Growing in grace. This is another way of saying growing in sanctification. (See 2 Peter 1:1-11.) Growing in grace is growing in sanctification and growing in love. As mentioned, love is the fountainhead for all of these graces.
5. The covenant of grace. Although God's grace has been provided for everyone, we still need to appropriate it "through faith." Romans 5:1 and 2 expresses this very thing: "Therefore being justified by faith, we have peace with God through our Lord Jesus Christ: By whom also we have access by faith into this grace." Thus, sinners must access the grace of Christ "by faith" (Rom. 5:2), i.e., "through faith" (Eph. 2:8).

Before discussing "faith," which is another necessary ingredient in our salvation, I want to briefly consider the "covenant of grace" a little further. The reason we need to include the "covenant of grace" is because I want to show how the "everlasting gospel" must include more than just the "objective" element of "justification by faith." In other words, the gospel cannot be the legal declaration that a sinner has imputed righteousness alone without the "subjective" transformation that occurs when the sinner has been "born again." God would not declare a sinner righteous without a corresponding conversion. And, since justification and sanctification cannot be separated, the gospel cannot be justification alone.

Now, let's consider the "covenant of grace." Everyone who would be saved must enter into a relationship with God. The covenant of grace was first established with Adam and Eve while they were still in the Garden of Eden. God promised to offer them redemption on conditions. These conditions included faith in a Promised Redeemer. This Redeemer would be Jesus, "THE LORD OUR RIGHTEOUSNESS" (Jer. 23:6 and Jer. 33:16). Thus, even Old Testament believers received righteousness by faith.

Notice what God promises in the everlasting covenant as taught in Jeremiah 31:31-34 and Ezekiel 36:23-28. We are taught that:
1. God's law is written upon our hearts.
2. The promise of Jesus' presence is within us.
3. A heavenly inheritance is waiting for us.

These promises are the essence of the gospel of righteousness by faith—justification and sanctification. Therefore, both justification and sanctification come by faith.

Now, let's consider faith. I want to begin by quoting Romans 1:16 and 17: "For I am not ashamed of the gospel of Christ: for it is the power of God unto salvation [Paul could have said, for it is the empowering grace of God unto salvation] to every one that believeth [i.e., to everyone that has faith]; to the Jew first, and also to the Greek. For therein is the righteousness of God revealed from faith to faith: as it is written, The just shall live by faith."

What does the expression "from faith to faith" actually mean? It means that when we receive the righteousness of God by faith it results in ever-increasing faith. As faith is exercised, we are able to receive more and still more of the righteousness of God until faith becomes a permanent attitude toward Him.

Here is a beautiful thought from *The Desire of Ages*: "through faith we receive the grace of God; but faith is not our Saviour. It earns nothing. It is the hand by which we lay hold upon Christ, and appropriate His merits, the remedy for sin" (p. 175). Here we see the role of faith that is expressed in Ephesians 2:8 and Romans 5:1 and 2.

And in *Faith and Works*, page 25, we read: "It [faith] is an assent of the understanding to God's words which binds the heart in willing consecration and service to God, Who gave the understanding, Who moved on the heart, Who first drew the mind to view Christ on the cross of Calvary. Faith is rendering to God the intellectual powers, abandonment of the mind and will to God."

Now, going back to Ephesians 2:8, we learn that grace is a "gift." Then in verse 9, Paul said: "Not of works, lest any man should boast." Is Paul really saying that works have nothing to do with the conditions of salvation? No, because in verse 10 he wrote, "For we are his workmanship, created in Christ Jesus unto good works, which God hath before ordained [margin, prepared] that we should walk in them." Thus, Paul agrees that "we are his workmanship, created in Christ Jesus unto good works."

Paul had much to say about "works of the law," which is different than works of faith, i.e., the fruit of walking in the Spirit. Many Evangelical scholars believe Paul was the supreme authority on the substance of the gospel. Furthermore, they limit Paul's gospel primarily to Romans 4, and especially verse 5, which says, "But to him that worketh not, but believeth on him that justifieth the ungodly, his faith is counted for righteousness." However, they fail to consider what Paul said in Romans 2:13, which says, "For not the hearers of the law are just before God, but the doers of the law shall be justified." Notice in Romans 16:26, Paul mentions "obedience of faith."

Paul is basically agreeing with James 2:17-26. James is very clear about the substance of dead faith. Let's read some selected verses from that portion of James. "Even so faith, if it hath not works, is dead, being alone. . . . But wilt thou know, O vain man, that faith without works is dead? . . . Seest thou how faith wrought with his [Abraham's] works, and by works was faith made perfect? . . . Ye see then how that by works a man is justified, and not by faith only. . . . For as the body without the spirit is dead, so faith without works is dead also."

Did you notice the words "by works a man is justified"? I believe Paul and James are in perfect agreement.

Author Ellen G. White offers us some inspirational thoughts about the role of faith, justification, and obedience in *Selected Messages*, book 1: "Genuine faith appropriates the righteousness of Christ, and the sinner is made an overcomer with Christ; for he is made a partaker of the divine nature, and thus divinity and humanity are combined. [Peter basically said the same thing in 2 Peter 1:4.]

"He who is trying to reach heaven by his own works in keeping the law, is attempting an impossibility. Man cannot be saved without obedience, but his works should not be of himself; Christ should work in him to will and to do of His good pleasure [see Philippians 2:12]. . . .

"When we seek to gain heaven through the merits of Christ, the soul makes progress. Looking unto Jesus, the author and finisher of our faith [see Hebrews 12:2], we may go on from strength to strength, from victory to victory; for through Christ the grace of God has worked out our complete salvation. . . .

"But while God can be just, and yet justify the sinner through the merits of Christ, no man can cover his soul with the garments of Christ's righteousness while practicing known sins, or neglecting known duties. God requires the entire surrender of the heart, before justification can take place; and in order for man to retain justification, there must be continual obedience, through active, living faith that works by love and purifies the soul [see Galatians 5:6 and 1 Peter 1:22]. . . .

"In order for man to be justified by faith, faith must reach a point where it will control the affections and impulses of the heart; and it is by obedience that faith itself is made perfect [see James 2:22]."

And, in *Faith and Works*, we read: "I ask, How can I present this matter as it is? The Lord Jesus imparts all the powers, all the grace, all the penitence, all the inclination, all the pardon of sins, in presenting His righteousness for man to grasp by living faith—which is also the gift of God" (p. 24).

Now, I want to more clearly emphasize what the author said in *Selected Messages*, book 1, on page 366: "God requires the entire surrender of the heart, before justification can take place." This "entire surrender of the heart" is a process of daily denying self and taking up the cross. Many words have been written explaining this important issue of salvation. I can only give a brief summary of how to surrender our lives to the Lord-ship of Jesus. Yes, He is our Savior, but Jesus is also our Lord and Master.

There is an excellent book on this subject, *Surrender: The Secret to Perfect Peace & Happiness*, by Pastor Gregory L. Jackson. Jackson uses the sanctuary model in his prayers, and he demonstrates how the process of surrender works in this model. He uses Luke 9:23 as his basic text in explaining what *surrendering* is all about. Let me quote this verse: "And he said to them all, If any man will come after me, let him deny himself, and take up his cross daily, and follow me." Then, on page 70, he makes the following point: "If we are to be successful in surrendering, we must do it at the right time. We have already discovered that Jesus got up a 'great while before day' and went to a 'solitary place, and there prayed' (Mark 1:35)."

Following these words, he quotes Isaiah 50:4 and 5, which says: "The Lord GOD hath given me the tongue of the learned, that I should know how to speak a word in season to him that is weary: he wakeneth morning by morning, he wakeneth mine ear to hear as the learned. The Lord GOD hath opened mine ear, and I was not rebellious, neither turned away back." The point Jackson makes is that we need to be prepared for any eventuality before the need arises. The only way we can do this is by early morning devotions. He states further, "the Lord wants to wake us up to speak to us, and if we don't rebel by turning over and going back to sleep, He'll speak to us personally, giving us the wisdom and strength we need for that day."

After Jackson is awakened, he uses the sanctuary model for prayer. Then, he noticed his prayers became more fervent and intimate. He knows that the power of God is in His Word, so he claims God's promises from the Bible. First, he gives praise and thanksgiving to God. Then, he confesses all of his sins that come to mind while he is meditating upon Psalm 139:23 and 24, which says, "Search me, O God, and know my heart: try me, and know my thoughts: And see if there be any wicked way in me, and lead me in the way everlasting." After repeating these verses, he reflects on the past 24 hours. It is when he is meditating that God shows him, not only his sinful acts, but also the sinful thoughts and motives that generated the sinful acts. As the Lord reveals "the wicked way in me," Jackson repents and asks for forgiveness and cleansing. The bottom line is that he searches with the Lord's help, repents, and surrenders at each step in this process.

However, Jackson freely admits that it is possible to be surrendering fully every day and still sin. Why? Because of ignorance. But, those who are surrendering daily won't stay in ignorance of truth indefinitely. As mentioned in Luke 9:23, denying self and taking up the cross is a daily activity.

In *Testimonies for the Church*, volume 2, we read the following from Ellen G. White: "None are living Christians unless they have a daily experience in the things of God and daily practice self-denial, cheerfully bearing the cross and following Christ. Every living Christian will advance daily in the divine life. As he advances toward perfection, he experiences a conversion to God every day; and this conversion is not completed until he attains to perfection of Christian character, a full preparation for the finishing touch of immortality."

You see, conversion is also a daily process, as well as sanctification. This comment explains why justification (i.e., conversion) is a daily process. Note what Paul stated in 1 Corinthians 15:31: "I die daily." In other words, Paul surrendered to Jesus every day, and he became converted daily.

Paul also wrote about surrender in Galatians 2:20: "I am crucified with Christ: nevertheless I live; yet not I, but Christ liveth in me: and the life which I now live in the flesh I live by the faith of the Son of God, who loved me, and gave himself for me." Therefore, justification (conversion) requires a full surrender daily to God's revealed will, which takes time, as the sins of ignorance are revealed to us. Thus, Jesus is being bestowed upon us, and possessed by us daily, in the processes of surrender, conversion, and sanctification. Also, only those who are obedient have true faith, and only those who have true faith are obedient.

In conclusion, I hope everyone recognizes that the gospel must include the subjective aspects of sanctification as well as justification. However, there is more than justification and sanctification as components of the everlasting gospel. I don't have the space to dwell on these other aspects of the gospel, other than to mention that the gospel also includes judgment, which is revealed in Revelation 14:6 and 7. Also, the gospel includes prophecy, as revealed in Revelation 1:1-3. "The Revelation of Jesus Christ" is the prophecy found in the last book of the Bible. Notice what Peter said in his first epistle, chapter 1, verse 25: "But the word of the Lord endureth for ever. And this is the word which by the gospel is preached unto you." Therefore, the gospel includes the words of Jesus and the words written by His prophets.

My fellow brothers and sisters, are we prepared to give the final message of righteousness by faith to a perishing world? What will it take for us to realize that Jesus is waiting for us to share this news with others? He wants to finish His final ministry of judgment, but He is waiting for a people whom He can use to proclaim His righteousness, by precept and example. I believe the secret is found in 1 Thessalonians 5:23: "And the very God of peace sanctify you wholly; and *I pray God* your whole spirit and soul and body be preserved blameless unto the coming of our Lord Jesus Christ."

Does Jesus have a people who are sanctified "wholly"? Are we "blameless"? Thank God for the wonderful promise in verse 24: "Faithful is he that calleth you, who also will do it." Not only will Jesus do this for us individually but He promises the same for His church.

In Ephesians 5:26 and 27, Paul says, "That he might sanctify and cleanse it with the washing of water by the word, That he might present it to himself a glorious church, not having spot, or wrinkle, or any such thing; but that it should be holy and without blemish." My prayer is for us to surrender all to Jesus, put on His robe of righteousness daily, receive His presence within, and be holy and without blemish so that we may reflect His character of love to the world.

Chapter 2

Can We Have Assurance of Salvation?

The purpose of this Bible study is to discover whether you and I can have assurance that we are saved. Can we really have this assurance of salvation? The answer is an emphatic yes! But I have learned that there is a caution that needs to be emphasized. Even though we can know in our hearts that we are saved, I don't believe it is a good idea to publicly announce the words, "I am saved." Why is this so? Because, when we say this, we can easily become overconfident. Furthermore, this is comparable to saying, "I am not sinning." It can also be misconstrued as boasting, and thus lacking in humility. Therefore, I believe our confidence that we are saved, should be kept to ourselves. Even if we preface this remark with "by the grace of God," I still believe it is presumptuous to say out loud. Instead, let's know in our hearts that we are saved and have eternal life now, but let's be careful about how we reveal this belief to others.

Notice what Paul said in 1 Corinthians 9:27: "But I keep under my body, and bring it into subjection: lest that by any means, when I have preached to others, I myself should be a castaway." In *Selected Messages*, book 1, we read: "We are never to rest in a satisfied condition . . . saying, 'I am saved.' When this idea is entertained, the motives for watchfulness, for prayer, for earnest endeavor to press onward to higher attainments, cease to exist. No sanctified tongue will be found uttering these words till Christ shall come, and we enter in through the gates into the city of God. Then, with the utmost propriety, we may give glory to God and to the Lamb for eternal deliverance. As long as man is full of weakness—for of himself he cannot save his soul—he should never dare to say, 'I am saved'" (p. 314).

In the previous chapter, I emphasized the "how to" have assurance of salvation. Now, I have decided to primarily give scriptural support to show that we can have assurance of salvation. But, it will be necessary to include some of the mechanics of "how to" have the assurance of salvation.

I don't want to come across as an authority on this very important matter, because I am not. So, I am reminded of a story, which I'm going to share with you.

A literary critic met a little girl on his way to the home of the well-known John Bunyan. "Do you know where John Bunyan lives?" he asked her.

"Yes," she replied as she started showing him the way to Bunyan's residence.

Walking along with the child, the man, who knew a lot about Bunyan's literary style, began to wax eloquent about allegory, metaphors, personification, etc. Caught up in literary topics, he unwittingly turned to face his young helper, asking her if she understood what he meant.

"No," she promptly answered.

Impulsively he shot back, "Then you don't know John Bunyan."

Astonished, the little girl replied emphatically and matter-of-factly, "But I do know him. He is my father."

I believe this story beautifully illustrates two important principles: 1) We can know a lot about God, like the literary expert, but not be personally experiencing Him in our lives. 2) We can know Him through child-like trust without understanding the steps involved in our salvation.

Let's turn to 1 John 5:11-13: "And this is the record, that God hath given to us eternal life, and this life is in his Son. He that hath the Son hath life; and he that hath not the Son of God hath not life."

Now, we come to a wonderful promise. Verse 13 says, "These things have I written unto you that believe on the name of the Son of God; that ye may know that ye have eternal life, and that ye may believe on the name of the Son of God."

In verse 13 I believe John is emphasizing two main thoughts: 1) He is writing to believers who believe. In other words, they have faith in Jesus as the Son of God. 2) He wants his readers to realize that by having faith in Jesus they should "know" that they have eternal life.

In the Greek, so I am told, this passage indicates a full conviction, or assurance of eternal life, when we have faith in Jesus. So, eternal life comes as a result of having a relationship—Jesus living within our hearts—"Christ in you, the hope of glory" (Col. 1:27).

Now, let us look at 1 John 4:13, which adds more detail. We read, "Hereby know we that we dwell in him, and he in us, because he hath given us of his Spirit." Brothers and sisters, John is telling us how we can "know" that there is a mutual relationship wherein we dwell in Jesus and He in us. How is this so? Because the Holy Spirit brings to us the presence of Jesus. (I will give support for this truth, later.) When Jesus is enthroned in our hearts, we will have full assurance that we are saved.

Another similar thought asserting the role of the Holy Spirit giving us assurance of salvation is found in Romans 8:16: "The Spirit itself beareth witness with our spirit, that we are the children of God." Therefore, the Holy Spirit "beareth witness," or assures us, "that we are the children of God." When we are converted and sanctified, through the power of the Holy Spirit, Jesus takes up residence in our hearts, and both Jesus and the Holy Spirit become our inner "witness" that we are God's children.

Furthermore, our heavenly Father even takes up residence in our hearts. Turning to John 14:23, we read, "Jesus answered and said unto him, If a man love me, he will keep my words: and my Father will love him, and we will come unto him, and make our abode with him." Thus, when we love Jesus and "keep his words," we have all three deities living in our hearts.

Now, let's turn to 1 John 3 and read a few passages. Verse 14 and 16 say, "We know that we have passed from death unto life, because we love the brethren. . . . Hereby perceive [i.e., know] we the love of God, because he laid down his life for us: and we ought to lay down our lives for the brethren."

Then, skipping down to verses 23 and 24, we read, "And this is his commandment, That we should believe on the name of his Son Jesus Christ, and love one another, as he gave us commandment. And he that keepeth his commandments dwelleth in him, and he in him. And hereby we know that he [Jesus] abideth in us, by the Spirit which he hath given us."

Therefore, Paul and, especially, John have both given us ample evidence that we can "know" that we have eternal life. This knowledge and assurance comes with experientially knowing Jesus. Furthermore, when we know Jesus experientially, He creates in us a "love for the brethren." However, there are some conditions that are required of us before we can have this assurance of salvation.

First, we must believe on Jesus as mentioned in 1 John 5:13. Note, in Greek there is only one word for believe—*pistis*. This same word means faith.

Second, through faith we access God's grace. God's grace equals His attributes, which are bestowed upon us when we are "born again," i.e., converted. (See Romans 5:2 or Ephesians 2:8.) Note, conversion involves daily surrendering to God's will. Remember, Luke 9:23 says, "If any man will come after me, let him deny himself, and take up his cross daily, and follow me."

Third, in order to retain faith, we must be obedient, otherwise our faith is dead. (See James 2:17-24 and Romans 1:5, margin.) In other words, living faith includes keeping God's commandments through the power of the Holy Spirit.

Fourth, repentance and forgiveness are given to us as gifts whenever we do our part by confessing our sins and turning away from them through the enabling grace of God. In 1 John 1:9 it says, "If we confess our sins, he is faithful and just to forgive us our sins, and to cleanse us from all unrighteousness."

Finally, we love God and one another. But, loving others comes naturally when we love God.

So, a condensed summary of these conditions is faith, grace, surrender, repentance, and love.

We discover more support for the role of love in the Christian's life from 1 John 4. Let's read selected sections beginning with verse 7: "Beloved, let us love one another: for love is of God; and every one that loveth is born of God, and knoweth God."

Then, in verses 12 and 13, we read the following: "No man hath seen God at any time. If we love one another, God dwelleth in us, and his love is perfected in us. Hereby know we that we dwell in him, and he in us, because he hath given us of his Spirit."

In verses 16 through 18, we read, "And we have known and believed the love that God hath to us. God is love; and he that dwelleth in love dwelleth in

God, and God in him. Herein is our love made perfect, that we may have boldness in the day of judgment: because as he is, so are we in this world. There is no fear in love; but perfect love casteth out fear."

The bottom line is that grace, faith, repentance, and love are all gifts of God. When we surrender our will to God, He supplies all these other conditions.

Later in this study, we will establish the truth that surrendering our will is a daily process. Thus, when we are "born again" daily and sanctified daily, we receive assurance that we are saved.

Now, let's go to Romans 5:1: "Therefore being justified by faith (i.e., being converted by faith), we have peace with God through our Lord Jesus Christ." Therefore, Paul is telling us that after we are converted we have peace. I believe this "peace" could not be present in our hearts if we were uncertain about our salvation. The greatest peace and joy for Christians is having the presence of Jesus in our hearts.

Continuing on to verse 2, we read, "By whom also we have access by faith into this grace wherein we stand, and rejoice in hope of the glory of God." This verse establishes the truth that we access grace by faith. Skipping down to verse 5, we read, "And hope maketh not ashamed; because the love of God is shed abroad in our hearts by the Holy Ghost which is given unto us."

One Bible commentary gives us an enlightening comment on this verse. It says, "This is no ordinary hope, for hope is often disappointed. This is the hope that is founded on the consciousness of justification and is endorsed by the presence of the Holy Spirit in the heart. Such hope cannot disappoint or put to shame."

The second part of verse 5, from the J.B. Phillips Translation says, "Already we have the love of God flooding through our hearts by the Holy Spirit given to us."

So, here are some questions we can answer for ourselves in order to know whether we have the assurance of salvation.

1. Do I love Jesus? I mean, really love Him more than life itself? In other words, have I surrendered my life to Jesus as my Lord and Master?
2. Do I love other people more than myself?
3. Do I have peace, joy, hope, and love daily in my heart?

4. Finally, am I growing in faith, love, and grace, which are the essentials of growing in sanctification?

I believe if we can answer yes to these four questions, then we can know that we are in a saving relationship with Jesus.

Let's turn to 2 Peter 1:1-4, wherein we find the formula for growing in grace, which is equivalent to growing in sanctification. We read, "Simon Peter, a servant and an apostle of Jesus Christ, to them that have obtained like precious faith with us through the righteousness of God and our Saviour Jesus Christ: Grace and peace be multiplied unto you through the knowledge of God, and of Jesus our Lord [I believe Peter is referring to experiential knowledge here].... Whereby are given unto us exceeding great and precious promises: that by these ye might be partakers of the divine nature..."

Question: Where do we find precious promises? Answer: From the Word of God—the Bible. John 17:17 gives us one of these promises. It says, "Sanctify them through thy truth, thy word is truth." In other words, we become sanctified by the Word of God.

Turning to 2 Peter 1:4, we read, "Whereby are given unto us exceeding great and precious promises: that by these ye might be partakers of the divine nature, having escaped the corruption that is in the world through lust." Therefore, when we are converted, we receive the divine nature, which is given to us by the Holy Spirit. Then, we are enabled to grow in grace and sanctification from the study of God's Word.

Have you noticed in Galatians 5:22 and 23 that the fruit of the Spirit is named in the singular form and begins with love? I believe the reason is because love is the fountain for all of the secondary graces (fruit) of the Spirit.

Let us turn to another wonderful promise found in Philippians 1:6, which reads, "Being confident of this very thing, [in other words, we know] that he which hath begun a good work in you will perform [margin says finish] it until the day of Jesus Christ."

In Hebrews 12:2, Paul tells us that we should be "looking unto Jesus the author and finisher of our faith."

Now, going back to 2 Peter 1:5-7, we find that Peter lists a number of graces. Even though "love" is listed last, it is also first and ever-present. Allow me to share a short passage from one of my favorite authors who wrote more than

Can We Have Assurance of Salvation?

100 years ago in a periodical titled *The Review and Herald*: "We are to add to faith, virtue; and to virtue, knowledge; and to knowledge, temperance; and to temperance, patience; and to patience, godliness; and to godliness, brotherly kindness; and to brotherly kindness, charity. You are not to think that you are to wait until you have perfected one grace before cultivating another. No; they are to grow up together, fed continually from the fountain of charity" (July 29, 1890).

At this time, I want to present an overview of the essentials of Christianity, which I have gleaned from my reading of the Bible and other sources. If we do these things, I believe we will have the assurance of salvation. Again, I must repeat, I am not an authority, as I fall far short of the ideal Pattern in the life of Jesus. I have labeled them the A, B, C's of living the Christian life.

A = "Alone" with God—prayer and devotions every morning with daily surrender included
B = "Bible" study
C = "Caring" for others—loving ministry or witnessing

I suspect some of our responses to these essentials may be: 1) I don't have time for devotions every morning; 2) I sometimes read my Bible, but not every day; 3) I don't know how to witness to others. We probably already know these basic principles, but the big question is, How are we going to implement these activities when the spirit is willing but the flesh is weak?

The answer may be found in the book *Steps to Christ*, pages 47 and 48: "Many are inquiring, '*How* am I to make the surrender of myself to God?' You desire to give yourself to Him, but you are weak in moral power, in slavery to doubt, and controlled by the habits of your life of sin. Your promises and resolutions are like ropes of sand. You cannot control your thoughts, your impulses, your affections. The knowledge of your broken promises and forfeited pledges weakens your confidence in your own sincerity, and causes you to feel that God cannot accept you; but you need not despair. What you need to understand is the true force of the will. This is the governing power in the nature of man, the power of decision, or of choice. Everything depends on the right action of the will. The power of choice God has given to men; it is theirs to exercise. You cannot change your heart, you cannot of yourself give to God its affections; but you can *choose* to serve Him. You can give Him your will; He will then work in you to will and to do according to His good pleasure. Thus your whole nature will be brought under the control of the Spirit of Christ; your affections will be centered upon Him, your thoughts will be in harmony with Him. . . . By yielding up your will to Christ, you ally yourself with the power that is above all principalities and powers. You will have strength from above to hold you steadfast, and thus through constant surrender to God you will be enabled to live the new life, even the life of faith."

The bottom line from this passage is that we must choose to fully surrender ourselves to Jesus on a daily basis. Then, when self is denied, we become filled with the Holy Spirit and have the presence of Jesus. In other words, we must choose daily to surrender our heart and will to Jesus in order to be daily "filled" by the Holy Spirit.

In Garrie F. Williams book *How to be Filled With the Holy Spirit and Know It*, page 65, he states, "I believe that the filling of a person's life with the Holy Spirit is actually another way of describing a life totally surrendered to God."

To help us better understand our hearts, let me provide you with an illustration. When the Bible uses the word "heart," it is referring to the inner person or the motives that actuate us. I believe our hearts are like a room, which can be cluttered with a lot of stuff, even idols, if you wish. However, the most important articles of furniture within each heart should be a throne and a cross. And, in order to surrender all of the clutter in our hearts, it requires a supernatural work. As mentioned, full surrender involves a supernatural work, a daily process, through prayer, wherein we surrender our selfish idols to the full control of the Holy Spirit. When we do this every morning, the Holy Spirit "fills" us, and we receive power to live the victorious Christian life.

Question: How many of us are on the throne in our hearts with Jesus still on the cross? We each should answer that question for ourselves. Even Jesus surrendered daily to His Father's will. In John 6:38 we read, "For I came down from heaven, not to do mine own will, but the will of him that sent me." Jesus didn't have to surrender any selfishness like we do, but He left us His example, and He commanded us to "deny" self and "take up" our "cross daily" and follow Him (Luke 9:23).

In 1 Corinthians 15:31 Paul says, "I die daily." In this verse, Paul is writing about making a full surrender to Jesus on a daily, or continual, basis.

Now, I want to share some passages on the "filling" or "baptism" of the Holy Spirit from the pen of Ellen G. White. In *The Great Controversy,* we read, "The Father gave His Spirit without measure to his Son, and we also may partake of its fullness" (p. 477). (See also Ephesians 3:19.)

In *The Acts of the Apostles*, page 50, we read, "If all were willing, all would be filled with the Spirit. . . . For the daily baptism of the Spirit every worker should offer his petition to God."

Turning to page 56 of the same book, we read, "Every worker who follows the example of Christ will be prepared to receive and use the power that God has promised to His church for the ripening of earth's harvest. Morning by morning, as the heralds of the gospel kneel before the Lord and renew their vows of consecration to Him, He will grant them the presence of His Spirit, with its reviving, sanctifying power. As they go forth to the day's duties, they have the assurance that the unseen agency of the Holy Spirit enables them to be 'laborers together with God.'"

These "heralds of the gospel" are not just the leadership of the church. These people are you and me, the laity. Did you notice the words "morning by morning" and "renew their vows of consecration to Him"? In other words, we need to re-consecrate ourselves "morning by morning," and then God will give us the "presence of His Spirit."

Furthermore, in *The Review and Herald*, November 29, 1892, edition, Ellen G. White wrote, "The Holy Spirit is the Comforter, as the personal presence of Christ to the soul." Paul essentially says the same thing in Galatians 4:6: "And because ye are sons, God hath sent forth the Spirit of his Son into your hearts, crying, Abba, Father."

Now, I want to re-emphasize that in order for us to have assurance of salvation and live a victorious Christian life we need to daily die to self. Since daily dying to self is a process, so also conversion is a daily process. In *Testimonies for the Church*, volume 2, Ellen G. White says,

"None are living Christians unless they have a daily experience in the things of God and daily practice self-denial, cheerfully bearing the cross and following Christ. Every living Christian will advance daily in the divine life.

As he advances toward perfection, he experiences a conversion to God every day; and this conversion is not completed until he attains to perfection of Christian character" (p. 505).

Another similar statement is made in *Testimonies to the Church*, volume 4, page 66:

"Selfishness must be put away, and we must overcome every defect in our characters as Christ overcame. In order to accomplish this work, we must die daily to self. Said Paul: 'I die daily.' He had a new conversion every day."

We have all seen the picture of Jesus standing at a door without a doorknob and knocking. Full surrender can be likened to this door into our hearts. Early every morning we can make the choice to open this door, through prayer, and thus surrender our lives to Jesus for that day alone. Then, as we re-consecrate our lives to Jesus during our devotional time, we are "filled" by the Holy Spirit. This "in-filling" brings us the sweet presence of Jesus and provides us the divine nature and the power we need to live a Christian life. I believe this "in-filling" of the Holy Spirit, and Jesus' presence, gives us assurance of salvation.

Now, the question naturally comes up, "Can this assurance be lost?" Most certainly this can happen. We all remember the story of King David, and the sin he caused with Bathsheba. This illustration shows that nobody can commit sin and expect the abiding presence of Jesus in his heart. When we commit knowledgeable sin, we lose our assurance of salvation. Thereafter, we must confess and forsake this particular sin. Jesus cannot abide in us when we have not confessed our sins of which we have knowledge and have not repented of these sins.

This is why David wrote Psalm 51. He had wandered far from God and had committed some terrible sins. He was deeply concerned about this when he prayed: "Have mercy upon me, O God, according to thy lovingkindness: according unto the multitude of thy tender mercies blot out my transgressions. Wash me thoroughly from mine iniquity, and cleanse me from my sin" (verses 1, 2).

Then in verses 10-12, he writes, "Create in me a clean heart, O God; and renew a right spirit within me. Cast me not away from thy presence; and take not thy holy spirit from me. Restore unto me the joy of thy salvation; and uphold me with thy free spirit."

Can We Have Assurance of Salvation?

So, considering David's fall from grace, are there any early warning signs we can heed before we lose the assurance of salvation? The answer is yes. In his book *Surrender: The Secret to Perfect Peace & Happiness,* Jackson wrote, "Eventually I hit a snag and began to miss the intimacy with the Lord that I had come to enjoy so much. I still got up early every morning and communed with the Lord through prayer and Bible study, but I didn't feel His presence as powerfully as in previous times. This greatly disturbed me, and I began to ask the Lord to show me the problem. This went on for a while until one day while talking to a doctor friend of mine, the Lord revealed the problem to me. In the past, God had used me to bless my friend, but this day God used him to bless me. As I shared my concern with him he said, 'Whenever that happens to me, it's always because there's some area in my life that God wants me to surrender to Him, and I'm holding back'" (p. 53).

At this time, Jackson made some interesting comments on the process of surrender. He said, "I had been surrendering more and more of my life to the Lord. As my walk with Him grew more intimate, His light of truth shone brighter and went deeper, revealing that the areas I had already surrendered needed to be surrendered on an even deeper level."

So, herein lies the problem that many of us face today. As our knowledge of God's will becomes more and more enlightened, we will also need to deepen the process of surrender of our hearts. When those sins which we once committed in ignorance become revealed and we fail to make a full surrender on a daily basis, we then fail to open the door of our heart again to the presence of Jesus.

Some other early warning signs include omission of secret fervent prayer and Bible study. In *Testimonies for the Church*, volume 1, we read, "Do not neglect secret prayer, for it is the soul of religion. With earnest, fervent prayer, plead for purity of soul. Plead as earnestly, as eagerly, as you would for your mortal life, were it at stake. Remain before God until unutterable longings are begotten within you for salvation, and the sweet evidence is obtained of pardoned sin" (p. 163).

Once we have lost the sweet presence of Jesus in us, it may take many days before the joy of salvation returns to us, with His presence in us. Remember the incident in the life of Jesus when He was about twelve years old. Mary and Joseph had lost track of Him for only one day, but they subsequently spent three days looking for Him. Notice this comment in *The Desire of Ages*: "By one day's neglect they lost the Saviour; but it cost them three days of anxious search to find Him. So with us; by idle talk, evilspeaking, or neglect of prayer, we may in one day lose the Saviour's presence, and it may take many days of sorrowful search to find Him, and regain the peace that we have lost" (p. 83).

Finally, we can lose our assurance of salvation if we neglect to witness for Jesus. The English word "witness" comes from the Anglo-Saxon word "witam," which means "I know." If we know and experience so little of Jesus in our hearts, we will eventually lose His presence. Then we cannot witness, because we have nothing of Jesus within our hearts for which we can witness.

Therefore, in summary, there are three major causes of losing our assurance of salvation: 1) neglecting secret prayer, 2) neglecting Bible study, 3) failure of having Jesus' presence within us, which negates our capacity to witness for Him.

Williams offers us this comment: "In front of television, not only does time for Bible study and prayer evaporate, but so does the desire to spend time in fellowship with God." So, if we are really serious about our salvation, then it's imperative that we spend quality time with Jesus and share Him with others. There is a cross involved in being a disciple of Jesus. Not only is He our Savior, but He should also be our Lord and Master. Jesus gave His all in order to save us. Are you willing to give Him all?

In conclusion, yes, we can have assurance of salvation. It requires us to spend time with God in secret prayer and Bible study. As we choose daily to surrender to His will, the Holy Spirit gives us a daily conversion, which includes the presence of Jesus in our hearts. At the same time, we also continue growing in grace and love, which is sanctification. Thus, we can have the assurance of salvation as long as we have the presence of Jesus in our hearts.

When we lose His presence, it's because we have failed to surrender on a deeper level or because we have not confessed our sins that need to be repented. So now, as we are nearing the close of this earth's history, let us seriously resolve to be faithful to Jesus and surrender our lives to Him, who is our Lord and Master.

Finally, knowing all the steps involved in having assurance of salvation does not, in itself, give us the joy of salvation. The steps must be implemented so that Jesus may work in us "both to will and to do of His good pleasure." We may not always be willing, but we can still ask Jesus to help us to be willing. He will do this for us if we sincerely desire to be like Him.

Genuine assurance is based upon one simple formula: we must give all to Jesus, in absolute surrender to His will, daily denying self. Then, He gives us His strength to make all the right responses to temptations, to overcome all of our sins, and even our inherent propensities to sin, and improve our usefulness to serve Him and others. After that, we can say with Paul, as in Galatians 2:20, "I am crucified with Christ: nevertheless I live; yet not I, but Christ liveth in me: and the life which I now live in the flesh I live by the faith of the Son of God, who loved me, and gave himself for me."

My prayer is for us to trust more in God's faithfulness to finish the good work that He has begun in us (Phil. 1:6). Amen.

Chapter 3

A Thief in the Night

The purpose of this Bible study will be to discover what exactly the Lord meant when He illustrated His second coming as a "thief" in Matthew 24:42-44. This same illustration, with the added thought, "a thief in the night," connected to "the day of the Lord," was used by Peter and Paul, in 2 Peter 3:10 and 1 Thessalonians 5:2, respectively.

First, let's read some verses from Matthew, then we will read a similar passage from Luke 17:30-36. Matthew 24:40-44 says, "Then shall two be in the field; the one shall be taken, and the other left. Two women shall be grinding at the mill; the one shall be taken, and the other left. Watch therefore: for ye know not what hour your Lord doth come. But know this, that if the goodman of the house had known in what watch the thief would come, he would have watched, and would not have suffered his house to be broken up. Therefore be ye also ready: for in such an hour as ye think not the Son of man cometh."

Now, let's read the other passage in Luke 17:30-36: "Even thus shall it be in the day when the Son of man is revealed. In that day, he which shall be upon the housetop, and his stuff in the house, let him not come down to take it away: and he that is in the field, let him likewise not return back. Remember Lot's wife. Whosoever shall seek to save his life shall lose it; and whosoever shall lose his life shall preserve it. I tell you, in that night [please notice that Jesus prefaced both "in that day" and "in that night" in this passage] there shall be two men in one bed; the one shall be taken, and the other shall be left. Two women shall be grinding together; the one shall be taken, and the other left."

So, is Jesus really telling us that His second coming will be a secret event?

A Thief in the Night

The answer is no. Then what is the meaning of these passages? Let's begin by reading two Bible passages wherein the phrase "a thief in the night" occurs. In 1 Thessalonians 5:2 Paul says, "For yourselves know perfectly that the day of the Lord so cometh as a thief in the night."

The second reference is found in 2 Peter 3:10-12: "But the day of the Lord will come as a thief in the night; in the which the heavens shall pass away with a great noise, and the elements shall melt with fervent heat, the earth also and the works that are therein shall be burned up. Seeing then that all these things shall be dissolved, what manner of persons ought ye to be in all holy conversation and godliness, Looking for and hasting unto the coming of the day of God, wherein the heavens being on fire shall be dissolved, and the elements shall melt with fervent heat?"

Note that the "day of God" in 2 Peter 3:12 is the same as the "day of the Lord" in verse 10. So, what conclusions can we draw from these verses?

1. The "thief in the night" is in some way connected to the "day of the Lord."
2. During the "day of the Lord . . . the heavens shall pass away with a great noise" and the earth and all that is on it "shall be burned up." Furthermore, "the heavens being on fire shall be dissolved."

But, before we finalize a conclusion, it is necessary to first do a systematic and comprehensive study of all related passages of scripture that mentions "a thief in the night" and "the day of the Lord."

First, let's read Isaiah 28:9 and 10, which establishes this principle. "Whom shall he teach knowledge? and whom shall he make to understand doctrine? them that are weaned from the milk, and drawn from the breasts. For precept must be upon precept, precept upon precept; line upon line, line upon line; here a little, and there a little." (See also Hebrews 5:11-14.)

In order for Christians to seriously engage in Bible study, they need a reliable Bible concordance. The reason I recommend this is because a concordance lists most of the important words of the Bible in an orderly fashion, allowing you to quickly find verses containing words you are looking for. *Strong's Exhaustive Concordance to the Bible*, *Young's Analytical Concordance to the Bible*, or *Cruden's Complete Concordance* are all good. Commentaries, on the other hand, may not be reliable, as they are human interpretations, expressing what the author believes to be the meaning of particular passages. Obviously these may be biased toward one's personal theology or that of his or her church.

In William Miller's book *Views of the Prophecies and Prophetic Chronology*, we have the following guidelines for Bible study, which I believe are helpful:

1. "Every word must have its proper bearing on the subject presented in the Bible."
2. "All Scripture is necessary, and may be understood by diligent application and study . . . to understand doctrine, bring all the Scriptures together on the subject you wish to know, then let every word have its proper influence; and if you can form your theory without a contradiction, you cannot be in error." [This is why a Bible concordance becomes necessary, in order to find these related verses.]
3. "Scripture must be its own expositor, since it is a rule of itself. If I depend on a teacher to expound to me, and he should guess at its meaning, or desire to have it so on account of his sectarian creed, or to be thought wise, then his guessing, desire, creed, or wisdom is my rule, and not the Bible."

This sounds like good advice to me. So again, beware of the commentaries. Following this advice, it makes sense to begin a study with the preceding and following verses that are included within the passage of scripture that you want to fully understand. The reason we should return to the primary passage is because we need to evaluate other words and ideas that are present within the contextual thought of that passage; in other words, we need to do a word study in the passage under question.

Now, let's go back to the two passages about "a thief in the night" that we read earlier. Returning to 2 Peter 3, we notice that verse 8 has an interesting comment. It says, "But, beloved, be not ignorant of this one thing, that one day is with the Lord as a thousand years, and a thousand years as one day." For now, just keep in mind that the "day of the Lord" may represent a period of time, and not one literal day.

Let's go back to 1 Thessalonians 5 and look at some other verses within the context of the "thief in the night" phrase connected with the "day of the Lord." In verses 3 through 8, we read,

"For when they shall say, Peace and safety; then sudden destruction cometh upon them, as travail upon a woman with child, and they shall not escape. But ye, brethren, are not in darkness, that that day should overtake you as a thief. Ye are all the children of light, and the children of the day: we are not of the night, nor of darkness. Therefore let us not sleep, as do others; but let us watch and be sober. For they that sleep sleep in the night; and they that be drunken are drunken in the night. But let us, who are of the day, be sober, putting on the breastplate of faith and love; and for an helmet, the hope of salvation." Then, in verse 9 we read, "For God hath not appointed us to wrath, but to obtain salvation by our Lord Jesus Christ."

At this time we could do word studies on the "day of the Lord," and even on God's "wrath." But, because of my limited space, I will simply present a summary of my research on these events. However, don't rely upon my research. Go and do your own word study.

The "day of the Lord" is mentioned numerous times in the Old Testament, and it refers to a period of time when God intervenes in this world's history to punish the wicked and deliver His people from their enemies. In many of these passages, the "day of the Lord" is also referred to as "in that day" or "in those days." We even find passages in the New Testament, wherein the "day of the Lord" is thus represented. For example, the passage in Luke 17:30 was referencing the "day of the Lord" when Jesus said "when the Son of man is revealed." Then in verse 31, He said, "In that day." I believe this "day" really covers a period of time, and it also begins with the "wrath of God." I will quickly explain how and why the "day of the Lord" begins with the "wrath of God." However, you can easily verify this by consulting your concordance.

What exactly is the "wrath of God"? Turn with me to Revelation 14:19. It says, "And the angel thrust in his sickle into the earth, and gathered the vine of the earth, and cast it into the great winepress of the wrath of God."

Now, skipping down to chapter 15, verse 1, we read, "And I saw another sign in heaven, great and marvellous, seven angels having the seven last plagues; for in them is filled up the wrath of God."

In summary, the "wrath of God" covers a period of time and is equivalent to the seven last plagues. Now, when we go back to 2 Peter 3:10-12 and consider what all is included in this "day of the Lord," I believe it is clear that the time frame includes the 1,000 year millennial judgment, the final destruction of the wicked, and the cleansing of this earth. (See also Revelation 20.)

In the New Testament, the "day of the Lord" is always connected with the *parousia* (Greek word for the "coming" of Jesus back to earth). But, one of the most dangerous deceptions in these last days is the "secret rapture" theory of Jesus' second coming. There is no biblical support for any secret second coming of Jesus. True, there is a "rapture" of sorts connected to the *parousia*, but it won't be in the manner that has been portrayed by the infamous "Left Behind" book and movie series.

So, what exactly is the "rapture"? The word "rapture" is not found anywhere in the Bible, but it has been coined by evangelical Christians for the words "caught up" when pertaining to the saints who they believe will vanish from this earth and meet Jesus in heaven.

Turn with me to 1 Thessalonians 4:16 and 17: "For the Lord himself shall descend from heaven with a shout, with the voice of the archangel, and with the trump of God: and the dead in Christ shall rise first: Then we which are alive and remain shall be caught up [rapture?] together with them in the clouds, to meet the Lord in the air: and so shall we ever be with the Lord."

The "secret rapture" theory is built upon the premise that there will be a seven year period of tribulation, preceded by a "secret rapture" and followed by the remainder of the saints being "caught up" (a visible rapture) at the end of the tribulation. Therefore, the theory really proposes two raptures. The first rapture would be secret, followed seven years later by the visible coming (*parousia*) of Jesus, wherein the remainder of the saints, many of whom are converted during the tribulation, are "caught up" or "raptured."

However, we find absolutely no proof of two "*parousias*" of Jesus' second coming within the Scriptures. If the invisible "rapture" is true, wouldn't the visible coming of Jesus really be His third coming?

At this time, I want to quote a short paragraph from Richard P. Lehmann's treatise on "The Second Coming of Jesus": "The NT characterizes the advent of Christ in various ways. Paul uses the expression 'the day of the Lord' as equivalent to parousia (1 Thess. 4:15; 5:2). Peter uses both terms together when he speaks about 'the parousia of the day of the Lord' (2 Peter 3:12). Thus, parousia becomes an eschatological term linked to the 'day of Yahweh' in the OT."

A Thief in the Night

If Bible students would carefully read 1 Thessalonians 4:16 and 17, along with 1 Corinthians 15:51 and 52, they would recognize that the second coming of Jesus will be a spectacular, noisy event, not a secret one followed seven years later by His visible coming.

The bottom line is this, "Will God rapture the church before the end-time tribulation, and then give a second chance for those left behind to be ready for His visible second coming?" The emphatic answer is no. Remember, wherever there are saints, there is a church. And God has not promised His church an escape clause from "the tribulation," including the fictitious "seven year tribulation" deception.

Yes, there will be a final tribulation, but God's people will be sheltered during this tribulation, which includes the seven last plagues. They will be delivered during the seventh plague when Jesus comes. The book of Revelation reveals that there will be 144,000 (symbolic) saints who will be alive on this earth when Jesus comes. (See Revelation 7 and 14:1-5.) Paul references this event in 1 Thessalonians 4:15, which says, "For this we say unto you by the word of the Lord, that we which are alive and remain unto the coming [*parousia*] of the Lord shall not prevent [precede] them which are asleep."

What is Paul really saying in this verse? In other words, Paul is reassuring the Thessalonians that their loved ones who have died will be resurrected and "caught up" at the same time the living saints are "caught up" to meet Jesus in the heavens. This statement clearly debunks the theory that many living saints will be "caught up" seven years before the resurrection of the righteous dead. Enthusiasts of the "rapture" neglect to include this scenario.

Now, let's go back to the "thief in the night" phrase and clarify what this sudden, unexpected event really is. In simple words, the "thief in the night" event is synonymous with the close of probation for all mankind. I realize a closing of probation is a new concept for evangelical Christians, but nevertheless, it is a biblical truth. *Webster's New World Dictionary* defines "probation" as "a testing or trial, as of a person's character, ability to meet requirements, etc." Throughout the history of man, probation has closed upon select individuals and populations. The "thief in the night" close of probation will be the final closing.

Let us return to Matthew 24 and look at some other verses. This is the same chapter in which Jesus was answering the disciples' questions about His second coming. Beginning with verse 36, we read, "But of that day and hour knoweth no man, no, not the angels of heaven, but my Father only. But as the days of Noah were, so shall also the coming of the Son of man be. For as in the days that were before the flood they were eating and drinking, marrying and giving in marriage, until the day that Noe entered into the ark, And knew not until the flood came, and took them all away; so shall also the coming of the Son of man be."

Now we come to one of the Bible passages that claimants of the secret rapture believe support their theory. Although we have already quoted these verses, I want to repeat them in order to make a significant point. "Then shall two be in the field; the one shall be taken, and the other left. Two woman shall be grinding at the mill; the one shall be taken, and the other left" (verses 40, 41). Then, in verse 42 Jesus says, "Watch therefore: for ye know not what hour your Lord doth come." Following His warning, He gives the analogy of the "thief," which we used at the beginning of this study. (See Matthew 24:43.)

Now, let's clarify what happened in "the days of Noah." There was a closing of probation at that time. Their destinies were "fixed." But exactly when were their destinies "fixed," their fates "sealed," and their probation "closed"? Remember, all the animals had entered the ark, followed by Noah and his family. Then the door of the ark was closed. Then nothing happened for seven days. Yet, those who were "left behind" still perished, beginning seven days after the door of the ark was closed.

The problem with using this passage in support for a secret rapture is that those left outside of the ark, i.e., those "left behind," all perished. There was no second chance. Therefore, their probation ended when the door of the ark closed. Jesus made the same point in Luke 17:37: "And they answered and said unto him, Where, Lord? And he said unto them, Wheresoever the body is, thither will the eagles [i.e. vultures] be gathered together."

So, in the final analysis, there will be a closing of probation for all mankind in the near future. At that time Jesus will have finished His heavenly sanctuary ministry of salvation, and He will declare the words found in Revelation 22:11 and 12: "He that is unjust, let him be unjust still: and he which is filthy, let him be filthy still: and he that is righteous, let him be righteous still: and he that is holy, let him be holy still."

Now, why would Jesus make an announcement like this? Because probation has closed for everyone—their destinies are fixed. As mentioned, Jesus has finished His ministry. Going on, we read, "And, behold, I come quickly; and my reward is with me, to give every man according as his work shall be."

Therefore, since probation has closed, there is no more salvation available for sinners, because Jesus has finished His High Priestly ministry. It is time for God to pour out His wrath in the seven last plagues.

Dear friends, can you see how the closing of probation comes suddenly and unexpectedly, as "a thief in the night"? Any student of the Bible who has contemplated the seventh plague realizes that Jesus' second coming won't be a silent, stealthy event. However, the close of probation will be sudden, silent, and unexpected. Also, can you see why the "day of the Lord" begins with the "wrath of God"? God has already "sealed" His saints upon finishing His ministry. Their destinies are fixed; they will be delivered from their enemies during the glorious second coming of Jesus. Of course, the destinies of the wicked have also become fixed.

Let's examine one of the parables of our Lord in Matthew 13:24-30 and learn about the sequence of the harvest of the world. This harvest includes both the wicked and the righteous. The parable tells the story of when the wicked will be separated from the righteous at the end of the world. In verse 30 we read, "Let both grow together until the harvest: and in the time of harvest I will say to the reapers, Gather ye together first the tares, and bind them in bundles to burn them: but gather the wheat into my barn."

Later, when His disciples asked the meaning of the parable, Jesus gave His answer in verses 37 through 43: "He that soweth the good seed is the Son of man; The field is the world; the good seed are the children of the kingdom; but the tares are the children of the wicked one; The enemy that sowed them is the devil; the harvest is the end of the world; and the reapers are the angels. As therefore the tares are gathered and burned in the fire; so shall it be in the end of this world. The Son of man shall send forth his angels, and they shall gather out of his kingdom all things that offend, and them which do iniquity; And shall cast them into a furnace of fire: there shall be wailing and gnashing of teeth."

In this parable, it is apparent that the wicked are "harvested" before the righteous.

Then, in a companion passage about the harvest, we get a more complete picture of when the harvest of the earth begins. Turn with me to Revelation 14:14-19. I will quickly summarize the information. In verse 15 we notice the words "for the harvest of the earth is ripe." In verse 18 the words are essentially repeated: "for her grapes are fully ripe." Then, in verse 19, which we quoted earlier, we notice that the wicked are punished during "the wrath of God." In summary, the wicked begin their punishment during the seven last plagues. Also, Jesus delivers His people at the culmination of the seventh plague.

When Jesus returns for the symbolic 144,000 church, He will resurrect His sleeping people, and they will be the first to meet Jesus. Then the translated saints will be "caught up" to meet Him in the sky. What a glorious reunion this will be. A grand finale of the "blessed hope."

But what happens to the wicked at the appearance of Jesus? Turn with me to Revelation 19:21 and read a parallel passage about Jesus' second coming: "And the remnant were slain with the sword of him that sat upon the horse." This "remnant" are the wicked survivors of the previous six plagues who are destroyed by the brightness of Jesus' coming.

In conclusion, I realize some advocates of the "secret rapture" will not be convinced, for this end-time scenario may be deeply rooted into their belief system. I haven't included some other verses that are used in defense of the "secret rapture" theory. For example, 1 Thessalonians 3:13 suggests that the "raptured" saints will return to earth with Jesus. (Jude 14 is used in a similar manner.) This is conjecture, as "saints" also include angels. The Greek word translated "saints" is *hagios*, which means "holy ones." Jesus tells us who these "holy ones" are in Matthew 25:31: "When the Son of man shall come in his glory, and all the holy angels with him, then shall he sit upon the throne of his glory." (See also Deuteronomy 33:2 and compare it to Psalm 68:17.)

The "seventieth week" of Daniel 9 has also been misunderstood, leading to a faulty exegesis used in support of the seven year tribulation theory. We will discuss this in a later chapter.

My prayer is that the Holy Spirit will convict us that the true explanation of the "thief in the night" comes suddenly and unexpectedly when our destinies are decided by divine fiat. Then, Jesus pronounces those words that we quoted earlier in Revelation 22:11. Probation has closed, and everybody's destinies are "fixed." Then, God pours out His wrath upon the wicked, which begins the "day of the Lord."

Dear friends, don't fall for Satan's lie about a "secret rapture" for God's church and a "second chance" for those "left behind" to receive salvation. Instead, there will be a silent, sudden, and unexpected closing of probation for everyone before Jesus' second coming. Furthermore, "Judgment must begin at the house of God" as brought out by Peter in 1 Peter 4:17. Peter says, "For the time *is come* that judgment must begin at the house of God." Please notice the words in the KJV Bible. The phrase "is come" is printed in italics and is not included in the Greek text. Thus, Peter is writing about a time in the future, and he continues his thought with these words: "And if it first begin at us, what shall the end be of them that obey not the gospel of God?"

Therefore, the Christian who is pure in heart will be found worthy in the judgment and be protected during the final tribulation. As clarified earlier, God's church will not be exempt from persecution, including the final tribulation, but He has assured us that He will be with us through it. The saints who are sealed will be protected from the plagues. And let us not be among those who are banking upon another chance for salvation after the "secret rapture," which is not going to happen.

May all of us make our calling and election sure by maintaining an abiding, trusting relationship with Jesus, who will be our constant companion until His glorious appearance at His second Advent.

Chapter 4

The Covenants

In this chapter, we will launch into an investigation of the covenants. I do not claim to be an authority on this subject, but that which I have learned from my Bible studies I want to pass on to you. There has been some misunderstanding and controversy about the covenants among Christians. The general idea has been that salvation was earned by God's people in Old Testament times by the "old covenant," while New Testament Christians are saved through the provisions of the "new covenant." This is a clear misunderstanding of the Scriptures. This misconception will be clarified in this study.

In addition, there is a controversy in Christianity about God's law and its place and function within the new covenant. There are many Christians who believe the Ten Commandments are no longer binding since we are now under the provisions of the new covenant. Still others are not so bold to do away with the Decalogue (Ten Commandments), but they see the Sabbath as a relic of the old covenant, which should be frankly discarded. In this study, we will address the covenants and the law. The next chapter will address the subject of the Sabbath; however, much of the groundwork for that will be laid in this study.

Let us begin with a dictionary definition of a covenant. *Webster's Dictionary* defines a covenant as "a binding agreement, or contract, between two or more persons." There is another word used in the Bible that is interchangeable with the word covenant. That word is "testament." The word testament is a Latin derivation of the word covenant. They are interchangeable; therefore, when the King James Version Bible uses testament in a passage, it is not a mistake, and we should understand that it is referring to a covenant. Furthermore,

The Covenants

the use of "Old Testament" and "New Testament" as the divisions of the Bible also signify the old and new covenants. However, this can be a little confusing to us, because the old covenant was not a vehicle for salvation for Old Testament "Christians."

The everlasting covenant has been the only vehicle for salvation in both the old and new dispensations. The everlasting covenant conveys God's purpose—that man be joined to Him in loving service and have eternal fellowship with Him through the redemption that is in Jesus Christ, our wonderful Lord and Savior.

The Bible uses other words that have a direct bearing on the meaning of the covenants. Let us turn in our Bibles to Exodus 34:28: "And he [Moses] was there with the LORD forty days and forty nights; he did neither eat bread, nor drink water. And he [God] wrote upon the tables the words of the covenant, the ten commandments."

In this verse, we are told that the "words of the covenant" are "the ten commandments." In verse 29 we read, "And it came to pass, when Moses came down from mount Sinai with the two tables of testimony in Moses' hand . . ." Stopping here, we can readily see that the "testimony" is equivalent to the "words of the covenant" and the Ten Commandments. Furthermore, the "statutes" and "judgments" are included as an extension of the "words of the covenant."

Let's examine Deuteronomy 4:13 and 14: "And he declared unto you his covenant, which he commanded you to perform, even ten commandments; and he wrote them upon two tables of stone. And the LORD commanded me at that time to teach you statutes and judgments, that ye might do them in the land whither ye go over to possess it."

Therefore, the "ten commandments" and God's "testimony," along with the "statutes and judgments," are really the conditions of the covenants.

Finally, in every covenant there were "promises" made by all the participants. Each party was binding itself to a promise to fulfill certain requirements and render specified services, much like a Last Will and Testament wherein the testator specifies the conditions for the bestowal of the inheritance.

In review, we see that a covenant is an agreement or contract, much like a Last Will and Testament, with promises and conditions. We see that God's covenants did indeed include conditions—His law, His testimony, His Word, and His statutes and judgments. (The latter are safeguards that expand and reinforce the Ten Commandments.) There were also promises, which we shall discuss a little further on.

Now, let's take a closer look at some of these Bible covenants. The first we will consider is God's everlasting covenant with Abraham and his seed. This was a covenant of grace. It is found in Genesis 17: "And when Abram was ninety years old and nine, the LORD appeared to Abram, and said unto him, I am the Almighty God; walk before me, and be thou perfect. And I will make my covenant between me and thee, and will multiply thee exceedingly. And Abram fell on his face: and God talked with him, saying, As for me, behold, my covenant is with thee, and thou shalt be a father of many nations. Neither shall thy name any more be called Abram, but thy name shall be Abraham; for a father of many nations have I made thee. And I will make thee exceeding fruitful, and I will make nations of thee, and kings shall come out of thee. And I will establish my covenant between me and thee and thy seed after thee in their generations for an everlasting covenant, to be a God unto thee, and to thy seed after thee" (verses 1-7).

Most Bible students agree that this covenant was initially introduced in Genesis 3:15: "And I will put enmity between thee and the woman, and between thy seed and her seed; it shall bruise thy head, and thou shalt bruise his heel." This, of course, was pointing to Christ. Jesus is the promised "seed" who would be born into the human family and who would eventually defeat the serpent (Satan). This same "seed" is brought to view in the covenant with Abraham. "Now to Abraham and his seed were the promises made. He saith not, And to seeds, as of many; but as of one, And to thy seed, which is Christ" (Gal. 3:16).

Returning to Genesis 17, we continue with verse 8: "And I will give unto thee, and to thy seed after thee, the land wherein thou art a stranger, all the land of Canaan, for an everlasting possession; and I will be their God."

Here we see that God has made some promises to Abraham. First, a promised land for an everlasting possession. Second, that this covenant would be made with his seed (his posterity, but chiefly Christ). And third, Jehovah would be their God; in other words, His presence would be with them.

We find a confirmation of these promises in Genesis 26. The Lord appeared to Isaac, the promised child of Abraham who was to be the immediate inheritor of the covenant and promises, and said to him, "And I will make thy seed to multiply as the stars of heaven, and will give unto thy seed all these countries; and in thy seed shall all the nations of the earth be blessed; Because that Abraham obeyed my voice, and kept my charge, my commandments, my statutes, and my laws" (verses 4 and 5).

Here we have introduced another dimension of the covenant with Abraham—the condition of obedience. Notice that God made the covenant with Abraham and his seed "because . . . Abraham obeyed my voice, and kept my charge, my commandments, my statutes, and my laws." Abraham walked with God and was called "the Friend of God" (James 2:23). He obviously had the law written in his heart—at the core of his being. Jesus, Abraham's seed, also had the law written in His heart (Ps. 40:8). We will discuss this more, later in this study.

The next covenant we will consider is man's covenant with God, generally referred to as "the old covenant." This, unfortunately, became a "works" oriented covenant ("works of the law," according to Paul) wherein the Jews believed they were saved by the law. The "old covenant" is a misnomer and should be more clearly identified as a covenant of works. There were three different covenants in effect at Mt. Sinai: 1) the everlasting covenant, which was still operative; 2) the old covenant of works made by the people to God; and 3) the Sinai covenant, which included the sanctuary services. The sanctuary services were added to point the Israelites to Jesus.

It is important to note that the Israelites were not being saved by either their works of the law under the old covenant or their performance of services under the Sinai covenant. They were to be saved by the provisions of the everlasting covenant. Therefore, the sanctuary services were temporary, for a temporary covenant. We will study this more later.

Reviewing the points we have discussed, we see that:
- The everlasting covenant was implemented in Eden (Gen. 3:15) and was renewed with Abraham.
- This covenant with Abraham—the everlasting covenant—is the new covenant, after being ratified by Jesus' death.

- Abraham's descendants made an old covenant of works with God at Sinai, which they soon broke.
- God gave the Israelites a sanctuary—its services pointed them to Christ.

Neither the old covenant of works nor even the sanctuary services had any saving virtue in themselves, but everyone who is saved is done so through the provisions of the everlasting covenant, which has always been operative, even at Sinai. The old covenant was even operative at the time of Abraham.

Let us now go to Galatians 4:21: "Tell me, ye that desire to be under the law, do ye not hear the law? For it is written, that Abraham had two sons, the one by a bondmaid, the other by a freewoman." Let us first identify what "law" Paul was referring to in this verse? He must be speaking of the Torah, or Penteteuch—the first five books of the Old Testament. He was not specifically speaking of the Decalogue, because there we find no mention of Abraham and his sons. Going on we read, "Which things are an allegory: for these are the two covenants." Stopping here, we notice in the margin of many KJV Bibles the word "testaments" is placed as a synonym for covenants.

We should also explain what an allegory is. An allegory is a parable or illustration that parallels the subject under discussion. Therefore, this allegory of Abraham and his two sons is illustrating these two covenants. We are all familiar with the story of Abraham and Sarah being promised a son. However, after many years without an heir, Abraham decided to take matters into his own hands. He fathers Ishmael (by Hagar) after the flesh—his own works. Later, Abraham realizes his mistake, and he casts out Hagar and Ishmael. Thus, we see that the principle of the old covenant was applied by Paul to Abraham when he went about to accomplish God's purposes through his own efforts.

The old covenant of works can even be applied to Cain's offering to God. It was the same principle of trusting in man's own ideas, good intentions, and works of the flesh rather than exercising true faith in, and obedience to, God.

Abel, on the other hand, was a partaker of the everlasting covenant. Thus, the old covenant runs contemporaneously with the everlasting covenant down through history. They are conditions of the heart. One is a ministration of death, while the other is a ministration of righteousness. One puts faith in what man can do, the other puts faith in the promises of God and what He can do.

Therefore, when we speak of the covenants, we should be thinking of the heart condition under each covenant, not merely to a time in history. People before the cross were not restricted to the old covenant.

Let us go to Hebrews 8:13. It says, "In that he saith, A new covenant, he hath made the first old. Now that which decayeth and waxeth old is ready to vanish away." Now, going to chapter 9, verse 1, we read, "Then verily the first covenant had also ordinances of divine service, and a worldly sanctuary." The writer of Hebrews combines the old covenant and the Sinai covenant together, referring to them collectively here as the "first covenant."

In his second epistle to the Corinthians, Paul says, "Not that we are sufficient of ourselves to think any thing as of ourselves; but our sufficiency is of God; Who also hath made us able ministers of the new testament [covenant]; not of the letter, but of the spirit: for the letter killeth, but the spirit giveth life. But if the ministration of death, written and engraven in stones, was glorious, so that the children of Israel could not stedfastly behold the face of Moses for the glory of his countenance; which glory was to be done away: How shall not the ministration of the spirit be rather glorious?" (2 Cor. 3:5-8).

What made the old covenant a ministration of death? Were the Ten Commandments really such a negative ministration? Notice that it was that which was "written and engraven in stones." This is the crux of the problem. The promise of the people to keep those commandments were like ropes of sand. As long as they were external, "engraven in stones," the people were destined to failure.

In the nineteenth century periodical *Signs of the Times*, Ellen G. White wrote, "If the transgressor is to be treated according to the letter of this [old] covenant, then there is no hope for the fallen race; for all have sinned, and come short of the glory of God. The fallen race of Adam can behold nothing else in the letter of this covenant than the ministration of death; and death will be the reward of everyone who is seeking vainly to fashion a righteousness of his own that will fulfill the claims of the law" (September 5, 1892).

Now, going back to 2 Corinthians 3, we read, "And not as Moses, which put a veil over his face, that the children of Israel could not stedfastly look to the end of that which is abolished. But their minds were blinded: for until this day remaineth the same veil untaken away in the reading of the old testament [covenant]; which veil is done away in Christ. But even unto this day, when Moses is read, the veil is upon their heart. Nevertheless when it [the heart] shall turn to the Lord, the veil shall be taken away" (verses 13-16).

Now the picture is becoming clearer. As long as the veil is upon the heart, there is no relationship with Christ. Paul is emphasizing that a relationship with Christ is essential, otherwise their "works" only lead to failure and death. The problem was with the heart. Paul covers this in detail in Romans 8: "There is therefore now no condemnation to them which are in Christ Jesus, who walk not after the flesh, but after the Spirit. For the law of the Spirit of life in Christ Jesus hath made me free from the law of sin and death. For what the law could not do, in that it was weak through the flesh, God sending his own Son in the likeness of sinful flesh, and for sin, condemned sin in the flesh: That the righteousness of the law might be fulfilled in us, who walk not after the flesh, but after the Spirit" (verses 1-4).

The only way for the righteousness of the law to be fulfilled in us is to have Christ abiding in us, leading us to walk after the Spirit. The problem is not with the law, but with the "weakness of the flesh," the carnal mind, the unrenewed heart, which can only lead to death. Note Paul's next words: "For to be carnally minded is death; but to be spiritually minded is life and peace. Because the carnal mind is enmity against God: for it is not subject to the law of God, neither indeed can be."

A chapter in the book *Patriarchs and Prophets* titled "The Law and the Covenants" does an excellent job of summarizing what we have presented so far. "The covenant of grace was first made with man in Eden . . . This same covenant was renewed to Abraham in the promise, 'In thy seed shall all the nations of the earth be blessed.' Genesis 22:18. This promise pointed to Christ. So Abraham understood it (see Galatians 3:8, 16), and he trusted in Christ for the forgiveness of sins. It was this faith that was accounted unto him for righteousness. The covenant with Abraham also maintained the authority of God's law. The Lord appeared unto Abraham, and said, 'I am the Almighty God; walk before Me, and be thou perfect.' Genesis 17:1. The testimony of God concerning his faithful servant was, 'Abraham obeyed My voice, and kept My charge, My commandments, My statutes, and My laws.' Genesis 26:5. And the Lord declared to him, 'I will establish My covenant between Me and thee and thy seed after thee in their generations, for an everlasting covenant, to be a God unto thee and to thy seed after thee.' Genesis 17:7.

"Though this covenant was made with Adam and renewed to Abraham, it could not be ratified until the death of Christ. It had existed by the promise of God since the first intimation of redemption had been given; it had been accepted by faith; yet when ratified by Christ, it is called a *new* covenant. The law of God was the basis of this covenant, which was simply an arrangement for bringing men again into harmony with the divine will, placing them where they could obey God's law.

"Another compact—called in Scripture the 'old' covenant—was formed between God and Israel at Sinai, and was then ratified by the blood of a sacrifice. The Abrahamic covenant was ratified by the blood of Christ, and it is called the 'second,' or 'new,' covenant, because the blood by which it was sealed was shed after the blood of the first covenant. That the new covenant was valid in the days of Abraham is evident from the fact that it was then confirmed both by the promise and by the oath of God—the 'two immutable things, in which it was impossible for God to lie.' Hebrews 6:18....

"The people did not realize the sinfulness of their own hearts, and that without Christ it was impossible for them to keep God's law; and they readily entered into covenant with God. Feeling that they were able to establish their own righteousness, they declared, 'All that the Lord hath said will we do, and be obedient.' Exodus 24:7. They had witnessed the proclamation of the law in awful majesty, and had trembled with terror before the mount; and yet only a few weeks passed before they broke their covenant with God, and bowed down to worship a graven image. They could not hope for the favor of God through a covenant which they had broken; and now, seeing their sinfulness and their need of pardon, they were brought to feel their need of the Saviour revealed in the Abrahamic covenant and shadowed forth in the sacrificial offerings. Now by faith and love they were bound to God as their deliverer from the bondage of sin. Now they were prepared to appreciate the blessings of the new covenant.

"The terms of the 'old covenant' were, Obey and live: 'If a man do, he shall even live in them' (Ezekiel 20:11; Leviticus 18:5); but 'cursed be he that confirmeth not all the words of this law to do them.' Deuteronomy 27:26.

The 'new covenant' was established upon 'better promises'—the promise of forgiveness of sins and of the grace of God to renew the heart and bring it into harmony with the principles of God's law" (pp. 370-372).

Thus, God did not abandon His people after they broke their covenant. He sought to lead them to Christ. This He did through the added sanctuary services. The sacrificial system had been in existence ever since the sin of Adam. Now it was formally instituted; however, the system—the services, the ceremonies, and the sacrifices—could never purify the conscience. All the dead animals in the world couldn't atone for sin. Christ, and Christ alone, was the answer. The sinner could believe on Christ and be forgiven and cleansed. Then he expressed his faith in Christ by means of the sanctuary service. Faith manifested itself through the God-ordained ministry of the sanctuary, but the sinner was in reality saved by the provisions of the everlasting covenant. Nobody would be saved under the provisions of the old covenant.

God brought the Israelites to Sinai in order to renew the same covenant He had made with Abraham. Had they received it with a hearty "amen," as did Abraham, the blessings of righteousness in Christ, with forgiveness of sin and obedience to the law, would have been theirs. Instead, they self-confidently proclaimed, "All that the LORD hath spoken we will do" (Ex. 19:8).

A natural question might be, Why would God allow the Israelites to make a covenant of works with Him? The answer is that this was allowed "for a witness against thee" as Moses testified in the "curses." Deuteronomy 31:26 says, "Take this book of the law, and put it in the side of the ark of the covenant of the LORD your God, that it may be there for a witness against thee."

This "book of the law" was the book of Deuteronomy, but it also included the Pentateuch. In other words, the first five books of the Bible, the writings of Moses, constituted the "book of the law." Therefore, the Mosaic writings, as an extension of God's law, were to be a witness against them.

Remember, after the first generation of Israelites died in the wilderness, Moses gathered their children together in the land of Moab, and before going into the land of Canaan, another "covenant" was implemented with them. Deuteronomy 29:1 says, "These are the words of the covenant, which the LORD commanded Moses to make with the children of Israel in the land of Moab, beside the covenant which he made with them in Horeb [Sinai]."

Apparently, God revealed to Moses that this "covenant" would be broken. Deuteronomy 31:29 says, "For I know that after my death ye will utterly corrupt yourselves, and turn aside from the way which I have commanded you; and evil will befall you in the latter days; because ye will do evil in the sight of the LORD, to provoke him to anger through the work of your hands."

Now, let's go back to the everlasting covenant as illustrated in God's covenant with Abraham. Recall that in Genesis 17:7 and 8, God promised to establish His covenant with Abraham and his seed. One of the promises under this covenant was the everlasting possession of the land of Canaan. Abraham did not receive this promise, nor have his descendants—at least not yet. In Hebrews 11:8-13 we read, "By faith Abraham, when he was called to go out into a place which he should after receive for an inheritance, obeyed; and he went out, not knowing whither he went. By faith he sojourned in the land of promise, as in a strange country, dwelling in tabernacles with Isaac and Jacob, the heirs with him of the same promise: For he looked for a city which hath foundations, whose builder and maker is God. . . . These all died in faith, not having received the promises."

So, when do God's people receive the inheritance as promised in the everlasting covenant? Let's include two more passages of scripture and shed more light on this. In Genesis 22, right after Abraham was about to offer Isaac as a sacrifice, verse 17 says, "That in blessing I will bless thee, and in multiplying I will multiply thy seed as the stars of the heaven, and as the sand which is upon the sea shore; and thy seed shall possess the gate of his enemies."

As we discovered earlier from Galatians 3:16, Jesus is the seed who shall possess the gates of His enemies. "Now to Abraham and his seed were the promises made. He saith not, And to seeds, as of many; but as of one, And to thy seed, which is Christ." When does Jesus " possess the gate of his enemies"? That takes place at His second coming when He returns as "KING OF KINGS AND LORD OF LORDS" (Rev. 19:16). Therefore, none of God's people will receive their inheritance until Jesus comes again. It is then that the kingdom is given to the saints (Dan. 7:27).

However, the other provisions of the everlasting covenant have been available since the Garden of Eden, and these promises were confirmed when Jesus ratified the new covenant by His blood. These other promises include forgiveness of our sins and justification and sanctification by Jesus' presence in us and His law in our hearts.

Returning to the book of Galatians, we find this comment in chapter 3, verse 15: "Brethren, I speak after the manner of men; Though it be but a man's covenant [or testament], yet if it be confirmed, no man disannulleth, or addeth thereto." Therefore, God's new covenant, which confirmed the everlasting covenant, cannot be changed in any way after Christ's death.

Now, let us include Hebrews 9:16 and 17, which makes this point more clearly. "For where a testament [or covenant] is, there must also of necessity be the death of the testator. For a testament is of force after men are dead: otherwise it is of no strength at all while the testator liveth."

So, we must conclude that the testament, or covenant, becomes confirmed at the time of the testator's death, and it cannot be changed in any way thereafter. Any changes in God's moral law would have to be made prior to Christ's death. Of course, since God's law is eternal, we should not expect to find any changes. Only the ceremonial law, that which prefigured Christ, could possibly be changed or passed away.

In Jeremiah 31:31-33 we read, "Behold, the days come, saith the LORD, that I will make a new covenant with the house of Israel, and with the house of Judah: Not according to the covenant that I made with their fathers in the day that I took them by the hand to bring them out of the land of Egypt; which my covenant they brake, although I was an husband unto them, saith the LORD: But this shall be the covenant that I will make with the house of Israel; After those days, saith the LORD, I will put my law in their inward parts, and write it in their hearts; and will be their God, and they shall be my people."

Jeremiah 32:40 says, "And I will make an everlasting covenant with them." Notice that Jeremiah uses the "everlasting covenant" as interchangeable with the "new covenant." The writer of Hebrews confirms that this promise is fulfilled in Jesus by quoting Jeremiah 31:33: "This is the covenant that I will make with them after those days, saith the Lord, I will put my laws into their hearts, and in their minds will I write them; And their sins and iniquities will I remember no more" (Heb. 10:16, 17).

Now, let us see what Ezekiel says about this same covenant in Ezekiel 36:23: "And I will sanctify my great name, which was profaned among the heathen, which ye have profaned in the midst of them; and the heathen shall know that I am the LORD, saith the Lord GOD, when I shall be sanctified in you before their eyes."

Dropping down to verses 26 through 28, we read, "A new heart also will I give you, and a new spirit will I put within you: and I will take away the stony heart out of your flesh, and I will give you an heart of flesh. And I will put my spirit within you, and cause you to walk in my statutes, and ye shall keep my judgments, and do them. And ye shall dwell in the land that I gave to your fathers; and ye shall be my people, and I will be your God."

Ezekiel has basically repeated the same promises of the everlasting covenant that were proclaimed earlier by Jeremiah. In conclusion, Christ had the law written in His heart (Ps. 40:8), and by His presence in our hearts, He has promised to write the law in us. The law is a transcript of His character. It encompasses all of God's revealed will, as found in "precepts," "statutes," and "judgments," and when we, as God's people, have internalized His law in our hearts, that law will be a transcript of our characters as well. When God's people have these two prerequisites—Christ's presence and the law in their heart—then Jesus can return to claim His own. May we all reflect Jesus, here and now, so He can come soon to take us home to our inheritance.

Bible Texts for the Covenants

Genesis 3:15	the first promise = rudimentary covenant
Genesis 17:7, 8	the everlasting covenant given to Abraham; land is promised as an inheritance in the everlasting covenant
Genesis 22:17	"thy seed [Jesus] shall possess the gate of his enemies"
Exodus 19:6 and 24:7	the old covenant of works
Exodus 34:28, 29	covenant = Ten Commandments = testimony
Deuteronomy 4:13, 14	statutes/judgments added to the covenant

Deuteronomy 29:1	another covenant in Moab which becomes a covenant of works
Deuteronomy 31:26	covenant conditions are a witness against them
Deuteronomy 31:29	Israelites predicted to break the covenant
Psalm 40:8	the law was written in Jesus' heart
Jeremiah 23:6	THE LORD OUR RIGHTEOUSNESS
Jeremiah 31:31-33, 32:40	the everlasting covenant
Ezekiel 36:23-28	the everlasting covenant
Romans 8:1-7	the carnal mind cannot keep the law, but Christ fulfills it in us
2 Corinthians 3:13-16	old and new covenants equal matters of the heart (the Sinai covenant becomes old)
Galatians 3:15	a confirmed covenant cannot be changed
Galatians 3:16	Paul explains the seed is Christ
Galatians 4:21-24	the old covenant illustration
Hebrews 8:13	the "first" (Sinai covenant) is replaced by the new covenant
Hebrews 9:1	the Sinai covenant had an earthly sanctuary service that was temporary
Hebrews 9:16, 17	a covenant (Last Will and Testament) is confirmed by the testator's death
Hebrews 10:16, 17	confirms Jeremiah's prophecy
Hebrews 11:8-13	Abraham and his descendants have not received the promised inheritance

Chapter 5

Jesus and His Sabbath

Many Christians don't realize that the Sabbath is intimately connected to the new covenant. These Christians recognize that salvation comes from having a covenant relationship with Jesus. They also realize their salvation involves the new covenant, but they don't know that the Sabbath is a necessary part of this covenant. In this study I want to show how the Sabbath is connected to the new covenant and why.

First, we need to define what a covenant is. A covenant is a binding agreement between two or more people. These covenants have conditions (rules and regulations) and promises made by all of the persons involved. There are several important covenants that have been made between God and His people. At this time, we will focus primarily on the Sabbath and its connection to the new covenant.

God has provided three main promises for His people in the new covenant. These promises include:
1. Our inheritance of a Promised Land
2. God's law written in our hearts, which includes the Sabbath, the fourth commandment of His law
3. Jesus living in our hearts, who imparts to us His holiness, i.e., sanctification

We see that God's law written in our hearts and Jesus living within us are two of the three promises of the new covenant.

There are two important truths we need to establish at the beginning of this study:

1. The Sabbath is God's "appointed time" to help us become holy. In other words, Jesus designed the Sabbath as a spiritual tool to help us become holy through the power of His Word and the Holy Spirit. Later in this study we will establish why we need the Sabbath to help us become holy by connecting the Sabbath to the new covenant and sanctification.
2. In order for us to keep the Sabbath holy, we need to be "wholly" sanctified. Only a wholly sanctified person can keep the Sabbath holy.

It works both ways—we need Jesus' holiness in order to keep the Sabbath holy, and we need the Sabbath to help us be holy. So, in summary, Jesus has "appointed" the Sabbath hours to help us become holy as we experience His presence within us during holy time. I suspect we have not yet internalized these important truths, but let us consider the promise that Jesus will "wholly" sanctify us if we allow Him. Turning to 1 Thessalonians 5:23 and 24, Paul writes, "And the very God of peace sanctify you wholly; and *I pray God* your whole spirit and soul and body be preserved blameless unto the coming of our Lord Jesus Christ. Faithful is he that calleth you, who also will do it."

Paul was telling not only the Thessalonians, but us as well, that God will do this for us if we allow it. While this would not be feasible by ourselves, it is not an impossibility with God.

Now, think back with me to the first week of Creation. Remember, the days were from evening to evening, not midnight to midnight. God created Adam and Eve near the end of the sixth day. They spent their very first evening, the Sabbath, in holy communion with their Maker. (Maybe we should rethink our understanding of the Sabbath as the beginning of the weekly cycle. Think about this as we continue our Bible study.)

Let's look at the importance of the Sabbath and how it relates to our walk with Jesus, i.e. our sanctification. Then I will discuss the significance of the Sabbath as it symbolizes important milestones in salvation's history. This secondary emphasis will make more sense as we continue. After this, I want to emphasize the Sabbath in its role of celebrating the finished works of Christ. In the near future, I believe the Sabbath will also be the final test that polarizes the world into one of two groups. In one group will be those who remain loyal to God during the final crisis, as opposed to the second group of people who will refuse, or neglect, the benefits of sanctification.

Many of us don't fully recognize the blessings we would receive from a 24-hour spiritual rest on the Sabbath day. Most Christians attend religious services for a few hours on Sunday. Then, following those services, they resume their secular activities for the remainder of what they believe to be "the Lord's day." Nevertheless, if Christians disregard God's purposes regarding His Sabbath, then they will lose these special blessings that He intends for them on this day.

As most of us know, the word "Sabbath" means rest. However, its deeper meaning includes a spiritual rest—a relationship with Jesus, i.e., our sanctification. Furthermore, the Sabbath and Jesus' presence are intimately connected. Let's reconsider Matthew 11:28. Jesus says, "Come unto me, all ye that labour and are heavy laden, and I will give you rest."

Yes, we can come to Jesus every day of the week, but in the language of our young people, the Sabbath is a weekly, prearranged "date" with Jesus. On this special day alone, we enter a "sanctuary of time" with Jesus. Let me repeat this thought. The Sabbath is a "sanctuary of time," and this "sanctuary time" is holy time.

Did you know that during the Sabbath hours we can receive a double blessing, no matter where we are? How is this so? Because, when we are sanctified, we have the number one blessing of Jesus' presence in us. The second blessing comes from having this presence of Jesus in us *during holy time*. Thus, we receive a double blessing as we experience Jesus' presence within us during holy time. Therefore, all of the blessings from the Sabbath come to us from having Jesus' presence within us during holy time.

Abraham Heschel, a prominent Jew who has passed away, once said, "Even when men forsake the Sabbath, its holiness remains." Sadly, many Christians are unaware of this truth that the Sabbath is holy, i.e., sacred.

Let's turn in our Bibles to Genesis 2:3: "And God blessed the seventh day, and sanctified it [i.e., God made it holy]: because that in it he had rested from all his work which God created and made."

Let's contemplate more on the thought that the Sabbath is a "sanctuary of time." A sanctuary is generally a place where we go to worship God. Likewise, the Sabbath is also a sanctuary. But instead of a designated place, the Sabbath hours are appointed to us as "sanctuary time." And this "sanctuary time" is holy time. Furthermore, there is yet another blessing for us, within the Sabbath hours. During these Sabbaths on earth, we can receive a weekly foretaste of our future restoration in heaven. I want to comment on this thought. Heaven is a place of holiness. But, where on earth can we find this holiness with Jesus? We find it in a sanctuary. During the week, we tend to mix together sacred and secular matters. During the Sabbath hours, we can exclude all the mundane affairs of this earth and be in a sanctuary with Jesus.

Furthermore, this spiritual rest and worship on the Sabbath will continue throughout eternity. Notice what Isaiah 66:23 says: "And it shall come to pass, that from one new moon to another, and from one sabbath to another, shall all flesh come to worship before me, saith the LORD."

Now, I want to include further significance of the seventh-day Sabbath. This next consideration will be a secondary emphasis in this study. It is this: the Sabbath memorializes the most important events in the history of mankind. Let me explain. Today, we set up memorials to commemorate important events. For example, we celebrate July 4 every year to commemorate our independence on July 4, 1776. So, likewise, Jesus established the Sabbath as a memorial of Creation. However, since Creation, the Sabbath has continued to undergo expanding significance. For example, after Adam's sin, mankind needed re-creation, in other words, sanctification.

Dear reader, I hope you are seeing the pattern. The idea of an expanded meaning, or significance, of the Sabbath isn't something new or unheard of. After the Israelites wandered for forty years in the wilderness, Moses repeated the Ten Commandments. How many of us have noticed the difference in the fourth commandment as recorded in Deuteronomy 5 with that in Exodus 20? Let's go to Deuteronomy 5:15, where Moses gives another reason for Sabbath observance. This reason is quite different from the fourth commandment as recorded in Exodus 20:8-11. Deuteronomy 5:15 says, "And remember that thou wast a servant in the land of Egypt, and that the LORD thy God brought thee out thence through a mighty hand and by a stretched out arm: therefore the LORD thy God commanded thee to keep the sabbath day."

Hence, the Sabbath had expanded in its significance from a memorial of Creation and re-creation to a sign of deliverance from bondage. The next milestone of salvation history becomes apparent as we contemplate the parallel of deliverance from physical bondage with that from spiritual bondage. Since Jesus' death on the cross, the Sabbath now symbolizes our redemption. Furthermore, Calvary represents the ultimate Sabbath significance. On that fateful Friday, Jesus finished His work of redemption. After His death, Jesus commemorated our redemption by resting in the grave during the hours of the Sabbath. Thus, the Sabbath now memorializes the finished work of Christ, which was our redemption and deliverance from the bondage of sin.

At this point it is necessary for us to examine a number of reasons Christians offer to excuse themselves from observing the Sabbath rest.

1. The Sabbath was a relic of the "old covenant" of the Jews and was done away with when Jesus died on the cross. Today, new covenant Christians observe Sunday as the "Lord's day" in commemoration of His resurrection.
2. All Christians who have been "saved" can "rest" every day in the Lord's work, which is being performed in them. This claim overlooks our personal accountability to God's command in the fourth commandment to keep the Sabbath day holy (Ex. 20:8-11).
3. It doesn't matter which day we keep as long as we keep one day every week for worship services.

Now let's answer the first objection, that the Sabbath was an institution for the Jews and belongs to the old covenant. As previously mentioned, the Sabbath was established at the end of creation week and, therefore, existed about 2,000 years before any Jew was ever born. By the way, the Sabbath is the "Lord's day," and not Sunday, as most Christians believe. Notice what Isaiah says in chapter 58, verses 13 and 14: "If thou turn away thy foot from the sabbath, from doing thy pleasure on my holy day; and call the sabbath a delight, the holy of the LORD, honourable; and shalt honour him, not doing thine own ways, nor finding thine own pleasure, not speaking thine own words: Then shalt thou delight thyself in the LORD."

Isaiah was speaking for the Lord; therefore, I believe the words "my holy day" provide conclusive evidence that the Sabbath is the "Lord's day." Further evidence is found in the New Testament in Mark 2:27 and 28. These verses say, "The sabbath was made for man, and not man for the sabbath: Therefore the Son of man is Lord also of the sabbath." Thus Jesus, as "Lord of the Sabbath," established the Sabbath as His holy day. He established it for our benefit at the end of creation week.

There is a book by J.N. Andrews titled *History of the Sabbath* from which, on page 515, I quote: "The importance of the Sabbath as a memorial of creation is that it keeps ever present the true reason why worship is due to God; for the worship of God is based upon the fact that he is the Creator, and that all other beings were created by him. The Sabbath, therefore, lies at the very foundation of divine worship, for it teaches this great truth in the most impressive manner, and no other institution does this . . . This great fact can never become obsolete, and must never be forgotten. To keep it in man's mind, God gave to him the Sabbath."

The objection that the Sabbath is associated with the old covenant is generally due to a misunderstanding about the nature of the old and new covenants. The fact is that all of the Ten Commandments, and especially the Sabbath, are the rules, regulations, and promises of both the old and the new covenants. We will discuss this further at a later point.

Now, let's answer the second objection to keeping the Sabbath holy: All Christians who have been saved can rest every day in the Lord's work, which is being performed in them. This assumption sounds really wonderful. So, they presume that Jesus has fulfilled the Sabbath rest for the benefit of all Christians, and therefore, they don't need to "work" at all toward their own sanctification.

Let's answer this assumption from 1 Thessalonians 4:3-7. "For this is the will of God, even your sanctification, that ye should abstain from fornication" (verse 3). Breaking into this thought, it is obviously God's will for Christians to be sanctified. Then, in verses 4 through 7, Paul tells us that we need to know "how to" live a life of sanctification. Verse 4 says, "That every one of you should know how to possess his vessel in sanctification and honour."

This "vessel" must refer to our minds and bodies. Since Paul said "you should know how to" in this verse, it is evident that we do have a function that pertains to our sanctification. Then, in verse 7 we read, "For God hath not called us unto uncleanness, but unto holiness." In other words, sanctification.

There are several verses that confirm that we have an obligation in the work of sanctification. In 2 Corinthians 7:1 we read, "Having therefore these promises, dearly beloved, let us cleanse ourselves from all filthiness of the flesh and spirit, perfecting holiness in the fear of God." The words "let us cleanse ourselves" point clearly to our cooperation in the work of sanctification.

Let us look at a couple of Old Testament passages which confirm that we have a part to perform in our sanctification. Leviticus 11:44 and 45 says, "For I am the LORD your God: ye shall therefore sanctify yourselves, and ye shall be holy; for I am holy . . . For I am the LORD that bringeth you up out of the land of Egypt, to be your God: ye shall therefore be holy, for I am holy."

While these verses may sound like we can sanctify ourselves, they do not give the complete picture as we see in Leviticus 20:7 and 8. There it says, "Sanctify yourselves therefore, and be ye holy: for I am the LORD your God. And ye shall keep my statutes, and do them: I am the LORD which sanctify you."

Therefore, our sanctification becomes a mutual endeavor as we partner together with God. These verses should suffice to put to rest the idea that Jesus has done "everything" for our sanctification. We must cooperate with Jesus and do our part. Our "work" is to allow Christ's presence and power in us, in order to continue our sanctification. Furthermore, it is God's will for us to be obedient to His laws. This must include the seventh-day Sabbath, since the fourth commandment is at the heart of God's Ten Commandments.

Let us now answer the third objection: It doesn't matter which day we keep, as long as we keep one day every week for worship services. At the same time, some may be asking the question, "Brother Alavezos, where is the biblical proof that the Sabbath is a sign (i.e., a memorial) of Creation, sanctification, and redemption?" To answer these issues, let's go to Exodus 31:13, where we read, "Speak thou also unto the children of Israel, saying, Verily my sabbaths ye shall keep: for it is a sign between me and you throughout your generations; that ye may know that I am the LORD that doth sanctify you."

In this verse we see the proof that the Sabbath is a sign of our sanctification. Ezekiel 20:12 and 20 are two more proof texts for this truth. "Moreover also I gave them my sabbaths, to be a sign between me and them, that they might know that I am the LORD that sanctify them. . . . And hallow my sabbaths; and they shall be a sign between me and you, that ye may know that I am the LORD your God."

Returning to Exodus 31:17, we read, "It [the Sabbath] is a sign between me and the children of Israel for ever; for in six days the LORD made heaven and earth, and on the seventh day he rested, and was refreshed."

The philosophy that it does not matter what day we keep is faulty for one obvious reason—it discards the memorial. For example, if a couple's marriage occurred on a certain date, would our wives appreciate it if we changed the anniversary celebration to a different day? I don't think so. The same logic applies to the Sabbath, which is a memorial of Creation—and also sanctification and redemption. God specified in the beginning that the Sabbath should be commemorated on the seventh day of every week.

In the last chapter, we discovered that everlasting covenant and new covenant are interchangeable terms. To Abraham and his seed was also given the everlasting covenant (Gen. 17:7). Galatians 3:29 says, "If ye be Christ's, then are ye Abraham's seed, and heirs according to the promise." Since the new covenant became ratified by Christ's death, then the Sabbath must truly memorialize our redemption. Therefore, the Sabbath is the memorial of the new covenant—*not* Sunday. I will give more proof that the Sabbath is the memorial of the new covenant further on. These are some of the biblical proofs that the Sabbath memorializes our redemption as well as Creation and our sanctification, but there is even more proof forthcoming.

In the book *The Desire of Ages*, we find this interesting observation: "To all who receive the Sabbath as a sign [a memorial] of Christ's creative and redeeming power, it will be a delight. Seeing Christ in it, they delight themselves in Him. The Sabbath points them to the works of creation as an evidence of His mighty power in redemption" (p. 289).

Again, the Sabbath has expanded to symbolize all of these milestones of salvation history. Bear in mind that although we have been redeemed we're not yet in the Promised Land. So, the Sabbath gives us spiritual rest, here and now. And it also gives us a foretaste of heaven when we will be completely restored to worship God "from one sabbath to another" (Isa. 66:23).

At this point, I want to include more about this "rest" that we have in Jesus on the Sabbath. Turn with me to Hebrews 4, where Paul continues on the theme of the "rest" that "remaineth to the people of God." Reading verses 6, 8, and 9, Paul wrote, "Seeing therefore it remaineth that some must enter therein, and they to whom it was first preached entered not in because of unbelief.... For if Jesus [Joshua in the margin] had given them rest, then would he not afterward have spoken of another day. There remaineth therefore a rest to the people of God."

A literal translation of Hebrews 4:9 says, "So then a Sabbath-keeping has been left behind for the people of God." ("Remaineth" literally means "has been left behind.") Also, Paul is using the Greek word "Sabbatismos" for "rest" in this verse. "Sabbatismos" is a unique, newly coined word that is not found anywhere else in Scripture. Then, in verses 10 and 11, Paul continues his thought, but he uses a different Greek word for "rest" for the remainder of these verses. This is significant. The point is that the seventh-day Sabbath is the Sabbath-keeping that has been left behind as the "rest" that we have in Jesus, not some substitute Sabbath or vague reference to any day that can be useful for worship services. Could Paul be endorsing a new kind of "rest" that has been instituted for new covenant Christians? Absolutely not! When something has been *left behind*, then it must have been a present reality for the people of God previously. Therefore, the early Christians and the Jews continued to worship their Creator on the seventh-day Sabbath as the Jews did previously.

Now, we need to re-emphasize a truth that was mentioned at the beginning of this chapter. The Sabbath celebrates all the finished works of Christ. We see this in the following:

1. When Jesus finished Creation, He established the Sabbath to celebrate it.
2. When Jesus finishes re-creation (i.e., sanctification for all of His creation), the Sabbath will celebrate it when we become restored to our inheritance, in the final fulfillment of the new covenant.
3. Since Calvary represents the pinnacle of Sabbath significance, the Sabbath now symbolizes our redemption, as we clarified earlier.

Should we throw out the Sabbath symbol for the substance of Christ's presence and redemption? No, of course not. God's purposes do not change. Each Sabbath, now and throughout eternity, we are reminded of the price of our redemption. Also, Jesus did not abolish His Sabbath. We can search the Scriptures from Genesis through Revelation, and nowhere can we find any mention of the Sabbath being abolished or exchanged for another day.

Jesus Himself kept the Sabbath day holy. However, He didn't keep it "holy" in the same manner as did the legalistic Jews. Furthermore, Jesus instructed His disciples in Matthew 24:20 to "pray ye that your flight be not in the winter, neither on the sabbath day." Wouldn't this be inappropriate advice if Jesus intended to abolish the Sabbath or exchange it for another day?

For centuries the Catholic Church has promoted the idea that weekly Sunday observance commemorates the resurrection of Christ, but Scripture clearly uses baptism to symbolize Christ's death and resurrection. The idea of a weekly commemoration of the resurrection evolved later in support for Sunday observance. Sunday keeping has no correlation at all with the work of sanctification in us. Furthermore, Sunday keeping cannot symbolize the "rest" of redemption that has been made available to us through Jesus' death on the cross and His presence within us. Remember, the Sabbath is the true symbol of our redemption.

Pope John Paul II claimed that Sunday is the "extension and full expression" of the Old Testament Sabbath. Granted, some may perceive this as a brilliant idea, but Sunday can never function for the same purposes as the Sabbath. They are two different days, with two different meanings and significance. As mentioned earlier, the Sabbath primarily symbolizes spiritual rest. The Sabbath is a holy day. Sunday is more like a man-made holiday. It can never be an "extension and full expression" of the Sabbath.

Truly, the seventh-day Sabbath was left behind for the people of God (Heb. 4:9). The bottom line is this: Sunday can never replace the Sabbath. Let us look at additional evidence for this conclusion. This will also fulfill my promise to give more information on the covenants.

Let us turn to Galatians 3:15. "Brethren, I speak after the manner of men; Though it be but a man's covenant, yet if it be confirmed, no man disannulleth, or addeth thereto."

A Last Will and Testament becomes confirmed at a person's death. Therefore, Jesus' new covenant was confirmed at His death and no man can set it aside or add anything to it. Bear in mind that "testament" is the Latin word for covenant, and they are interchangeable. The Greek word *diatheke* is translated both ways in the New Testament.

Hebrews 9:16 and 17 confirm the same as the above text: "For where a testament [*diatheke* = covenant] is, there must also of necessity be the death of the testator. For a testament is of force after men are dead."

Therefore, a natural conclusion would be a "testament," which includes God's covenant with man, was "confirmed" (ratified) at the time of Christ's death, and hence it cannot be changed in any particular thereafter. So again, what is the "sign" or "memorial" of the new covenant? The seventh-day Sabbath.

As we are nearing the conclusion of this study, I want to include an important function of the Sabbath. The Sabbath has always served as a sign of man's allegiance and loyalty to God. Very soon, however, the Sabbath will be God's test of loyalty for the whole world.

After the passage of Sunday laws, the Sabbath will be the catalyst that polarizes everyone into one of two groups. In one group will be those who obey God's command to keep the Sabbath day holy. This group of people will be experiencing Jesus' presence and power in their lives. The other group will be comprised of those who accept the false day of worship. Let us not be found in this latter group. Many of these people will accept the false day of worship because of terrible circumstances in the final conflict.

The good news is that there is hope for everyone who understands more fully *how* the Sabbath can help prepare us, through sanctification, for Jesus' second coming. Today, may we be living witnesses of the power of Christ, which lifts us above the storms of life. When the time comes for the outpouring of the Holy Spirit, may we be ready to proclaim the Sabbath more fully.

In conclusion, I want to briefly list the blessings we can receive from the spiritual rest of the Sabbath. In general, we receive a double blessing:

- When we are in Christ. In other words, when converted, we receive the blessing of sanctification, which is Christ living in us.
- When we enter into His "sanctuary of time." Jesus has already bestowed a blessing upon the Sabbath day itself. During this "sanctuary of time" we receive spiritual rest. The Sabbath is the time when we recharge our spiritual batteries. The Sabbath prepares us for the fulfillment of the new covenant promise to have God's law written in our hearts and Jesus' presence within us. There is no greater joy for

Christians than having the presence of Jesus within us, especially as we enter into His "sanctuary of time."

There is yet another blessing within the Sabbath day experience. The Sabbath is a weekly foretaste of our future restoration. When we enter into that heavenly rest, we shall see Him face to face.

My sincere desire is for a closer walk with Jesus. I want to invite you, dear reader, to share with me this same desire. We need to appropriate more fully the blessings of the Sabbath during the "sanctuary of time" that we spend with Jesus. And, with His presence within us, we can share Him with others. It is only when we experience Jesus within that we can proclaim the Sabbath more fully in a way that will disarm prejudice and draw others to the truth.

Chapter 6

Modern Bible Versions

How many of us have ever used a parallel Bible? I did, and guess what I discovered? There were many verses saying different things from the two versions. The purpose of this Bible study will be to reveal some facts that are little known by Christians. These facts concern the origin and true nature of the modern Bibles that we have today. Although I am not an authority, I have re- searched the writings of notable scholars of Hebrew and Greek languages who had access to the ancient manuscripts. These scholars discovered the facts, which I want to share with you. So, please keep an open mind as I share with you these findings.

Basically, we have two groups of English Bibles being used by Christians. In one group, there are more than 5,200 ancient witnesses found in manuscripts, portions of manuscripts, cursives, and lectionaries that support what is called the received text. The received text was the foundation from which our King James Version Bible was translated.

The second group is supported by a much smaller number of ancient witnesses. They include less than 1 percent of the total Greek sources, yet are the foundation for nearly all of the modern Bibles in use today. However, only three of these were primarily used to translate the first New Testament Revised Version of 1881. These manuscripts were the codices Vaticanus, Sinaiticus, and Alexandrian.

Little is known about these manuscripts, except some Christians recognize that they came from Alexandria, Egypt. One was found in the pope's library, and another was discovered in a wastebasket at St. Catherine's convent near Mt. Sinai.

A Primer on Salvation and Bible Prophecy

How many of us suppose that Satan wouldn't dare tamper with God's Word? Would Satan do such a thing? Would he influence his agents to change some of God's words? The answer should be obvious. We all recognize that Satan misrepresented God's words when he tempted Eve to eat of the forbidden fruit. In other words, he deceived her. In this study, I am going to show you some deceptions that have slipped into our modern Bibles.

Webster's New World Dictionary and Thesaurus gives us some synonyms for "deception." These include the words "trickery, double-dealing, craftiness, disinformation and duplicity."

There are several questions we should seek to answer about these modern versions. For example, what do we really know about the translators of the first Revised Version of the English Bible. It may come as a surprise to find that one was a Unitarian who denied the divinity of Jesus. Another was an open lesbian. Did you know that Bishop Hort, one of the two leaders of the revision, referred to the King James Version Bible as "vile"? He actually put this in print. Hort and Bishop Westcott, the other leader of the revision, were pro-Roman Catholic. In other words, they were "closet" Catholics, both having come out of the Oxford Movement. These two clergymen were trying to bring the Church of England back to Rome.

Wescott and Hort were also spiritualists. They founded the "ghostly guild" for the study of paranormal experiences. Both of them denied the literal stories of Genesis chapters 1 through 3. Furthermore, these two men had an agenda, and they succeeded. They were determined to get rid of the authorized version (KJV) and establish a new revision of the Bible. (See "Sequel to Modern Bible Versions" - Appendix F)

All of the revisers were instructed to "correct" what they perceived to be errors in the KJV Bible, but they were told to use the "received text," which was the basic text for the KJV Bible. However, they disregarded this advice. With the insistence of Wescott and Hort, they mainly used two ancient Greek manuscripts, which had already been discarded by the churches of the east. Namely, they used the codices Vaticanus and Sinaiticus as the basis for their biblical text.

What do we know about these two ancient manuscripts? As mentioned previously, they originated from Alexandria, Egypt, but very few Christians today realize that they were altered by Origen and other heretics in the early centuries. Through the providence of God, the eastern churches continued to use the Greek Byzantine text, which later became known as the received text.

Bible scholar John W. Burgon, dean of Chichester University, made an interesting comment that I want to share with you. He said, "Who but those with Roman Catholic sympathies could ever be pleased with the notion that God preserved the true New Testament text in secret for almost one thousand years and then finally handed it over to the Roman pontiff for safe-keeping? Surely every orthodox Protestant will prefer to think with Burgon that God preserved the true text of the Greek New Testament in the usage of the Greek-speaking Church down through the centuries and then at length delivered it up intact to the Protestant reformers."

Burgon also tells us some little known facts about these two ancient manuscripts. He said, "The impurity of the text exhibited by these codices is not a question of opinion, but fact . . . In the Gospels alone, Codex B (i.e. Vaticanus) leaves out words or whole clauses no less than 1,491 times. It bears traces of careless transcriptions on every page. Codex Sinaiticus abounds with errors of the eye and pen to an extent not indeed unparalleled, happily rather unusual in documents of first-rate importance. On many occasions 10, 20, 30, 40 words are dropped through very carelessness. Letters and words, even whole sentences, are frequently written twice over, or begun and immediately cancelled; while that gross blunder whereby a clause is omitted because it happens to end in the same words as the clause preceding, occurs no less than 115 times in the New Testament."

This sounds unbelievable, doesn't it? But, Dr. Frederick H.A. Scrivener, the most learned scholar of the revision committee, wrote *A Full Collation of the Codex Sinaiticus*. In his introduction he said, "The Codex is covered with such alterations brought in by at least ten different revisers, some of them systematically spread over every page, others occasional or limited to separate portions of the manuscript, many of them being contemporaneous with the first writer, far the greater part belonging to the sixth or seventh century."

Scrivener also comments on Codex B (Vaticanus). He said, "One marked feature characteristic of this copy, is the great number of its omissions, which has induced Dr. Dobbin to speak of it as presenting an abbreviated text of the

New Testament: and certainly the facts he states on this point are startling enough. He calculates that Codex B leaves out words or clauses no less than 330 times in Matthew, 365 in Mark, 439 in Luke, 357 in John, 384 in the Acts, 681 in the surviving Epistles; or 2,556 times in all. That no small proportion of those are mere oversights of the scribe seems evident from the circumstance that this same scribe has repeatedly written words and clauses twice over."

Herman C. Hoskier, another Bible scholar, did a thorough study on these same two manuscripts, and he confirmed both Burgon's and Scrivener's reports. He documented his findings in a two-volume book titled *Codex B and Its Allies: A Study and an Indictment*. This is the full title of his two-volume book, which is more than 900 pages. Hoskier lists 3,036 references where Vaticanus and Sinaiticus contradict each other in the four gospels alone. In other words, in more than 3,000 instances in the four gospels, they didn't even agree with each other. It is all clearly documented, but how many Christians realize the deception that has been foisted upon us? Today, our world is flooded with modern Bibles that are founded upon these two faulty manuscripts.

Let's turn in our Bible to Psalm 12:6: "The words of the LORD are pure words: as silver tried in a furnace of earth, purified seven times."

Then in the next verse, my KJV reads, "Thou shalt keep them, O LORD, thou shalt preserve them from this generation for ever."

It is contextually clear that the Psalmist declared that the Lord would preserve His words forever. But now we have a problem, because most translations read differently. Many of our modern translations have changed the word "them," which refers to God's words, with "him" or "us." The New Revised Standard Version, for example, says, "You, O LORD, will protect us; you will guard us from this generation forever."

Granted, both statements are correct, for God will surely preserve His people and His words, but in this passage, God is giving assurance that His Word will be preserved. This example is only one of thousands of the differences found in the translations of God's Word.

Perhaps we should ask why the translators would make such a change in this passage. One apparent reason was because the translators were making numerous changes to God's words, and this verse, as it appears in the KJV, would be an indictment against them. Another underlying reason was because modern translators believed that many of God's words had been lost, and they were in the business of restoring His words. They proposed to do this by using the older Greek manuscripts, namely the Vaticanus and the Sinaiticus, which they claimed to be the "oldest and best."

Please note that this claim is often found in our modern Bibles to defend the use of the Greek manuscripts they employ, but is this a true claim? Regarding this, let me cite more information from Burgon: "I am utterly disinclined to believe, so grossly improbable does it seem—that at the end of 1800 years 995 copies out of every thousand, suppose, will prove untrustworthy; and that the one, two, three, four or five which remain, whose contents were till yesterday as good as unknown, will be found to have retained the secret of what the Holy Spirit originally inspired."

Furthermore, he comments, "We suspect that these two manuscripts are indebted for their preservation, solely to their ascertained evil character; which has occasioned that the one eventually found its way, four centuries ago, to a forgotten shelf in the Vatican Library; while the other, after exercising the ingenuity of several generations of critical Correctors, eventually got deposited in the wastepaper basket of the Convent at the foot of Mount Sinai."

Returning to Psalm 12:7, how may we determine which of these words, namely, *them*, *him*, or *us*, is the correct translation of this verse? The answer may be found in the Masoretic Hebrew manuscripts, which upon investigation, we find never use *him* or *us* in this verse. They all used *them*, which refers to God's words. There are still some Masoretic Hebrew and English Interlinear Old Testament Bibles available. Why use a Masoretic Hebrew text? We can recommend these texts because the Hebrew scribes who copied the Old Testament were extremely accurate in their work. They counted the letters from the top of every page, down and back up to top of the page, for exactness.

At this juncture, some may question if a translation of these words into another language may still be considered "pure words." The answer, thankfully, is yes!

Let's consider what Jesus said in Matthew 24. Jesus wanted the people to understand what was written in the book of Daniel. Turning to Matthew 24:15, we read, "When ye therefore shall see the abomination of desolation, spoken of by Daniel the prophet, stand in the holy place, (whoso readeth, let him understand:)."

We acknowledge that Jesus intended Daniel's words to be understood in every generation when He said "whoso readeth," and not exclusively for their own time. But how many people today understand the Hebrew or the Aramaic languages that Daniel used? Fortunately, there is internal evidence in the Bible that translations are still inspired. For example, there are many verses in the New Testament that are Greek translations of the Hebrew Old Testament. In other words, some New Testament writers translated the Old Testament Hebrew sentences into the Greek language, which was the universal language in the days of the apostles. Furthermore, they even added Greek words that weren't included in the Hebrew passages. Anyone who has ever translated from one language to another knows that words must be added to the finished work to complete the sentence structure of the new language. All translators do this when translating the Bible. However, the KJV translators were men of integrity, designating the added words with italics.

Let's look at an example where a translation is employed by a Bible writer. Turning to Acts 21:40 and 22:1, 2, it says, "And when he had given him license, Paul stood on the stairs, and beckoned with the hand unto the people. And when there was made a great silence, he spake unto them in the Hebrew tongue, saying, Men, brethren, and fathers, hear ye my defence which I make now unto you. (And when they heard that he spake in the Hebrew tongue to them, they kept the more silence: and he saith,)."

At this point, Paul continued to speak in the Hebrew language on through verse 21, yet when Luke wrote Acts, including this discourse, he did so in the Greek language. This Greek translation of Paul's words in Hebrew is still considered a part of Scripture. Granted, the words were previously spoken in Hebrew by Paul, but it is the thoughts of the writer of Scripture that are inspired, and not necessarily the words, unless these words are a direct quote from God.

Let's turn to Acts 2:16: "But this is that which was spoken by the prophet Joel." Then Peter quotes from Joel 2:28-32. When comparing this passage in Acts with the one in Joel, we find that Peter made minor changes in the words. He left out a few of the words, but the thoughts were the same. Therefore, we need translations that express the correct thoughts of the original writers.

Modern Bible Versions

In 2 Timothy 3:15-17, it says, "And that from a child thou hast known the holy scriptures, which are able to make thee wise unto salvation through faith which is in Christ Jesus."

Breaking into this passage, let us ask a pertinent question. Was Timothy reading the original autographs that were written in Hebrew? No, of course not. And we certainly don't have any original autographs of the Old Testament Hebrew scriptures, either. Please note, however, that Paul referred to the copy that Timothy possessed as "holy scriptures." We may feel confident that a reliable copy of Scripture is still considered "holy scriptures" in our day.

Going on, we read, "All scripture is given by inspiration of God, and is profitable for doctrine, for reproof, for correction, for instruction in righteousness: That the man of God may be perfect, thoroughly furnished unto all good works."

In the New American Standard Bible, verse 17 reads as follows: "That the man of God may be adequate, equipped for every good work."

Please tell me honestly, are these two Bible versions saying the same thing? Is "adequate" equivalent to "perfect"? The Greek word *artios* means complete or perfect, not just adequate.

Now, let's turn to 2 Peter 1:20: "Knowing this first, that no prophecy of the scripture is of any private interpretation."

Brothers and sisters, this verse is loaded with important truth. Many of us don't realize that "private interpretation" includes any comments in the body of the "holy scriptures" that are written by uninspired men or women. Such comments are really interpretations and should be placed somewhere separate from the "holy scriptures." I will say more on this later.

In verse 21, Peter gives us more insight on prophecy: "For the prophecy came not in old time by the will of man: but holy men of God spake as they were moved by the Holy Ghost." Translators should not add or take away from what those "holy men of God spake."

As we summarize the information covered so far in this Bible study, we have:

1. "Holy men" inspired by the Holy Spirit gave us the "holy scriptures."
2. They used their own words, but the thoughts came from God.
3. God's thoughts can be translated into another language and still be

considered "holy scriptures."
4. The original autographs are lost, but faithful copies were made and circulated throughout the churches of the east.
5. These copies, found in the Hebrew Masoretic and Greek Byzantine texts exhibit remarkable uniformity in the thoughts of more than 5,000 extant witnesses.
6. God has kept His promise to preserve His words "for ever," as foretold in Psalm 12:7.

Now, let us consider the importance of God's words. Following are a variety of passages taken from the King James Version Bible:

- "Sanctify them through thy truth: thy word is truth" (John 17:17).
- "Thy word have I hid in mine heart, that I might not sin against thee" (Ps. 119:11).
- "For ever, O LORD, thy word is settled in heaven" (Ps. 119:89).
- "Thy word is a lamp unto my feet, and a light unto my path" (Ps. 119:105).
- "Every word of God is pure: he is a shield unto them that put their trust in him. Add thou not unto his words, lest he reprove thee, and thou be found a liar" (Prov. 30:5, 6). So, Solomon is telling us, and especially those who translate Scripture, not to add any unnecessary words to God's Word.
- Thus saith the LORD; Stand in the court of the LORD'S house, and speak unto all the cities of Judah, which come to worship in the LORD'S house, all the words that I command thee to speak unto them; diminish not a word" (Jer. 26:2). Jeremiah was told to give all of the words of the Lord to the people, and he was told not to subtract any words that God had given him.
- "Behold, the days come, saith the Lord GOD, that I will send a famine in the land, not a famine of bread, nor a thirst for water, but of hearing the words of the LORD" (Amos 8:11).
- "For I testify unto every man that heareth the words of the prophecy of this book, If any man shall add unto these things, God shall add unto him the plagues that are written in this book: And if any man shall take away from the words of the book of this prophecy, God shall take

away his part out of the book of life, and out of the holy city, and from the things which are written in this book" (Rev. 22:18, 19).

Dr. Francis Steele, in his booklet *Translation or Paraphrase*, gives us a definition for what should be considered proper translation technique. He says, "A translation should convey as much of the original text in as few words as possible yet preserve the original atmosphere and emphasis. The translator should strive for the nearest approximation in words, concepts, and cadence. He should scrupulously avoid adding words or ideas not demanded by the text. His job is not to expand or to explain, but to translate and preserve the spirit and force of the original—even, if need be, at the expense of modern colloquialisms—so long as the resultant translation is intelligible."

He goes on to say, "We expect in a translation the closest approximation to the original text of the Word of God that linguist and philological science can produce. WE WANT TO KNOW WHAT GOD SAID- NOT WHAT DOCTOR SO- AND-SO THINKS GOD MEANT BY WHAT HE SAID."

As mentioned before, what makes the King James Version Bible stand apart from all the modern Bibles was the translators use of italics whenever words were added that were not present in the Hebrew and Greek texts.

Now, let's compare some words of "holy scripture" as found in the King James Version Bible with some of these other Bible versions.

Mark 7:18 and 19 in the KJV Bible says, "And he saith unto them, Are ye so without understanding also? Do ye not perceive, that whatsoever thing from without entereth into the man, it cannot defile him; Because it entereth not into his heart, but into his belly, and goeth out into the draught, purging all meats?"

If you have a modern Bible version, you might want to examine it to see what the translators may have added. The New International Version (NIV) encloses in parentheses the following words: "(In saying this, Jesus declared all foods 'clean.')." The Revised Standard Version (RSV) says basically the same thing. Weymouth's New Testament goes even one step further. It reads, "By these words Jesus pronounced all kinds of food clean."

This incorrect interpretation of Mark 7:18 and 19 is teaching error. All foods are not clean. Furthermore, clean or unclean food is not even the point of this passage. The subject was eating with unwashed hands (verse 5) and pots and cups (verse 8), things the Pharisees were very strict about.

In 2 Peter 2:9 we find these words in the KJV: "The Lord knoweth how to deliver the godly out of temptations, and to reserve the unjust unto the day of judgment to be punished."

This verse is straight forward in declaring that punishment begins at the day of judgment, but let us read what the pro-Catholic Bibles say in their translation of the last part of this verse:

- NIV – ". . . and to hold the unrighteous for the day of judgment, while continuing their punishment."
- RSV – ". . . and to keep the unrighteous under punishment until the day of judgment."
- New American Standard Bible (NASB) – ". . . and to keep the unrighteous under punishment for the day of judgment."
- The Living Bible (TLB) – ". . . and continue to punish the ungodly until the day of final judgment comes."
- New King James Version (NKJV) – ". . . and to reserve the unjust under punishment for the day of judgment."

By modifying this verse, these modern Bibles offer support for Purgatory.

While we are in 2 Peter, let's go back to chapter 1 and read verse 19 from the KJV: "We have also a more sure word of prophecy; whereunto ye do well that ye take heed, as unto a light that shineth in a dark place, until the day dawn, and the day star arise in your hearts."

Jesus makes it clear that He is the Morning Star in Revelation 22:16: "I Jesus have sent mine angel to testify unto you these things in the churches. I am the root and the offspring of David, and the bright and morning star."

The NIV and many other versions agree with the application that Jesus is the Morning Star. The NIV says, "I am the Root and the Offspring of David, and the bright Morning Star." The NIV translators even capitalized Morning Star. Notice, however, what this same version says in Isaiah 14:12 about Lucifer (Satan): "How you have fallen from heaven, O morning star, son of the dawn! You have been cast down to the earth, you who once laid low the nations!"

The KJV correctly translates this verse as follows: "How art thou fallen from heaven, O Lucifer, son of the morning! how art thou cut down to the ground, which didst weaken the nations!"

Lucifer is the "son of the morning," not the Morning Star as the NIV indicates. In Hebrew, the word "star" is not even mentioned in Isaiah 14:12.

It's amazing how the NASB version even goes so far as to place 2 Peter 1:19 as a cross reference to Isaiah 14:12, to solidify the notion that the passage refers to Jesus rather than Lucifer.

One of the best verses in the Bible that clearly identifies Jesus as God is found in 1 Timothy 3:16. It reads thus in the KJV: "And without controversy great is the mystery of godliness: God was manifest in the flesh . . ."

How do we find modern Bibles translating this verse?

NASB – "He who was revealed in the flesh . . ."

RSV – "He was manifested in the flesh . . ."

NIV – "He appeared in a body . . ."

There is absolutely no excuse in confusing the Greek word hos, which means "he," with the Greek word theos, for God. This translation comes primarily from the Sinaiticus, since the Vaticanus doesn't even have 1 Timothy in it.

Many Christians don't realize that Origen, who was largely responsible for the Egyptian manuscripts, was an Arian. In other words, he didn't believe Jesus was God. That was one of the reasons Origen and other heretics altered the manuscripts coming from Alexandria, Egypt.

Mark 10:24 in the KJV reads as follows: "Children, how hard is it for them that trust in riches to enter into the kingdom of God!"

For a gross distortion of Bible truth, we now quote from the NIV, RSV, and NASB for the same verse: "Children, how hard it is to enter the kingdom of God."

Is this truly the Word of God? Would Jesus tell His disciples, or anyone else for that matter, that it is hard to be saved? Yet, the NIV is the recommended version to be read in our churches!

Now, let's turn to 2 Corinthians 2:17 and read from the KJV. It says, "For we are not as many, which corrupt the word of God: but as of sincerity, but as of God, in the sight of God speak we in Christ."

In the margin, an alternate translation for the word corrupt, says, "or, deal deceitfully with." I believe either way, corrupt or deal deceitfully, express the thought Paul was conveying in 2 Corinthians 2:17. We have the same thought just two chapters later. In 2 Corinthians 4:1 and 2, we read, "Therefore seeing we have this ministry, as we have received mercy, we faint not; But have renounced the hidden things of dishonesty, not walking in craftiness, nor handling the word of God deceitfully."

I want to stop here and go back to 2 Corinthians 2:17 and read from the NIV, which is typical of the RSV and others. I acknowledge Paul used a different Greek word in chapter 4 than what he used in chapter 2, verse 17. However, both Greek words are connected to deception.

Now, let's read 2 Corinthians 2:17 from the NIV. It says, "Unlike so many, we do not peddle the word of God for profit." And the RSV says, "For we are not, like so many, peddlers of God's word."

Dear friends, I hope you can see from this abbreviated study that our modern Bibles are not being faithful in their translation of God's Word. As we near the conclusion of this study, I realize some Christians will conclude that I am biased toward the KJV Bible. And, I freely admit that this is true. However, I have researched this information for myself, and I believe if a Christian uses a modern Bible he or she won't be able to discern, or even correctly understand, some of the time prophecies found in God's Holy Scriptures. For examples, see Daniel 8:14, Daniel 9:24-27, Revelation 9:14, 15, and compare the KJV with our modern Bibles.

I have presented only a few of the facts, but I will add the little known fact that the Nestle/Aland Greek New Testament text, which was used in all of our modern Bibles, has undergone twenty-seven revisions. This translates into twenty-seven different times that there have been multiple changes in the words of their New Testament text. Furthermore, the translators of the revised version based their translation on the classical Greek language instead of the common Koine Greek language used by the writers of the New Testament.

Also, there are two basic Hebrew texts still available for our use today. One is genuine and the other is inaccurate. The true text is the Masoretic text. One is Daniel Bomberg's manuscript, edited by Ben Chayyim—the *2nd Rabbinic Bible* of 1524-1525. The other inaccurate Hebrew text was edited by Ben Asher. It is the *Biblia Hebraica* by Kittel.

Now, I want to expose the deceptive statement made in many modern Bibles on "the oldest and best" manuscripts. While it is true the Vaticanus and

Sinaiticus manuscripts are the oldest Greek manuscripts in existence today, they are not the best, as we have already demonstrated, nor are they the oldest manuscripts available when we include versions in the other languages. For example, the Waldensian old Latin Italic version is 200 years older than both the Vaticanus and the Sinaiticus. Another older translation is the Antioch, Syrian Peshitta translation, which was in use about the same time as the old Latin version. (The old Latin is not the same as Jerome's Latin Vulgate version.)

Guess what my friends, both of these older foreign translations, i.e., the Italic and the Peshitta, are in agreement with the received text that underlies the KJV Bible! So please go and research for yourselves the history that has been presented today. But don't depend upon the advice of a theologian or even your minister.

I believe we are nearing the close of this earth's history, and Satan has used his deceptive tactics of undermining God's Word by the translators of our modern Bibles. If you are not yet convicted, at least compare what your modern Bible says with the KJV Bible. I believe the Holy Spirit will gradually convince you of the truth, which I have just shared with you.

Again, reading from John 17:17, Jesus says to us: "Sanctify them through thy truth: thy word is truth." We become sanctified through the hearing or reading of God's Word.

And again, in Psalm 119:11, it says, "Thy word have I hid in mine heart, that I might not sin against thee."

Yes, there are many of God's words present in our modern Bibles, but there are also many uninspired errors of interpretation found in these Bibles, as well. So, I personally consider God's "Holy Scriptures" to be found in the King James Version Bible. Although I occasionally use the other translations as reference material, my private devotional studies come from the KJV.

Also, I find it much easier to memorize verses from the KJV than from any modern Bible. Hence, these verses are more easily recalled so that I can meditate upon God's Word as I go about my daily activities.

In conclusion, I am not convinced that we can be sanctified by meditating upon any uninspired thoughts that have been planted into the paraphrased Bibles, such as "all foods are clean." Many Christians don't realize that what we eat has a direct bearing upon our health, and our sanctification. God has declared some meats "unclean," not for arbitrary reasons but because some flesh food is injurious to our health. Our bodies are supposed to be a temple for the indwelling of the Holy Spirit. In 1 Corinthians 3:16, 17 it says, "Know ye not that ye are the temple of God, and that the Spirit of God dwelleth in you? If any man defile the temple of God, him shall God destroy; for the temple of God is holy, which temple ye are."

In Deuteronomy 14:3, we are told, "Thou shalt not eat any abominable thing." And, in verse 8, swine is specifically mentioned as "unclean unto you: ye shall not eat of their flesh, nor touch their dead carcase."

God hasn't changed His mind about what is abominable or unhealthy for human consumption. No matter what uninspired translators say, we need to meditate upon what God has declared in His Word.

I conclude this chapter with an earnest appeal: Please, seriously reconsider using God's "holy scriptures" that have been faithfully translated into the English language and found in the King James Version Bible. You won't be disappointed as you discover God speaking to your soul. Yes, there are some archaic words present, but they are often clarified within the context of the passage you are reading. If still in doubt about the meaning of a word, consult a concordance or dictionary, a practice that will strengthen and expand your vocabulary and your mind.

May God bless and sanctify us as we become more and more like Him by reading and hearing His word.

Chapter 7

History Repeats Itself

In this chapter, I want to demonstrate how the "classical" prophets, especially Isaiah and Ezekiel, as well as some of the minor prophets, spoke more for our time than the days in which they lived. It is the belief of many that each of the ancient prophets spoke less for their own time than for ours.

Here is a comment from one of my favorite authors: "The last books of the Old Testament show us workers taken from the laborers in the field. Others were men of high ability and extensive learning, but the Lord gave them visions and messages. These men of the Old Testament spoke of things transpiring in their day, and Daniel, Isaiah, and Ezekiel not only spoke of things that concerned them as present truth, but their sights reached down to the future, and to what should occur in these last days" (*Selected Messages*, book 3, p. 419).

With these words in mind, you are probably familiar with the truism "history repeats itself." In other words, events in the past are repeated in the future. Once again, from the same book, page 339, we read, "The Bible has accumulated and bound up together its treasures for this last generation. All the great events and solemn transactions of Old Testament history have been, and are, repeating themselves in the church in these last days."

A good example of this is that ancient Israel wandered in the wilderness, and today, modern Israel is likewise wandering in a spiritual wilderness. Let's read what Paul says pertaining to the children of Israel and their wilderness wanderings: "Now all these things happened unto them for examples: and they are written for our admonition, upon whom the ends of the world are come" (1 Cor. 10:11).

We also have Peter, another New Testament writer who agrees with Paul, as he writes in his first epistle. In 1 Peter 1:12 he writes, "...not unto themselves, but unto us they did minister the things, which are now reported unto you by them that have preached the gospel unto you with the Holy Ghost sent down from heaven; which things angels desire to look into."

While it is true these Bible verses don't explicitly state that future generations will go through similar experiences as did the children of Israel, one only needs to study history for this truth to become obvious. It is important for us to recognize that the prophets did not use modern examples to portray future events. In other words, they used local events and topography to symbolize what would occur in the future. Because "history repeats itself," these Old Testament prophets were essentially outlining our history today.

Let's look at a good example. The prophets often spoke about the "day of the Lord," which is a phrase that has a dual application, but it primarily applies to these last days when God intervenes in our history, beginning with the seven last plagues. This phrase, "the day of the Lord" or "in that day," is found in numerous places in the Old Testament. It is often connected with the destruction of Israel's enemies. Babylon is a good example of an enemy of Israel. In the book of Revelation, modern Babylon is destroyed during the fifth, sixth, and seventh plagues. Furthermore, modern Babylon is composed of three entities: the dragon, the beast, and the false prophet (Rev. 16:13, 19). In the last remnant of time, all three of these powers will be enemies of God's people.

The Old Testament prophets did not have the same dragon power, beast (Papacy), or false prophet (apostate Protestantism) as enemies of literal Israel, but they often had a three-fold enemy that attacked ancient Israel. This warfare was often couched in the setting of the "day of the Lord" or "in that day."

We need to establish some fundamental principles. The principle of repetition tells us how we can know when an important truth has been established. When God repeats a message more than once, we know this is something of special importance. This repetition, which establishes an important truth, is well supported in 2 Corinthians 13:1: "This is the third time I am coming to you. In the mouth of two or three witnesses shall every word be established." When we hear, for example, the same words from two or three Bible prophets, we can know that the Lord is establishing a truth that we are to give special attention to.

Yet, there is another basic principle that is directly related to the principle that "history repeats itself." Perhaps you are familiar with the law of the "first and last mention." The law of the "first mention," simply put, means the first time any subject, or fact, is mentioned in the Bible. Obviously, the "last mention" is the last time this same subject appears in the Bible.

A short passage from Australian writer Louis Were may help to clarify further what this principle of "first and last mention" involves. In his book *The Certainty of The Third Angel's Message*, we read, "Like the books of the Bible, and the various features of Divine truth, the laws governing the understanding of the Bible are definitely connected and at times interwoven. Thus the law of the first and the last mention is connected with the law of repetition and the law of enlargement. The enlargement comes by the repetition, and the repetition repeats that which is first mentioned—and naturally, the enlargement and the repetition are found in the last mention, for it is in the last mention that things are enlarged to their fullest sense . . . As in the human anatomy all the nerves lead from the extremities to the brain, so, in the Bible, all the threads of truth, all the laws of interpretation, meet in one splendid union in the Book of Revelation" (p. 157).

To simplify what Were is saying, let us consider the last sentence quoted: "All the threads of truth, all the laws of interpretation, meet . . . in the Book of Revelation." Any significant prophetic truth found in the book of Revelation will be a repetition and enlargement of a subject found elsewhere in Bible prophecy, and this "last mention" will have the most complete description of the prophecy.

For an example of this "first and last mention," let us go back to the subject of Babylon. Babylon is first mentioned in Genesis 10. Turning there, we will begin reading at verse 8: "And Cush begat Nimrod." Now, dropping down to verse 9, we read, "He was a mighty hunter before the LORD." (The word "before" in Hebrew actually means "against," so Nimrod was a mighty hunter against the Lord.)

In verse 10, we read, "And the beginning of his kingdom was Babel." Babel also means Babylon, which was "in the land of Shinar" (verse 10). This is the first mention of Babylon. The last mention is in the book of Revelation, which enlarges upon the first mention. However, the Bible mentions Babylon many times in between the first and the last mention. The work of a student of prophecy is to trace the history of Babylon from its infamous, singular beginning to its final, complex three-fold entity in Revelation.

Remember, Babylon was initially a pagan entity that attempted to defy God with its tower reaching to heaven. Later, Babylon became a great city that ruled the then-known world and made war against God's people. In the book of Revelation, we find another entity, papal Rome, added to the makeup of Babylon. It, too, wars against God and His people and is described as "the mother of harlots." Her daughters (apostate Protestantism) also become the third part of the makeup of "Babylon the great."

Hopefully you are now seeing the law of the first and the last mention and how it is related to the law of repetition and enlargement. As we continue on, we will see how these principles are also related to that of history repeating itself.

The principle of repetition and enlargement can be very easily demonstrated in the book of Daniel. The second chapter of Daniel gives us a sketchy outline of prophecy. Then, the seventh chapter repeats the same outline but uses different symbols. Furthermore, it adds more details to the prophecy. Thus, Daniel 7 enlarges what was previously said in Daniel 2. Chapters 8 and 9 go over much of the same history, but again, these two chapters add more details. Finally, chapters 10 through 12 repeat and enlarge on the previous three parallel prophecies. This is an illustration of the law of repetition and enlargement.

Where this differs from the law of the "first and last mention" is in the fact that these repeated and enlarged events may or may not be the first and last mention of the subject under study. For example, Daniel repeats and enlarges on the four kingdoms, but it is neither the first or last time the kingdoms are mentioned in the Bible. Since all the prophets were writing their prophecies with the last days in mind—essentially telling our story—we want to combine not only the first and last mentioned, but the repetition and enlargement of all the prophets between the first and last mention.

Imagine a series of transparencies such as you may have seen in an anatomy class in school. You begin with the first basic picture and then add more details with each successive transparency until the full and complete picture is presented.

Now, with these preliminary rules in mind, let us go to the Scriptures. In Isaiah 2:2 and 3 we read, "And it shall come to pass in the last days, that the mountain of the LORD's house shall be established in the top of the mountains, and shall be exalted above the hills; and all nations shall flow unto it. And many people shall go and say, Come ye, and let us go up to the mountain of the LORD, to the house of the God of Jacob; and he will teach us of his ways, and we will walk in his paths: for out of Zion shall go forth the law, and the word of the LORD from Jerusalem."

Here is a good example of one of Isaiah's prophecies for the "last days." Notice that Isaiah mentions literal Jerusalem. However, since the Jews rejected Christ, the promises given to literal Israel were inherited by the church—"spiritual Israel."

Let us go on to fully establish that Isaiah is truly writing about the last days. Verse 12 says, "For the day of the LORD of hosts shall be upon every one that is proud and lofty, and upon every one that is lifted up; and he shall be brought low." Now, skipping down to verse 17, we read, "And the loftiness of man shall be bowed down, and the haughtiness of men shall be made low: and the LORD alone shall be exalted in that day."

Did you notice the phrase "in that day"? This is referring back to the "day of the Lord." Continuing on with verses 19-21, we read, "And they shall go into the holes of the rocks, and into the caves of the earth, for fear of the LORD, and for the glory of his majesty, when he ariseth to shake terribly the earth. In that day [again, referring to the day of the Lord] a man shall cast his idols of silver, and his idols of gold, which they made each one for himself to worship, to the moles and to the bats; To go into the clefts of the rocks . . . for fear of the LORD, and for the glory of his majesty, when he ariseth to shake terribly the earth."

Dear reader, should any of us be in doubt that Isaiah is describing end-time events when Jesus comes again? But let us go on, for perhaps some are not yet convinced that the "day of the Lord" primarily applies to events connected with Christ's second advent. Turn to Revelation 16:14, which is dealing with the sixth plague. There we read, "For they are the spirits of devils, working miracles, which go forth unto the kings of the earth and of the whole world, to gather them to the battle of that great day of God Almighty." In other words, the great "day of the Lord."

Furthermore, Peter, in his second epistle, chapter 3, is even more convincing. Verse 10 says, "But the day of the Lord will come as a thief in the night; in the which the heavens shall pass away with a great noise, and the elements shall melt with fervent heat, the earth also and the works that are therein shall be burned up."

A few years ago, I gave a presentation using 2 Peter 3:10, wherein I demonstrated that the day of the Lord is 1,000 years long. It begins with the seven last plagues, known as the "wrath of God," and extends through the 1,000 years during which the "books are opened" and the saints are involved in the judgment of the wicked. When we consider that it begins as a "thief in the night," which more accurately describes the general close of probation, and ends with everything being "burned up," what else could this day of the Lord represent? This is even clearer when we factor in verse 8, which says, ". . . that one day is with the Lord as a thousand years, and a thousand years as one day."

Now, returning back to Isaiah, let's look at chapter 4. The first verse of that chapter says,

"And in that day seven women shall take hold of one man, saying, We will eat our own bread, and wear our own apparel: only let us be called by thy name, to take away our reproach."

I am going to break in here to propose a spiritual application to this verse. What does a woman represent in prophecy? A church (Jer. 6:2; 2 Cor. 11:2; Rev. 12:1; etc.). What does the number seven represent? Completeness or the total number. What does bread represent? Doctrine (Matt. 16:11, 12). Could Isaiah be illustrating the same confederation of churches as described by John the Revelator, in Revelation 17? Think about it. Very soon, all the Protestant churches will be in a confederation with the "mother" church, but they will be allowed to retain most of their own doctrines.

Now, let us continue on with Isaiah 4:2-4: "In that day shall the branch of the LORD be beautiful and glorious, and the fruit of the earth shall be excellent and comely for them that are escaped of Israel. And it shall come to pass, that he that is left in Zion, and he that remaineth in Jerusalem, shall be called holy, even every one that is written among the living in Jerusalem: When the Lord shall have washed away the filth of the daughters of Zion, and shall have purged the blood of Jerusalem from the midst thereof by the spirit of judgment, and by the spirit of burning." I believe this passage clearly portrays God's end-time church undergoing a purification "in that day."

You should recognize by now that God uses repetition and enlargement, as illustrated in Daniel and Isaiah, to enhance our understanding of Bible prophecy. In addition, God also uses the principle of the first and last mention, with all the history in between these two extremes, to demonstrate the principle that history repeats itself. Serious Bible students can get the "big picture" by tracing what the other prophets wrote about a particular prophecy. We must keep in mind, however, that Old Testament prophets used local events in such a way as to symbolize future history.

Now, let's go to Isaiah 10, where he begins discussing Assyria first—Assyria was the dominant empire during Isaiah's day. However, his vision sees into the future, as evidenced by his portrayal of Jesus in chapter 11. In chapter 13, Isaiah sees Babylon in the setting of the "day of the LORD." Scattered throughout chapters 10 through 14, we notice many references to "in that day." We have two references to the "day of the LORD" in chapter 13. So, what is Isaiah telling us, beginning with the kingdom of Assyria, in Isaiah 10? Remember, Nimrod also founded Assyria, as well as Babylon, and both of these kingdoms were enemies of Israel.

Let's read Isaiah 10:20-23: "And it shall come to pass in that day, that the remnant of Israel, and such as are escaped of the house of Jacob, shall no more again stay upon him that smote them; but shall stay upon the LORD, the Holy One of Israel, in truth. The remnant shall return, even the remnant of Jacob, unto the mighty God. For though thy people Israel be as the sand of the sea, yet a remnant of them shall return: the consumption decreed shall overflow with righteousness. For the Lord GOD of hosts shall make a consumption, even determined, in the midst of all the land."

Evidently, this passage primarily applies to us today more than it applied for the ancient Israelites. A "consumption" is literally a burning that consumes the wicked. Fortunately, during this "consumption," the righteous will be living in the full blaze of God's glory.

In Isaiah 28:21 and 22, we read, "For the LORD shall rise up as in mount Perazim, he shall be wroth as in the valley of Gibeon, that he may do his work, his strange work; and bring to pass his act, his strange act. Now therefore be ye not mockers, lest your bands be made strong: for I have heard from the Lord GOD of hosts a consumption, even determined upon the whole earth."

Now, we need to consider some of the history that transpired during Isaiah's ministry. It was during his ministry that the northern kingdom of Israel was taken into captivity. Shortly after that, 185,000 Assyrians who had encamped around Jerusalem were put to death by one angel. We see in these events 1) a purification of God's church, as the northern kingdom of Israel was purged from the southern kingdom of Judah, and 2) a deliverance of God's people by the "consumption" of their enemies.

Translated to our days, there will be a future purification of the church and a "consumption" that will be "determined upon the whole earth."

Let us look at a couple of verses in the New Testament that confirm that this "consumption," which is "determined upon the whole earth," involves a fire that destroys the wicked. In Hebrews 12:29, it says, "For our God is a consuming fire." Turning to 2 Thessalonians 2:8, it says, "And then shall that Wicked be revealed, whom the Lord shall consume with the spirit of his mouth, and shall destroy with the brightness of his coming." And finally, in Revelation 19:20 and 21, we read, "And the beast was taken, and with him the false prophet that wrought miracles before him, with which he deceived them that had received the mark of the beast, and them that worshipped his image. These both were cast alive into a lake of fire burning with brimstone. And the remnant were slain with the sword of him that sat upon the horse." It should be clear that Isaiah was also describing this future destruction of the wicked.

Now, let's turn back to Isaiah 13:9-11, where we read of judgment against ancient Babylon. "Behold, the day of the LORD cometh, cruel both with wrath and fierce anger, to lay the land desolate: and he shall destroy the sinners thereof out of it. For the stars of heaven and the constellations thereof shall not give their light: the sun shall be darkened in his going forth, and the moon shall not cause her light to shine. And I will punish the world for their evil, and the wicked for their iniquity."

These verses are describing the seventh plague. Now, going on to verse 13, we read,

"Therefore I will shake the heavens, and the earth shall remove out of her place, in the wrath of the LORD of hosts, and in the day of his fierce anger." Again, these verses are describing the day of the Lord.

Because of my limited space, we cannot go into depth with Ezekiel's prophecies, so I will just summarize how Ezekiel prophesied more for our time than his own. Ezekiel was in the group of captives by the river Che'bar. He was in the land of Babylon, and he was given visions concerning the siege at Jerusalem. The Lord showed him a judgment falling upon the Israelites who were left behind in Jerusalem. The shocking part of his story concerns a revelation from the Lord about the abominations done by God's own people.

Today, as we analyze the first nine chapters of Ezekiel, we realize God was purging His church, similar to the purging that occurred in Isaiah's day, when God purged out the ten northern tribes of Israel. Since history repeats itself, shouldn't we expect another purging, or purification, of God's church today? Think about it.

There is no serious argument that Ezekiel chapters 36 through 39 speak for our time. We have the new covenant realized in God's people in chapter 36. Then in chapter 37, we read about the valley of dry bones coming to life. Surely this portrays the latter rain coming upon God's end-time church. And, finally, in chapters 38 and 39, there is Gog and Magog, which portrays earth's final battle before Jesus comes.

At this point, we should include a few of the so-called "minor" prophets to complete our study. Again, we are demonstrating that other prophets, besides Daniel and John the Revelator, wrote for our benefit, also. Although they pronounced judgments against the enemies of Israel and Judah in their day, they placed these local events in an end-time setting. How did they do this? They did it by pronouncing judgments against their enemies in the context of the "day of the LORD." As we clarified earlier, the "day of the LORD" or "in that day" are phrases referring to end-time events, which begin with the seven last plagues.

With the understanding that these "minor" prophets also wrote for their

own times, I believe they can be grouped into one of three groups:
7. The earliest group of "minor " prophets lived during the Assyrian supremacy. These prophets primarily included Hosea, Joel, Amos, and Micah.
8. The second group of prophets lived during the supremacy of Babylon. These prophets included Nahum, Habakkuk, and Zephaniah.
9. The third group prophesied during the post exile period of time, when Persia was the ruling empire. These prophets included Haggai, Zechariah, and Malachi.

Now, let's go back to the first group of prophets. When Assyria was the dominant empire, Hosea and Amos, along with Isaiah, portrayed Assyria in an end-time setting, when God punishes modern Babylon. In other words, Assyria prefigured modern Babylon. We find this to be true from a careful study of Isaiah, chapters 10, 11, and 12. Let us go to Isaiah 10 and look at a few verses. Verse 12 says, "Wherefore it shall come to pass, that when the Lord hath performed his whole work upon mount Zion and on Jerusalem, I will punish the fruit of the stout heart of the king of Assyria, and the glory of his high looks."

Breaking into this passage, the question naturally arises: What is the "whole work" of the Lord in regards to His people "upon mount Zion and on Jerusalem"? This is describing the purification of His church. Then going forward to verse 20, which we read earlier, we read again:

"And it shall come to pass in that day, that the remnant of Israel, and such as are escaped of the house of Jacob, shall no more again stay upon him that smote them; but shall stay upon the LORD."

Now, dropping down to verses 25 and 26, we read, "For yet a very little while, and the indignation shall cease, and mine anger in their destruction. And the LORD of hosts shall stir up a scourge for him according to the slaughter of Midian at the rock of Oreb."

Stopping here, I want to bring up an important point. This "slaughter of Midian" is referring back to the "first mention" of a battle involving the enemies of Israel, wherein God intervened and slaughtered the Midianites. In Judges 5 we find recorded the song of Deborah, the prophetess, after that first victory of the Israelites in the valley of Megiddo. In Judges 5:20 we read, "They fought from heaven; the stars in their courses fought against Sisera."

Therefore, this first battle prefigures the last battle of Armageddon, which is the "last mention" of Megiddo. "Armageddon" is a compound name combining *Har* and *Megiddo*, which may be translated as "mountain of slaughter," depicting the final battle when God destroys all the enemies of His people.

Going now to the "minor" prophets, allow me to share a passage from the book, *Prophets and Kings*: "The prophecies of judgment delivered by Amos and Hosea were accompanied by predictions of future glory. To the ten tribes, long rebellious and impenitent, was given no promise of complete restoration to their former power in Palestine. Until the end of time, they were to be 'wanderers among the nations.' But through Hosea was given a prophecy that set before them the privilege of having a part in the final restoration that is to be made to the people of God at the close of earth's history, when Christ shall appear as King of Kings and Lord of lords. . . . In symbolic language Hosea set before the ten tribes God's plan of restoring to every penitent soul who would unite with His church on earth, the blessings granted Israel in the days of their loyalty to him in the Promised Land" (p. 298).

Now, going forward to Zephaniah, who lived and prophesied during the kingdom of Babylon, we find more than a few references to the "day of the Lord." In chapter 2, verses 1-3, Zephaniah makes an appeal to seek the Lord while probation lingers: "Gather yourselves together, yea, gather together, O nation not desired; Before the decree bring forth, before the day pass as the chaff, before the fierce anger of the LORD come upon you, before the day of the LORD'S anger come upon you. Seek ye the LORD, all ye meek of the earth, which have wrought his judgment; seek righteousness, seek meekness: it may be ye shall be hid in the day of the LORD'S anger."

In my opinion, this "decree" represents Jesus' declaration in Revelation 22:11, which refers to the close of probation, when Jesus declares: "He that is unjust, let him be unjust still: and he which is filthy, let him be filthy still: and he that is righteous, let him be righteous still: and he that is holy, let him be holy still."

Thereafter, the "day of the LORD'S anger," as mentioned in Zephaniah 2:2, commences with the seven last plagues.

Finally, in the third group of prophets, we have Malachi. Let's turn to

Malachi 4:1. It says,

"For, behold, the day cometh, that shall burn as an oven; and all the proud, yea, and all that do wickedly, shall be stubble: and the day that cometh shall burn them up, saith the LORD of hosts, that it shall leave them neither root nor branch."

And if there is any question about what day is being portrayed here, dropping down to verse 5 we read: "Behold, I will send you Elijah the prophet before the coming of the great and dreadful day of the LORD."

Who represents Elijah today? The people proclaiming God's final warnings to the world, and to Christendom, are they who fulfill the role of Elijah.

In conclusion, I hope this study has helped the reader to realize that all of God's prophets, in addition to Daniel and John, wrote their prophecies for our benefit, as well as for ancient Israel.

I realize that we have covered a lot of doom and gloom in this study, but we are reminded of a purification process that the Lord permitted to come upon His people of ancient Israel. I believe this purification has already started with us who are living today. Day after day, we are witnessing the closing scenes of this earth's history. It doesn't take a rocket scientist to see that Jesus will soon finish His work in the heavenly sanctuary. Now is the time to make our calling and election sure. Now is the time to ask ourselves the following three questions:

1. Are all my sins confessed to my Savior?
2. Do I love Jesus more than my life itself?
3. Have I surrendered all to Jesus—my Lord and Master?

My appeal and prayer is that you will answer yes to all three of these questions. Let us spend more time with Jesus in His Word. Then He will reveal to us more and more treasures of truth, which we can share with our loved ones and neighbors. May God's grace sustain us, and perfect us, until we meet in heaven.

Chapter 8

Daniel's Prophecies for Today

Pastor Bruce Nicola Jr. mentioned an important truth that I want to repeat at the beginning of this study. He made it clear that the God of prophecy is more important than the prophecies themselves. With this in mind, we must first focus upon Jesus and His role as the Alpha and Omega, the word of Scripture.

A careful reading of 2 Peter 1:19-21 reveals to us that all Scripture may be considered prophecy, in the sense that all Scripture comes from the mind and counsel of God, which has been communicated to His prophets for the benefit of His people. Peter said, "We have also a more sure word of prophecy; whereunto ye do well that ye take heed, as unto a light that shineth in a dark place, until the day dawn, and the day star arise in your hearts: Knowing this first, that no prophecy of the scripture is of any private interpretation. For the prophecy came not in old time by the will of man: but holy men of God spake as they were moved by the Holy Ghost."

The Old Testament prophets gave many of these prophecies to literal Israel, but as we discovered in the last chapter, they also prefigured promises and threats that would be applied to spiritual Israel in our days. Prophecy in the Greek often means "to foretell," in other words, a foretelling or a prediction. Foretelling types of prophecies contain a message about what God will do in the future. There is also a broader meaning of prophecy. Here is a definition of the word prophecy from *Bullinger's Lexicon and Concordance*: "Prophetic declarations, exhortations, warnings, uttered by the prophets while under divine influence, and referring either to the past, the present, or the future."

A Primer on Salvation and Bible Prophecy

In other words, there is a type of prophecy that contains a message for the living generation when the prophet spoke to the people, but often has a broader application for God's people in the future. This is what Paul was saying in 1 Corinthians 10:11: "Now all these things happened unto them for examples [i.e., types]: and they are written for our admonition, upon whom the ends of the world are come."

A *type* or symbol has its counterpart in the *anti-type*, or its reality. As we noted in the previous chapter, events of the Old Testament were often types that will have their anti-type in the New Testament, such as the battle at Megiddo in Judges 5 compared with the battle of Armageddon in Revelation 16. Therefore, the Bible may be considered a book of prophecies.

Jesus was typified by the various sacrifices in the Old Testament. He was "the Lamb slain from the foundation of the world" (Rev. 13:8). In addition to types, we often see Jesus in various dimensions. In the book of Daniel, for example, we find Jesus is revealed in numerous different roles as the Benefactor of His people.

In Daniel 3 we find Him portrayed as the Son of God. In chapter 7 He is revealed as the Son of man, in the context of a judgment scene. He is described as the Prince of the Host and the Prince of Princes in chapter 8. In this same chapter, He functions as our High Priest. In chapter 9 Jesus is designated as the Messiah, the Prince, the One who is "cut off," i.e., sacrificed. In chapter 10 He is mentioned in the role of Michael, who assists Gabriel in his spiritual battle against the "prince of Persia," who most likely represents one of Satan's angels (this "prince" is contrasted with the "kings of Persia" mentioned in verse 13).

Finally, in Daniel 12:1 Jesus is again portrayed in his role as Michael, who "stands up" at the completion of His High Priestly ministry. It is Michael—one like God—who is the Commander of His armies in heaven. (See Revelation 12:7, 19:11-14.) *Archangel* literally means "chief of the angels," which Christ is, but not a created angel, for He was the Creator. Michael is the one who resurrects His righteous saints who have died. (See Jude 9 and 1 Thessalonians 4:16, 17.)

Since 1798, knowledge and understanding of the prophecies of Daniel have increased. I believe Christians of all Protestant denominations today generally accept this statement. Daniel 12:4 reads, "But thou O Daniel, shut up the words, and seal the book, even to the time of the end: many shall run to and fro, and knowledge shall be increased."

Verse 7 points to the appointed time when knowledge would be on the increase. The angel said, "That it shall be for a time, times, and an half." This is the same prophetic time prophesied in Daniel 7:25. (See also Revelation 12:14, 13:5.) It pointed to the 1260 years (each day represents a year; see Numbers 14:34 and Ezekiel 4:6) that the Papacy would reign, which began in AD 538 and concluded in 1798. Thus 1798 marked the time appointed in God's prophetic time clock when He determined that there would be increased "knowledge" (understanding) of the prophecies.

The year 1844 is another "time appointed" (Dan. 8:19) date which marked the end of two time prophecies, the 2300 days of Daniel 8:14 and the seven "times" of Leviticus 26. Space will not allow for us to go into the time prophecy of Leviticus 26. Our focus here is on Daniel's prophecies. You can find information on this time prophecy in "Principles of Prophetic Interpretation," which is located in the appendices of this book.

Some people relegate Daniel's prophecies into the scrap pile of fulfilled history with very little new information for our present-day enlightenment, but this is not true, as we shall learn from our study. Those who believe they already understand the book of Revelation may come to the conclusion that since the book of Revelation is an unfolding of Daniel's prophecies, which it is, then Daniel doesn't add much more to our understanding of end-time events. With this kind of reasoning, some would be satisfied reading the last chapter of a book, or in the case of a study of end-time events, they would be content reading the book of Revelation. However, I think you will agree with me that when we focus on the conclusion alone we will be deficient in our understanding of God's full revelation.

Therefore, my purpose here will be to first present the "big picture" in broad strokes, as found in the book of Daniel, and then we will explore some new insights in Daniel's prophecies that are not found in any other book of the Bible.

At the beginning of this study, we need to symbolically remove our western glasses. This is important because the writers of the Bible were predominantly of an eastern, oriental culture. Furthermore, translating the Bible into a modern format, as the new versions often do, loses some of the original writers' intent. We must bear in mind that Hebrew thinking, and consequently their writings, were different than ours. For example, they wrote from the right side to the left, which is opposite of English writing. Also, typical Hebrew thoughts focused first upon the consequence, or the result of an action. Then the Hebrew mind would reason backwards (at least to our way of thinking) to its cause.

In the book of Daniel, the story begins with a terrible consequence; in other words, God's people are exiled from their homeland. Daniel later reveals the reasons for the exile, and he also provides the reader future history; in other words, apocalyptical prophecy wherein he reveals God's interactions in the affairs of future nations. Furthermore, Daniel, like other Hebrew writers, often wrote parallel thoughts. This is similar to some of our poetry, wherein we rhyme the end words of parallel phrases or sentences. For example, in the song *Home on the Range*, , we have the words: O give me a home, where the buffalo roam. Thus, home and roam rhyme.

Hebrew poetry is different in that instead of rhyming words they often wrote parallel, harmonizing thoughts. Please understand, I'm just giving one simplified example of Hebrew poetry. So, Hebrew writers have a kind of poetry wherein the second thought paraphrases the first one. In other types of Hebrew poetry, the second thought contrasts, or even enlarges the first thought.

Have you ever wondered why there is a lot of repetition in the Bible? Repetition and enlargement during the second, third, and even fourth paraphrase are valuable teaching tools, and it was used by Daniel for the four parallel prophecies found in his book.

With this background information on Hebrew thought and poetry, let us now turn to Daniel 2. The prophecy of Daniel 2 was first given in a dream to King Nebuchadnezzar of Babylon. In verse 4, we notice that the Chaldeans (Babylonians) spoke to the king in Syriack (Aramaean), which is the language of Syria. Daniel continues to use the Aramaean language on through this chapter, until the end of chapter 7. This first prophecy of an image is the basic skeletal outline of the four world empires that would impact God's people until the second coming of Jesus.

The other three parallel prophecies are found in Daniel 7, wherein Jesus officiates in His role during a pre-advent judgment; Daniel 8 and 9, which reveals Jesus as our High Priest and our Sacrifice; and finally, chapters 10 through 12, which portrays Jesus as the "great prince which standeth for the children of thy people" (Dan. 12:1). He is Michael, our mighty Warrior, who not only saves us but also fights for us against all the agencies of Satan.

Daniel 10 is included here as part of the last prophecy, as it provides the introduction to the last prophecy, as well as reveal the invisible forces of good and evil involved in the great controversy between Christ and Satan.

All of the prophecies after the first one in Daniel 2, repeat some of the details of Daniel 2, but then they expand on the basics by adding more details. This is the application of the important principle of repetition and enlargement. Also, because we acknowledge that Daniel used parallelism, we are enabled to align the four parallel prophecies and thereby determine where added details, or events, occur in the stream of time. This knowledge of the timing of certain events is very important. Hopefully this will become more apparent later in this presentation.

By applying the principle of parallelism, we can refute those who are critical of the historicist method of Bible interpretation. Most modern evangelicals belong to the group of Bible expositors known as futurists. (Please excuse me for using a generalization, as I realize some exceptions occur.) Futurists, in general, espouse some wild and fanciful theories of Bible interpretations. One example would include the "gap" theory. In this theory they remove the last week of time from the "seventy weeks" of Daniel 9:24-27. Then they introduce this prophetic week of time as seven literal years of tribulation, some time in the future, just before Jesus comes. There are numerous books and movies that portray end-time events in this fashion. There are many Christians who teach some variations of this theory. With the understanding of parallelism and the "big picture," we stand on vantage ground as we defend our position using the historical method of Bible interpretation.

Now, let us turn in our Bibles to Daniel 2:31: "Thou, O king, sawest, and behold a great image." Then Daniel describes the dream on through verse 35. Beginning in verse 36, Daniel proceeds with the interpretation of the dream. The book of Daniel uses this same format—prophecy followed by its interpretation—for the first three prophecies in chapters 2, 7, and 8, with the completion of the chapter 8 prophecy in chapter 9, because Daniel "fainted" before

A Primer on Salvation and Bible Prophecy

the full interpretation in chapter 8. (Daniel 8:27 says, "And I Daniel fainted, and was sick certain days.")

The fourth and final prophecy of Daniel 10 through 12 does not begin with a new prophecy, but instead, it gives a more detailed explanation of the former vision of Daniel 8. This understanding becomes apparent when we carefully consider Daniel 10:1: "But the time appointed was long: and he [Daniel] understood the thing, and had understanding of the vision." The astute Bible reader recognizes that there wasn't another new vision between Daniel chapters 8 and 10; therefore, the same vision of chapter 8 is the subject of Daniel 10:1.

Now, let's consider the word "vision" as used in the book of Daniel. There are two different words in Hebrew that are translated into the same English word "vision." These two Hebrew words are hazon (sometimes spelled chazon), a generic word which indicates a full or complete vision, and mareh, a specific part, or snapshot part of the whole vision. Mareh can also be used for an apparition, or an appearance of a heavenly being.

The reason I am bringing this matter to your attention is because a misunderstanding of the true meaning of the Hebrew writer's intent, in the meaning of his words, introduces confusion for those of us who are trying to understand exactly what the writer was conveying. For example, when *vision* is used in Daniel 10:1, the Hebrew word *mareh* is used. Therefore, a specific part (*mareh*) of the whole vision (*hazon*) is being referred to, i.e., the time prophecy of Daniel 8:14, which caused Daniel to faint. This was the part of the prophecy which Daniel did not fully understand until the angel Gabriel revealed it to him about twelve years later in Daniel 9. In Daniel 10:7 and 8, the word vision (*mareh*) refers to the apparition, or appearance of the heavenly being: "And I Daniel alone saw the vision [*mareh*] for the men that were with me saw not the vision [*mareh*]; but a great quaking fell upon them, so that they fled to hide themselves. Therefore I was left alone, and saw this great vision [*mareh*]."

However, in Daniel 10:14, the Hebrew word for vision is hazon, which refers back to the whole prophecy of Daniel 8. Let's read Daniel 10:14: "Now I am come to make thee understand what shall befall thy people in the latter days: for yet the vision [hazon = the whole vision] is for many days."

Another distinction of this last prophecy (chapters 10-12) is the omission of animal symbols to portray world empires. Instead, there is an unfolding of the kingdoms of the North versus the kingdoms of the South. Because of space limitations, I cannot get into a detailed account of this prophecy, but it outlines subsequent history after the breakup of the Grecian empire, and on through both phases of Rome (pagan and papal) until modern times.

Now, I want to present some typology found in Daniel's prophecies that is applicable for us today.

1. In Daniel 3 we find the story of the three Hebrew worthies who refused to worship the golden image built on the plain of Dura by King Nebuchadnezzar of Babylon. This history will be repeated in our days, when Sunday laws will be enforced worldwide, as the "image to the beast" is set up. Thus the type will be fulfilled by the anti-type.
2. In Daniel 5 King Belshazzar of Babylon lost his kingdom to Cyrus, a type of Christ (Isaiah 44:28, 45:1), thus fulfilling the fall of literal Babylon. This type will be fulfilled in our days when the anti-typical, spiritual Babylon falls during the battle of Armageddon when Jesus appears as "King of kings and Lord of lords."
3. Daniel 8:14 portrays the anti-type of the earthly Day of Atonement of the Jews.

Shortly, I want to present some of the inter-relationships between chapters 7, 8, and 9. I believe that when we understand these inter-relationships, we can better understand the heavenly sanctuary message introduced in Daniel 8:14—the cleansing of the sanctuary in heaven and the pre-advent judgment. First, however, I need to make some introductory remarks.

Hebrews 8:5 tells us that the heavenly sanctuary is the "pattern" for the earthly sanctuary and that the ministry of the priests served "unto the example and shadow of heavenly things." While this constitutes sufficient evidence for the two-phase ministry of Jesus, first in the "holy place" and the second in the "Most Holy Place," this may not be clear enough to many Christians who have not studied much into the subject of the heavenly sanctuary. The best way to understand this two-phase ministry is to gather together the information from the following books of the Bible:

1. Leviticus – especially chapter 16
2. Exodus – chapter 25, especially verses 8, 9, and 40

3. Hebrews – chapters 8-10
4. Revelation – the first four sanctuary scenes help in that they describe Jesus' activities within the heavenly sanctuary (Rev. 1:12-20; 4; 5; 8:2-6; and 11:19)
5. Daniel – chapters 7, 8, and 9

The reader would do well to read the first four above, which explain the Old Testament sanctuary ministrations and those same ministrations in the New Testament. As space will not allow us to cover all that material here, we will focus on the last one—Daniel chapters 7, 8, and 9—and their inter-relationships.

In your mind picture the earthly tabernacle/sanctuary with its outer court surrounded by a curtain. Within this courtyard sets the sanctuary with two apartments, commonly known as the "holy place" and the "Most Holy Place." They are connected together with only a curtain separating these two apartments. Now, imagine a high priest who officiates in the court every day, and he even enters the first apartment, the holy place, on a daily basis. This high priest is forbidden to enter the second apartment, the Most Holy Place, until the once-a-year special service on the Day of Atonement.

Keeping this imagery in our minds, let us turn in our Bibles to Daniel 7. Beginning with verse 9, we read, "I beheld till the thrones were cast down [set in order], and the Ancient of days did sit, whose garment was white as snow, and the hair of his head like the pure wool: his throne was like the fiery flame, and his wheels as burning fire. A fiery stream issued and came forth from before him: thousand thousands ministered unto him, and ten thousand times ten thousand stood before him: the judgment was set, and the books were opened."

Here in this passage we have "judgment" and "books" mentioned. Going down to verse 13, we read, "I saw in the night visions, and, behold, one like the Son of man came with the clouds of heaven, and came to the Ancient of days, and they brought him near before him."

Skipping down to verses 21 and 22, we read, "I beheld, and the same horn made war with the saints, and prevailed against them; Until the Ancient of days came, and judgment was given to the saints of the most High; and the time came that the saints possessed the kingdom."

Finally, in verse 26 we read, "But the judgment shall sit, and they shall take away his dominion, to consume and to destroy it unto the end."

In a brief overview of Daniel 7, we have the four sequential empires that would arise and fall, but another "horn" power would arise out of the fourth empire that would persecute God's people. History reveals that the four world empires, beginning with the time of Daniel, are the following: 1) Babylon, 2) Medo-Persia, 3) Greece, and 4) Rome. And, out of the ruins of pagan Rome, ecclesiastical Rome (papal Rome) assumed power and held undisputed control over the nations of the medieval world for 1260 years (AD 538 to AD 1798). Furthermore, all dissenters from the established religion were consigned to death by the agents of the papal empire unless these so-called "heretics" recanted.

But, God had an "appointed time" when the papal power would be removed. This appointed time was delineated in cryptic words in Daniel 7:25. The same period of time has been revealed in six more passages of scripture. (See Daniel 12:7 and Revelation 11:2, 3; 12:6, 14; and 13:5.) At the termination of the 1260 years, the pope was removed from his kingdom in 1798 by Napoleon's General Berthier.

In addition, there is another "appointed time" when the events described in verses 9 and 26—the "judgment" and the opening of the "books"—will take place. This "investigative judgment" will lead up to the destruction of the blasphemous, persecuting papal power. The precise time of this second "appointed time"—the time for the cleansing of the sanctuary (the anti-typical Day of Atonement)—is not revealed until we come to Daniel 8:14, which reads, "And he said unto me, Unto two thousand and three hundred days; then shall the sanctuary be cleansed."

In summary, Daniel 7 portrays a pre-advent "judgment" in heaven, wherein "books" are investigated (investigative judgment). And Daniel 8 tells us there would be a cleansing of the sanctuary, after 2300 days. Since the visions of Daniel 7 and 8 are parallel, then in simple language, the investigative judgment and the cleansing of the sanctuary are simultaneous events. Furthermore, Jesus began His second apartment ministry in 1844 at the termination of the 2300 years (457 BC to AD 1844—see "Principles of Prophetic Interpretation" in the appendices for more information on these time prophecies).

In Daniel 9:26 we have mentioned that the "Messiah" would "be cut off," i.e., sacrificed. So now, let's recall the imagery of the high priest, which we mentioned earlier, and his activities in the court and the sanctuary. He first enters the court where sacrifices are performed. Then he takes the blood of the sacrificial lambs, etc., and ministers within the first apartment, the holy place, of the sanctuary on a daily basis. Finally, on one day of every year (the Day of Atonement), the high priest entered the Most Holy Place. Now, let's draw some conclusions:

- Daniel 7 = Jesus as our High Priest, and He is involved in judgment as our Judge/Advocate ("one like the Son of man," verse 13)
- Daniel 8 = Jesus' ministry in the first apartment, holy place, until 1844
- Daniel 9 = Jesus became our sacrifice

When we consider the sequence of activities of the earthly high priest, we have the following:

1. Outer court activities (sacrifices)
2. First apartment/holy place ministry
3. Second apartment/Most Holy Place ministry (judgment)

Notice that in Daniel 7, 8, and 9 the sequence of activities are in reverse order: judgment, first apartment ministry, and sacrifice. Why is this?

Perhaps we can find the answer in the words of William Shea, M.D., Ph.D.: "We may have failed to readily recognize this progression due to the fact that these prophecies are presented in Semitic thought order, that is, in an order that reasons from effect back to cause. In modern western European thought processes, we reason from cause to effect. The ancients could do that too, but they commonly thought and wrote in the reverse of this order. This feature explains much about the connections between these prophecies and why they appear in the order that they do. When we understand this feature of these prophecies, the logical progression in the work of Christ the Messiah becomes clear."

As we near the conclusion of this presentation, there is one more principle that needs to be clarified in order to correctly understand the prophecies in the book of Daniel. Recognizing this principle requires, once again, taking off our western glasses and opening our spiritual eyes. When the nation of literal Israel rejected Jesus and authorized His crucifixion, the privileges and promises offered to them were transferred to the church, i.e., spiritual Israel. This same principle applies in the interpretation of all apocalyptic prophecies. Therefore, after AD 31, whenever Israel is mentioned in an end-time context, such as pertaining to its inheritance, etc., the Bible is referring to spiritual Israel. The same principle applies to literal Babylon, which is no more the subject of prophecy after AD 31, but instead, spiritual Babylon is intended.

So now, I want to apply this principle to the last prophecy in Daniel, specifically in regards to the kings of the North and the kings of the South in Daniel 11. From our vantage point of fulfilled prophecy, we know the recorded struggles of the nations that were literally north and south of Palestine. However, we also realize that during the middle ages it was the Papacy/ papal Rome who waged war against God's people. Therefore, the Papacy was the spiritual king of the north/Babylon during this period of time. Even during apostolic times, Peter referred to Rome as Babylon (1 Peter 5:13). Also, God's people were spiritual Israelites and were not confined within the boundaries of literal Palestine but were scattered all over the world.

You may have also noticed that there is no mention of the king of the south in chapter 11, from verse 31 through 40. The reason for this silence on the king of the south during this period of time was because the Papacy, as the spiritual king of the north, held undisputed sway for 1260 years. Then in verse 40, the king of the south makes an appearance at the beginning of the "time of the end." This would be in 1798 with the termination of the 1260 years of papal supremacy. It is important to remember that the "time of the end" does not refer to the end of time, but rather the end of a prophecy, i.e., the "time appointed."

In conclusion, a proper understanding of the prophecies of Daniel, using the proper principles of interpretation, such as "repeat and enlarge" and a day representing a year in prophecy, will reveal that Daniel prophesied not only for his day and time but for ours as well at "the time of the end." These truths will keep us from being deceived by erroneous interpretations, such as Antiochus Epiphanes of the Selucid (Syrian) nation being the "little horn" of Daniel 8, or interpreting the time prophecies of Daniel 12 as literal days. In the former, Antiochus Epiphanes does not meet the "time appointed," nor does he reach the magnitude of the "little horn" in terms of power and dominion. Only the Papacy has fulfilled that role. In the latter case, switching to a day-for-a-day in Daniel 12 would be to "repeat and diminish," throwing confusion into the prophecy.

There are many other important details in the book of Daniel that I could not include in this presentation due to limited space. You can find some of these details in a later chapter titled "Movement of Destiny," and in the appendix titled, "Principles of Prophetic Interpretation.".

We need to be firmly grounded in the truth, from our Bibles, so that we can give to others the reasons for our faith. We must also nurture our relationship with Jesus and sense His sweet, abiding presence within us every moment of every day. Let us cooperate with Him while He is in the Most Holy Place doing His special work of cleansing the sanctuary. This work also requires a cleansing of our soul temples, through the power of the Holy Spirit. The cleansing of the heavenly sanctuary and the cleansing of our soul temples go together. Let us ask the Holy Spirit to reveal any deep-rooted, hidden sins, so we can be cleansed and ready for Jesus to come and take us home.

Chapter 9

Jesus in the Book of Revelation

In light of the broad range of material discussed in the previous chapter, I will endeavor to simplify the "big picture" on the prophecies of both Daniel and Revelation. In this chapter my purpose will be to give an overview of the book of Revelation in a manner that, I hope, you will easily understand.

As mentioned in the introduction of the previous chapter, Pastor Nicola, Jr. suggested we should focus more on the God of prophecy than on the prophecies themselves. So, with this advice in mind, I have titled this study "Jesus in the Book of Revelation."

There are many deeply buried treasures of truth in the book of Revelation. The word "revelation" means revealed, and therefore, we know it is meant to be understood. At the beginning of this Bible study, I want to emphasize that this "prophecy" is " the revelation of Jesus Christ." Its focus is on Jesus—what He is saying, and what He is doing in heaven and in earth for our salvation. Furthermore, the "revelation of Jesus," which includes prophecy, is, in its broadest sense, the "gospel" of Jesus Christ.

In the January 14, 1904, issue of the *Pacific Union Recorder*, Ellen G. White wrote, "Our lesson for the present time is, How may we most clearly comprehend and present the gospel that Christ came in person to present to John on the Isle of Patmos—the gospel that is termed, 'The revelation of Jesus Christ, which God gave him, to show unto His servants things which must shortly come to pass.'"

Revelation 1:3 says, "Blessed is he that readeth, and they that hear the words of this prophecy, and keep those things which are written therein: for the time is a hand."

Here we find a wonderful promise—a blessing is pronounced upon those who read, or hear, and keep those things that are written within it. Let us claim this promise right now as we study this precious book.

The book of Revelation expands upon the book of Daniel. This is especially true of Daniel 7, 8, and 9, where Jesus is portrayed in different roles for our salvation. We noted in the previous study that in chapter 7 Jesus is portrayed as our Judge/Advocate, in chapter 8 He is introduced as our High Priest, and in chapter 9 He is revealed as our Sacrifice.

The book of revelation may be considered a "love letter" from Jesus. Note Revelation 1:5, which says, "And from Jesus Christ, who is the faithful witness, and the first begotten of the dead, and the prince of the kings of the earth. Unto him that loved us, and washed us from our sins in his own blood."

Yes, Jesus did all of His work for our salvation, because of His love for us, and we will never completely comprehend it. This love letter expresses His pastoral care for all His sheep and His untiring work to nurture and protect us.

Let's notice some of the different names and titles that are applied to Jesus:
1. Faithful Witness – Revelation 1:5
2. Prince of the kings of the earth – Revelation 1:5
3. Alpha and Omega – Revelation 1:8, 11; 22:13
4. The Almighty – Revelation 1:8
5. Son of man – Revelation 1:13; 14:14
6. Lamb – this symbol is used twenty-eight times in Revelation, portraying Jesus as our Savior. Revelation 5:6 and 9 portray Him as "a lamb as it had been slain" and our Redeemer.
7. Lion – Revelation 5:5
8. Bridegroom – Revelation 18:23
9. KING OF KINGS AND LORD OF LORDS – Revelation 19:16

All of these names and titles, just in the book of Revelation alone, point to the multiple roles that Jesus performs for us. Let us briefly consider some of these names and titles:

"The faithful witness" phrase must also include more than Jesus being a truthful witness. It must also surely refer to the witness, or example of His perfect life, which He exchanges for our "filthy rags." By virtue of His life, death, and resurrection, He has "washed us from our sins in his own blood" (Rev. 1:5).

The "Lamb" representation is the most common one used in the book of Revelation. Jesus is the sacrificial Lamb, "which taketh away the sin of the world" (John 1:29).

A "Lion" represents His kingship and power.

"Alpha and Omega" are the first and last letters of the Greek alphabet. Revelation 1:8 says,

"I am Alpha and Omega, the beginning and the ending, saith the Lord, which is, and which was, and which is to come, the Almighty."

These words remind us of some verses in the Old Testament. In Psalm 90:1 and 2, we read, "Lord, thou hast been our dwelling place in all generations. Before the mountains were brought forth, or ever thou hadst formed the earth and the world, even from everlasting to everlasting, thou art God."

Now, turning to the next chapter, Psalm 91:1 and 2 says, "He that dwelleth in the secret place of the most High shall abide under the shadow of the Almighty. I will say of the LORD, He is my refuge and my fortress: my God; in him will I trust."

Therefore, I believe this title, Alpha and Omega, refers to Jesus as the originator and finisher of our salvation, from "the beginning and the ending." We find Alpha and Omega repeated in Revelation 1:11, and also at the end of Revelation in chapter 22, verse 13. Thus we see "the beginning and the ending" mentioned at the beginning and ending of the book of Revelation.

I want to consider one more title applied to Jesus in Revelation 1:12 and 13. There we read,

"And I turned to see the voice that spake with me. And being turned, I saw seven golden candlesticks; And in the midst of the seven candlesticks one like unto the Son of man, clothed with a garment down to the foot, and girt about the paps [the chest] with a golden girdle."

This title, "the Son of man," was a favorite one used many times by Jesus in reference to himself. Jesus became "like unto his brethren." He became a man, like us, so that He would be "a merciful and faithful high priest in things pertaining to God, to make reconciliation for the sins of the people" (Heb.

2:17). This same title, "the Son of man," is used in Revelation 14:14, where John sees Jesus coming back to earth wearing a "golden crown" on His head.

It is important to recognize the seven candlesticks as belonging to the first apartment, or holy place, of the sanctuary (Ex. 25:31-33; Heb. 9:2). This sanctuary imagery, with Jesus attired in a high priestly robe, provides us the first of seven introductory sanctuary scenes found in the book of Revelation. Furthermore, each one of these seven sanctuary scenes are connected to the beginning of one of the seven major prophecies in the book of Revelation. In other words, each sanctuary scene serves as a backdrop or background setting for the prophecy it serves.

For example, imagine a theatrical play with the backdrop setting behind the stage. This backdrop provides a setting, which helps the audience understand what is going on. We will list these seven sanctuary scenes later in this study. It would be helpful to copy these seven sanctuary scenes somewhere in the margin of your Bibles at the beginning of Revelation.

As we contemplate these seven sanctuary scenes, we will notice a progression in Jesus' ministry in the first apartment, and then into the second, or Holy of Holies, for the judgment phase of His ministry. Therefore, these seven introductory sanctuary scenes are like windows through which we can gaze upon Jesus' heavenly ministry from beginning to end. Thus, Revelation supports a two-phase sanctuary ministry in heaven.

When we understand that Jesus' work for our full atonement—i.e., our AT-ONE-MENT with God—is still in process, it becomes clear that everything was not finished on the cross. Don't make a mistake here. Yes, His sacrificial atonement was full and complete at Calvary, but sin will not be completely removed from His believers until the benefits of His sacrificial atonement have been applied to all of His followers. This was the lesson taught by the *type*, the Old Testament sanctuary services. Jesus returned to heaven to fulfill His role as our High Priest in His heavenly ministry. His death laid the foundation for our salvation, but before a full restoration can be possible, the sanctuary services in "the true tabernacle, which the Lord pitched" (Heb. 8:2) must be completed.

This is expressed well by Ellen G. White in the best-selling book *The Great Controversy*: "The sanctuary in heaven is the very center of Christ's work in behalf of men. It concerns every soul living upon the earth. It opens to view the plan of redemption, bringing us down to the very close of time and revealing the triumphant issue of the contest between righteousness and sin. It is of the utmost importance that all should thoroughly investigate these subjects and be able to give an answer to everyone that asketh them a reason of the hope that is in them. The intercession of Christ in man's behalf in the sanctuary above is as essential to the plan of salvation as was His death upon the cross. By His death He began that work which after His resurrection He ascended to complete in heaven" (pp. 488, 489).

Let us briefly consider the earthly tabernacle services, which were typical of the heavenly. When the sinner brought his sacrifice into the courtyard and it was slain, was this the full solution to the problem of his sin? No! The sin was symbolically transferred into the sanctuary by a priest, via the blood, and a record of it was entered in the different books of record. Daily, all of the sins that were confessed accumulated within the sanctuary until the Day of Atonement. On that one day of the year, these sins were taken out of the earthly sanctuary and placed upon the head of the scapegoat. This act was to make an atonement for the people (Lev. 16:10). This was also known as the "cleansing of the sanctuary." Therefore, the atonement wasn't completely finished until all of the confessed sins were erased from the books of record and the sanctuary was cleansed of the accumulated sins.

These earthly services were only symbolic representations of the future, anti-typical, heavenly sanctuary services. So, in like manner, Jesus will bring the atonement to completion when His heavenly ministry is finished, and subsequently, when sin has been removed from the universe. Hebrews 9:22-24 says, "And almost all things are by the law purged with blood; and without shedding of blood is no remission. It was therefore necessary that the patterns of things in the heavens should be purified with these; but the heavenly things themselves with better sacrifices than these. For Christ is not entered into the holy places made with hands, which are the figures of the true; but into heaven itself, now to appear in the presence of God for us."

The sanctuary in heaven is God's command center, where His throne is located and from where He rules the universe. Psalm 20:1 and 2 says, "The LORD hear thee in the day of trouble; the name of the God of Jacob defend thee; Send thee help from the sanctuary, and strengthen thee out of Zion." Psalm 77:13 says, "Thy way, O God, is in the sanctuary." Also, the prophet Asaph was troubled when he witnessed ungodly people who were prospering, but hear what he concluded in Psalm 73:17: "Until I went into the sanctuary of God; then understood I their end."

Sometimes Jesus' footsteps through the heavenly sanctuary are obscure, but nevertheless, they can be discerned by the careful reader of Revelation.

Many Bible scholars perceive more than seven visions in the book of Revelation; however, they still fall into seven main, distinct groups of visions. Kenneth Strand, Ph.D., and Mervyn Maxwell, Ph.D., outlined eight different visions, but further study by Jon Paulien, Ph.D., and others, led to the realization that two of these "visions" were only parts of one vision. The *Daniel and Revelation Committee*, in association with the *Biblical Research Institute*, now recognize only seven major visions.

At this juncture, we should reiterate the principle taught in earlier studies—that of "repetition and enlargement"—and the role it plays in the composition of Daniel and Revelation. In the book of Daniel, we have four parallel prophecies. Each one of these prophecies has a beginning, and they end with Jesus' second coming. After the first prophecy (Daniel 2), each subsequent prophecy expands on the previous prophecy. We saw this in the preceding chapter.

Revelation is the complement of Daniel, and it also has four essentially parallel, long-range prophecies. The principle of repetition and enlargement is seen throughout Revelation, but here we see, perhaps more than in Daniel, the principle of progression. Thus, the first four prophecies in Revelation have a common beginning (see the appendices), and they end at Jesus' second coming. (The seven trumpets are a minor exception, as the seventh trumpet ends after the millennium.) The fifth prophecy, however, moves forward in the timing of its starting point, as it begins with the seven last plagues. Likewise, the sixth prophecy and, finally, the seventh continue to move forward in their starting point in time until the establishment of the New Jerusalem, at the end of the millennium.

The four long-range prophecies are located in the "historical" first part of Revelation. They are as follows:

Jesus in the Book of Revelation

1. The seven churches – Revelation 1-3
2. The seven seals – Revelation 4-8:1
3. The seven trumpets – Revelation 8:2-11:18
4. The great controversy between Christ and Satan – Revelation 11:19–14

The last three major prophecies are:

5. The seven last plagues and fall of Babylon – Revelation 15-18
6. Christ's second coming and Satan's confinement – Revelation 19 and 20
7. The New Jerusalem – Revelation 21 and 22

Please notice the progression in the starting times within the last three prophecies. Also, many Bible readers have noticed that Revelation is organized into a historical division followed by future prophetic divisions. In other words, Revelation chapters 1 through 14 appear to be historical, although each one of these prophecies still include future events. However, we must realize that when John wrote Revelation, nearly all of it was future.

One valid reason to divide Revelation into historical and future sections is that historical time ends with the close of human probation. After the close of probation, the seven last plagues begin (Rev. 15). But, as mentioned, it is apparent that there is information concerning the future within each of the four historical sections. Therefore, when we read each historical prophecy to its conclusion, we learn more and more about end-time events.

Now, I want to introduce another important feature found in the book of Revelation. It is a book of contrasts. These parallel contrasts permeate the book of Revelation. Here are a few examples:

1. We have two classes of people – the saved and the lost
2. There are two contrasting leaders – the Lamb and the dragon
3. There are two contrasting women – the bride and the harlot
4. There are two contrasting capital cities – the New Jerusalem and Babylon

Now, let's list the seven introductory sanctuary scenes that make up the beginning of each major prophecy:

1. Revelation 1:12-20 – the introduction to the seven churches
2. Revelation 4-5 – the introduction to the seven seals

3. Revelation 8:2-5 – the introduction to the seven trumpets
4. Revelation 11:19 – the introduction to the great controversy theme
5. Revelation 15:5-8 – the introduction to the seven last plagues and the fall of Babylon
6. Revelation 19:1-10 – the introduction to Jesus' second coming and Satan's confinement for 1,000 years.
7. Revelation 21-22:5 – the New Jerusalem becomes established on earth

As mentioned earlier, these sanctuary scenes form the beginning of each of John's seven major visions. Also, each introductory sanctuary scene provides some of the events and the time frame of the prophecy that follows. Now we are ready to go into some of the details of the seven introductory sanctuary scenes. Remember, these sanctuary scenes provide a sketchy overview of the prophecy that follows. Also, the sanctuary is God's command center—the throne room—from where He rules the universe.

In the first sanctuary scene, we discover Jesus is in the midst of "seven golden candlesticks." In Revelation 1:20 we learn that each of the seven candlesticks represent one of the seven churches. In the earthly sanctuary, a seven branched golden lamp provided lighting for the sanctuary. Since Jesus is the "Light" and "Life" of the world (John 8:12), then He provides the light of truth for His churches.

It is interesting that in the subsequent letters to the churches, one of the names, or titles, pertaining to Jesus is taken from this first sanctuary scene and included in the letter to that church. For example, in the letter to the church of Ephesus, Jesus uses the "seven stars" and the "seven golden candlesticks" in His introduction. Then Jesus uses the expression "the first and the last, which was dead, and is alive" in His address to the Smyrna church. For the church at Pergamos, Jesus uses the "sharp two-edge sword," etc.

Although Paul established these seven (and more) churches in Asia Minor, it is well recognized that these letters can also be applied to seven sequential eras of time throughout the history of Christ's church, from its inception during apostolic time, until the close of history. We'll discuss this more in the next chapter.

At this time let's take a closer look at Revelation 3:21. It says, "To him that overcometh will I grant to sit with me in my throne, even as I also overcame, and am set down with my Father in his throne." This verse, along with many other verses in the Bible, tells us that only those who overcome will be included in Jesus' kingdom. It also tells us there are two thrones in heaven—one for the Father and another for Jesus—in His kingdom, wherein we have a share of His throne. Note also that the twenty-four elders also have "seats" about one of these thrones (Rev. 4:4).

The second sanctuary scene is found in two whole chapters of Revelation, in which we have a description of the inauguration of Jesus as our High Priest. This sanctuary scene is in Revelation 4 and 5. It has the most extensive sanctuary imagery in the book of Revelation. In chapter 5 we have Jesus represented as "the Lion of the tribe of Judah" (verse 5) and "a Lamb as it had been slain" (verse 6).

In this sanctuary scene, Jesus opens the seven seals, which had previously been closed. Therein, we are introduced to the seven seals. These seven seals are another long-range prophecy, covering the entire age of the Christian Church. This prophecy parallels the seven churches. Due to limited space, I apologize for not going into the details of this second sanctuary scene. Many sermons could be given from just these two chapters of Revelation.

The third sanctuary scene begins in chapter 8, verse 2, and continues on through verse 5. Notice that the first verse of the eighth chapter really belongs to the previous prophecy of the seven seals. Remember, the chapters and verses were added later, and sometimes they were not properly aligned, as in this case. Note the transition from the seals to the trumpets in verse 2.

Now, moving on to verse 3, we read, "And another angel came and stood at the altar." Notice the word "altar." This altar is the altar of incense that was part of the furniture within the first apartment of the sanctuary. However, even though this altar was located within the first apartment, it also functioned during the second apartment ministry of the high priest. Remember, the incense from this altar rose over the top of the curtain, filling the Most Holy Place as well.

Proceeding on in verse 3, we read, ". . . having a golden censer, and there was given unto him much incense, that he should offer it with the prayers of all saints upon the golden altar which was before the throne." The altar of incense can be considered "before the throne" because of its function, even though its physical location was in the first apartment "before the veil" that faced the second apartment. The high priest would fill his censer with incense as he ministered before the ark (Ex. 30:1, 6; Heb. 9:3, 4). The "angel" represents our Savior, as it is He who offers incense mixed with "the prayers of all saints" during His intercessory ministry.

Going on to verse 5, we read, "And the angel took the censer, and filled it with fire of the altar, and cast it into the earth: and there were voices, and thunderings, and lightenings, and an earthquake." This scene aptly describes the close of probation and subsequent events. Thus, this third sanctuary scene portrays Jesus' intercessory ministry, from its beginning to the end. Therefore, the prophecy of the seven trumpets is long-range prophecy, covering the time frame of Jesus' ministry in both apartments of the heavenly sanctuary.

Now, the fourth introductory sanctuary scene is only one verse, and it is found in Revelation 11:19. Here again, this verse really belongs to the fourth long-range prophecy of the great controversy theme beginning in chapter 12. Let us first glance at Revelation 11:18. Please notice that verse 18 summarizes the seventh trumpet prophecy and also previews the rest of the book of Revelation (chapters 12 through 22). Revelation 11:18 says, "And the nations were angry, and thy wrath is come [the "wrath of God" begins with the seven last plagues, as brought out in Revelation 15:1], and the time of the dead, that they should be judged, and that thou shouldest give reward unto thy servants and prophets, and to the saints, and them that fear thy name, small and great; and shouldest destroy them which destroy the earth." Therefore, the seventh trumpet includes the seven last plagues and extends until the end of the millennium.

We are now ready to read Revelation 11:19: "And the temple of God was opened in heaven, and there was seen in his temple the ark of his testament: and there were lightnings, and voices, and thunderings, and an earthquake, and great hail."

Notice the word "ark." This ark is located within the Most Holy Place of the sanctuary in heaven. It contains the "testament," which is God's Ten Commandments, the gold standard used for judgment of the living and the dead. Since "the temple of God was opened" and the ark is visible, we must be gazing into the Most Holy Place. Thus, this sanctuary scene, and its prophecy of the great controversy between Christ and Satan, is a long-range prophecy. Notice that the last words in the sanctuary scene are "great hail." In Revelation 16:18-21 there is mentioned "voices, and thunders, and lightnings; and there was a great earthquake . . . and great hail." These are events transpiring during the seventh plague.

Moving forward to Revelation 15, we come to the fifth sanctuary scene. It begins with verse 5 and runs through verse 8. This sanctuary scene introduces us to the seven last plagues and is obviously a short-range one. Also, please notice that this sanctuary scene, with its prophecy, has progressed forward in time. Verse 5 says, "And after that I looked, and behold, the temple of the tabernacle of the testimony in heaven was opened."

The phrase "tabernacle of the testimony" means the "house of the law." The phrase "the temple of the tabernacle" must refer to that part of the sanctuary where the "testimony" was located. Thus, the "temple" of the "tabernacle" that was "opened" must refer to the Most Holy Place of the heavenly sanctuary. Although it was opened, it was to allow the exit of the seven angels who were to execute the seven last plagues. This must be the correct conclusion, as these angels do not execute the seven last plagues until probation has closed and Jesus has finished His second apartment ministry. In addition, the sanctuary is opened to the spiritual gaze of the serious Bible student, that he/she may understand the ministry of Jesus as our High Priest in the "true tabernacle, which the Lord pitched, and not man" (Heb. 8:2).

Let us read Revelation 15:8, which says, "And the temple was filled with smoke from the glory of God, and from his power; and no man was able to enter into the temple." One Bible commentary indicates this is a cryptic reference to the end of Jesus' intercessory ministry; thus probation has closed. Note that the fifth prophecy also includes chapters 17 and 18, which detail the fall of Babylon during the fifth through seventh plagues.

The sixth sanctuary scene introduces us to Jesus' second coming and the confinement of Satan for 1,000 years. The sanctuary scene is in Revelation 19:1-10. Let's notice verse 2, wherein God has finished His judgment. In verse 2 we read, "For true and righteous are his judgments: for he hath judged the great whore, which did corrupt the earth with her fornication, and hath avenged the blood of his servants at her hand."

The only sanctuary furniture in this sanctuary scene is a "throne" (verse 4). But there is a worship service in progress and the marriage of Jesus is consummated (verses 4-8). This corresponds precisely with Daniel 7:9-11, where thrones are "cast down" (literally, put in place) and the judgment is in session—a judgment that takes away the beast's dominion and condemns the beast to the flames. The marriage of the Lamb parallels the Son of God receiving His dominion in Daniel 7:14. Whereas Daniel's vision is an overview of the entire investigative judgment, this sixth sanctuary scene in Revelation is the consummation of that investigative judgment and the commencement of the executive judgment. This sixth prophecy can be considered another long-range one, as it includes Satan's 1,000 year confinement during the millennium.

Finally, the seventh sanctuary scene is found in Revelation 21 and runs through chapter 22, verse 5. It introduces the final prophecy, which portrays the New Jerusalem with the Father and the "Lamb" becoming our sanctuary. "And I saw no temple therein: for the Lord God Almighty and the Lamb are the temple of it" (Rev. 21:22).

Although we have completed the seven sanctuary scenes in the book of Revelation, we haven't gone into any deeper details in the substance of any of these seven major prophecies. That would be too large an undertaking and would be beyond the purpose of this overview of Revelation. However, we will highlight some of the details in the prophecies themselves.

The prophecy of the seven churches has not presented any major problems for our understanding, although we have by no means mined all of its treasures. Herein, Jesus gave promises to those who have overcome sin in their lives. In Revelation 21 and 22, we see a foretaste of the fulfillment of these promises to those who overcome. We also have a fair understanding of the great controversy found in Revelation 12-14. Chapters 15-20—the seven last plagues, a spotlight on the fall of Babylon, and Satan's 1,000-year confinement—are also generally understood by the churches. However, the prophecies of the seals and the trumpets have presented a number of problems for many of us. Without going into any details of these two prophecies, I would like to present some simple generalizations.

The seals and trumpets both span the entire Christian Church era. As we have seen, the seventh trumpet encompasses the plagues. The major difference between the seals and the trumpets pertains to the different classes of people targeted in their judgments. In the seals, the judgments are directed at the professed people of God. Most of God's righteous people were sealed by death, with the exception of the 144,000 saints who will be alive at the end of the sixth seal. In Revelation 6:17, a question is asked by those witnessing Christ's second coming: "For the great day of his wrath is come; and who shall be able to stand?" The answer is given in the seventh chapter. If we would carefully read the sixth seal (Rev. 6:12-17), it becomes apparent that this scene primarily refers to events connected with Jesus' second coming.

Now, some may raise the question, "Why would God allow the judgments of the seals to be inflicted upon His professed people?" Consider the experience of Israel just before they entered the Promised Land. Moses told them they would receive "blessings" or "curses," depending upon whether they obeyed or disobeyed His commandments. These blessings and curses are recorded in Leviticus 26 and Deuteronomy 28-32. The same principle applies to the New Testament church. Therefore, the warning judgments of the seals began with a pure New Testament church. During the first seal, this pure church proclaimed a pure gospel. As centuries passed, however, the Christian Church drifted into apostasy. Thus, God allowed the judgments of the seals to afflict His professed people. Nevertheless, during the centuries, God had a minority of faithful Christians who were martyrs, and these righteous ones were sealed by death.

Another important feature pertaining to the seals is that the first five seals began at different times, but they all continue on together until the close of probation and Christ's second coming. That is why the question, "How long, O Lord, holy and true, dost thou not judge and avenge our blood on them that dwell on the earth?" (Rev. 6:10), is followed with the answer, "that they should rest yet for a little season, until their fellow servants also and their brethren, that should be killed as they were, should be fulfilled" (verse 11).

Now, I just want to make a summary statement on the seven trumpets. As mentioned, the trumpets are judgments also, but they target the wicked, especially the enemies of God's people. The first four trumpets cover the fall of the Pagan Western Roman Empire, while the fifth and sixth trumpets inflicted judgments, first upon eastern Imperial Rome, then upon Western papal Rome.

God used the Muslim nations as His instrument to render these judgments upon the Eastern Roman Empire, as well as on the apostate Papal Roman Empire. Furthermore, I believe God will signally use the Muslim nations again, during the third "woe" of the seventh trumpet, to bring an apostate world into judgment. The fifth and sixth trumpets contain two time prophecies that provided great impetus in the beginning of the Millerite movement, especially the second one ending on August 11, 1840. We will discuss these prophecies in a later chapter.

As we near the conclusion of this study, I need to introduce two interludes found in the book of Revelation. Interludes are essentially inclusions of information that may be placed in parenthesis, i.e., a change in emphasis. These interludes can be considered "expanding spotlights on the final events of the church age." Therefore, both of these interludes include events connected with the "final crisis."

The first interlude spans a short time from the close of the sixth seal through the culmination of the seventh seal. It is found in Revelation 7. This chapter introduces the 144,000 saints who are sealed during the end-time sealing. Dear reader, we are nearing this period of time. We are nearing the turbulent hour when the end-time sealing will be placed upon God's faithful people. This time will come upon us as an overwhelming surprise when the Sunday Law has been passed. We need the showers of the early rain now, before the Sunday Law is passed, in order to be ready for the refreshing showers of the latter rain when it comes.

The second interlude is found during the sounding of the sixth trumpet. This interlude is in Revelation 10 and continues on into chapter 11, verse 14. The time frame begins around 1798 (the time of the deadly wound) and focuses upon God's end-time movement. This interlude also includes a judgment against the nation of France, the atheistic power brought to view in chapter 11. We will discuss this further in the chapter on the trumpets. This history extends to 1844, which marks the beginning of the seventh trumpet and the beginning of the investigative judgment.

As we conclude this overview, my hope and desire is that you will go back into Revelation, as a devotional study, and find what a blessing may be received as we contemplate all that Jesus does for us, because of His love for us.

Focus upon Jesus, and not upon the soon coming crisis. Do you really believe in your heart that Jesus is coming soon? Our actions will demonstrate what we truly believe. Time is truly short, so let us re-consecrate our lives to Jesus on a daily basis, so that we may be prepared to meet Him.

In closing, consider this short passage from the book Ministry of Healing: "In all your work remember that you are bound up with Christ, a part of the great plan of redemption. The love of Christ, in a healing, life-giving current, is to flow through your life. As you seek to draw others within the circle of His love, let the purity of your language, the unselfishness of your service, the joyfulness of your demeanor, bear witness to the power of His grace. Give to the world so pure and righteous a representation of Him, that men shall behold Him in His beauty" (p. 156).

Chapter 10

The Churches of Revelation

I hope you will agree with me that the book of Revelation is a prophecy. We find this stated in verse 3 of the first chapter: "Blessed is he that readeth, and they that hear the words of this prophecy, and keep those things which are written therein: for the time is at hand."

Yes, Revelation is a prophecy, but in a broader sense, the whole Bible contains prophecy. Peter expressed this truth when he wrote his second epistle. In 2 Peter 1:21 we read, "For the prophecy came not in old time by the will of man: but holy men of God spake as they were moved by the Holy Ghost."

Of course, he was referring to the prophecies of the Old Testament, which are a revelation of Jesus from the Holy Spirit. The Old Testament presents prophecies concerning Jesus through the typology of the sanctuary services and the testimonies of the prophets. In fact, Jesus Himself communicated to His prophets through spoken words, visions, and dreams.

Going further with this same line of reasoning, you will, hopefully, agree with me that "the revelation of Jesus Christ," as mentioned in the first verse, could also be considered the gospel. Ellen G. White understood this concept and wrote about it in the *Pacific Union Recorder*, January 14, 1904: "Our lesson for the present time is, How may we most clearly comprehend and present the gospel that Christ came in person to present to John on the isle of Patmos—the gospel that is termed, 'the Revelation of Jesus Christ," which God gave him, to show unto His servants things which must shortly come to pass."

We will begin this discussion with some repetition of the preceding chapter on Jesus in the book of Revelation and some earlier chapters. About 1900 years ago, Jesus' beloved disciple John was exiled to the isle of Patmos. This small island of volcanic rock is located in the Aegean Sea about 37 miles from the mainland of Asia Minor. John was banished there because of his bearing "record of the word of God, and of the testimony of Jesus Christ, and of all things that he saw." Emperor Domitian, however, could not destroy him, even in a caldron of boiling oil, so he sent him to Patmos in order to silence his "testimony." However, he was far from silenced.

Jesus honored His aged disciple by revealing to him "things which must shortly come to pass" (Rev. 1:1). While "in the Spirit on the Lord's day" (verse 10), John had a series of visions that he recorded in Revelation. The phrase "in the Spirit" means that he was either in vision, "walking in the Spirit," or both. The "Lord's day" must refer to the "Sabbath of the Lord thy God," as proclaimed in the fourth commandment (Ex. 20:8-11). In Mark 2:28, Jesus claims that He is "Lord also of the Sabbath." Isaiah 58:13 is even more conclusive, wherein God calls the Sabbath, "My holy day." As no other day is designated by the Lord in this manner, it leaves no other reasonable alternative.

Many Christians believe that Revelation is a sealed book, but this is not so. The word "revelation" means something that is revealed. Granted, there are symbols and imagery that require comparing scripture with scripture, but with the aid of the Holy Spirit, Jesus wanted this information to be understood. In verses 4 and 11, John specifically addresses his letter to "the seven churches which are in Asia." Beginning at Ephesus, a mailman would deliver the letters in a loop-like route to the seven churches. Using the existing Roman roads, he would travel about 300 miles in order to make the entire loop. We acknowledge that John intended his letters to first go to the seven churches mentioned, but these cities were not the only ones with churches in Asia Minor.

For example, there was a church at Colossae, for whom Paul wrote his epistle to the Colossians. Colossae was located about seven miles from Laodicea. Why, then, were these seven particular churches selected? Think about it. While the messages must have applied literally to each of those seven churches, it is generally agreed that these seven were representative of the Christian Church, reaching down through the centuries, until Jesus' second coming. In other words, the local church at Ephesus was representative of the church during the first Christian era. Following the first era, the local church at Smyrna was typical of the second Christian era, and so on.

Specific characteristics of each church can be found to correspond precisely with characteristics of different ages of the church. There is at least one more application possible, and that is that there are professed Christians who have the typical characteristics, and are undergoing the same circumstances of any one of the seven churches during any era. For example, during our Laodicean church era, we have groups of professed Ephesian Christians who have lost their first love for Jesus. Also, there are others in our Laodicean era who are Smyrna Christians and are facing persecution, etc. In Revelation 1:5 we read, "And from Jesus Christ, who is the faithful witness, and the first begotten of the dead, and the prince of the kings of the earth. Unto him that loved us, and washed us from our sins in his own blood." Thus, Revelation is a "love letter" from Jesus to His church in every age. Wonder of wonders! How can we ever comprehend the sacrifice Jesus made for our salvation? It will be the wonder of the redeemed through endless ages.

It is interesting that in the letters to each of the churches that one of the names, titles, or actions pertaining to Jesus is taken from the first sanctuary scene and is included in the letter to that church. For example, in the letter to the church of Ephesus, Jesus identifies Himself as He who holds the "seven stars" and walks in the midst of the "seven golden candlesticks." Then Jesus uses the title "the first and the last, which was dead, and is alive" in His address to the church of Smyrna. For the church at Pergamos, Jesus uses the "sharp two-edge sword," etc. All of this imagery is found in the first introductory sanctuary scene of verses 12 through 20.

Now, let's take a closer look at each of the seven local cities, with their respective churches.

EPHESUS

Ephesus means desirable. This city was a vacation paradise, where the pleasures of sin could be indulged in by the first century Hedonist. It was a large city with a harbor where ships were docked. These ships brought merchandise from the East and the West. Ephesus had a magnificent temple for their goddess, Diana (Acts 19). This temple was one of the seven wonders of the ancient world.

The Churches of Revelation

The church of Ephesus had a rich heritage, being founded by Paul, with Aquilla and Priscilla. This was about AD 53, when Paul was returning from his second missionary journey. During Paul's third missionary journey, he spent about three years in Ephesus, nurturing the church.

We are informed by tradition that John and Mary, the mother of Jesus, both moved to Ephesus just before the destruction of Jerusalem. John became known as John the Elder. John knew firsthand that this desirable church of Ephesus had lost its first love for Jesus. We also learn from tradition that Paul's epistle to the Ephesians was circulated to all of the other churches.

Eventually, after the first century Ephesus surpassed Antioch as the center or cradle of Christianity.

SMYRNA

Smyrna was about 25 miles north of Ephesus. It boasted a better harbor than Ephesus and also rivaled Ephesus in commercial activity.

During the first century AD, there was a large Jewish population living in Smyrna. There were also many Romans living there who enforced worship of the emperor. The church struggled against both of these hostile factions and thus became a persecuted church.

Smyrna is thought to mean "crushed myrrh," which is a fragrant odor produced from crushing the plant. This would be a fitting portrayal of the martyrdom of Christians in this city. We learn from tradition that Polycarp, the bishop of Smyrna, died a martyr's death there. Apparently, the Jews were foremost in gathering firewood for his martyrdom.

PERGAMOS

Pergamos, which is further north, was the capital city of the entire Roman province of Asia Minor. This ancient city was built upon a hill, raised up about 1,000 feet above the surrounding countryside. Pergamos was a very fitting name, meaning "elevation" or "exaltation."

It had a large school of medicine named after Asclepius, the god of healing. The city also erected a massive altar on a hill to the pagan god Zeus. It was in Pergamos that the Babylonian priests relocated after the fall of Babylon, so in addition to the false gods the city worshipped, the Babylonian religion was present.

Pergamos also had a reputable library, nearly equal to the one in Alexandria. Parchment, which comes from leather, was invented and first used for writing in the city of Pergamos.

The church at Pergamos compromised the principles of Christianity in order to gain favor with the Roman government. Thereafter, the church hierarchy became popular and exalted.

THYATIRA

The letter to Thyatira was the longest of the seven letters to the churches. Thyatira boasted no claim to fame, but it was established upon an important trade route, using existing Roman roads. It was a workingman's town and had many trade guilds for the manufacturing and dying of clothes. When Paul was evangelizing in Philippi, he baptized Lydia, a prominent woman merchant from Thyatira who sold purple dye (Acts 16:14).

The church in Thyatira had only a remnant of Christians who avoided the false teachings of "Jezebel." That remnant is referred to in Revelation 2:24 as the "rest," but we will go into this later after we finish the local history of the seven cities and their churches.

SARDIS

Sardis was initially built on a high mountain ridge, but it was later relocated down in the valley below. During John's youth, Sardis was being rebuilt after a large earthquake destroyed it in AD 17. It is important that we recognize that Sardis' golden years were in the past. Earlier, it was a very wealthy city. Its riches were legendary when the city was the capital of the Lydian kingdom.

Like Thyatira, the church at Sardis had only a remnant who were righteous. In Revelation 3:4, Jesus said, "Thou hast a few names even in Sardis which have not defiled their garments." Please notice that God's faithful people were few in numbers, in both the churches of Thyatira and Sardis.

PHILADELPHIA

Philadelphia was the youngest of the seven cities. It was located upon a broad hill with volcanic cliffs situated between two fertile valleys. This city had famous vineyards in red soil, similar to those in Napa Valley, California.

The city, and its church, were known for brotherly love. In fact, Philadelphia means "brotherly love." This affectionate term came from a king who renamed the city in loyalty to his older brother who had died.

LAODICEA

Laodicea was the wealthiest of the seven cities during the first century. It was well-known for banking and commerce. The city was located in a valley near some mountains, which towered to 9,000 feet in altitude. In AD 60, a large earthquake destroyed most of the city; however, the citizens of Laodicea, proud of their affluence, refused Roman help and rebuilt the city using their own resources.

They had a medical school that rivaled the one in Pergamos. They also produced a famous Phrygian powder that was used as eye-salve for healing eye problems. The city had large flocks of black sheep, from which they produced black woolen clothing. These clothes were exported to many other countries.

But Laodicea had a problem with its water supply. Some hot springs from the mountain above the city flowed down into the valley of Laodicea. By the time it reached the city below, the water was—you guessed it—lukewarm.

With this background information complete, we need to look at the content of these seven letters. It should be noted that these letters followed a regular format. First, Jesus would address the angel (the messenger) to that particular church. This person was probably the leading minister. Next, He would include a description of Himself taken from the first sanctuary scene, which we mentioned earlier. After describing some of His attributes, Jesus would give the church a commendation. He did this for the first six churches, but there was no commendation given to the church of Laodicea. Following the commendation, Jesus gave reproofs to all the churches, with the exceptions of Smyrna and Philadelphia. These two churches received only commendations, no reproofs. Finally, Jesus gave His counsels and warnings, followed by His promises to those who overcome. We will now consider some the spiritual content of each letter.

EPHESUS

Now, let us return to Revelation 2:1, where we read, "Unto the angel of the church of Ephesus write; These things saith he that holdeth the seven stars in his right hand." If we go back to the first sanctuary scene (Rev. 1:16), we read, "And he had in his right hand seven stars." I point this out to re-emphasize that the first sanctuary scene serves as a backdrop setting for the prophecy to the seven churches. All of the sanctuary scenes serve their prophecies in the same manner throughout the book of Revelation.

Going forward in chapter 2, John continues his narration of Jesus in verse 1. He says, "Who walketh in the midst of the seven golden candlesticks." Thus, Jesus is in direct communication with all of His churches, as the number seven represents completeness.

Following His commendations, a reproof comes in verse 4. "Nevertheless I have somewhat against thee, because thou hast left thy first love." In this reproof, the church with many advantages and virtues has eventually lost the essence of Christianity, which is love for Jesus and humanity. (Later, when we come to Laodicea, we'll notice a striking resemblance to another love-deficient church.) Then, Jesus counsels the church of Ephesus to repent "and do the first works." Therefore, Jesus is looking for good works of love, which are the fruit of the Spirit.

SMYRNA

Moving on to the church at Smyrna, we read in verse 8, "And unto the angel of the church in Smyrna write; These things saith the first and the last, which was dead, and is alive." Once again, as we refer to the first sanctuary scene in Revelation 1:17 and 18, we find this description, "the first and the last." Then, in verse 18 Jesus says, "[I] was dead; and, behold, I am alive for evermore."

Hereafter, we will skip over the descriptive sanctuary scene portrayals of Jesus given to the remaining churches, but please notice them in your study of these churches.

Let's now look at Revelation 2:9, where Jesus says, "I know thy works, and tribulation, and poverty." And in parentheses He states, "but thou art rich."

The Churches of Revelation

What a marvelous commendation Jesus gives to this church of Smyrna! Jesus gave no rebuke, nor even counsel to repent. (By the way, the church of Philadelphia likewise received only praise, and no rebuke.)

Jesus counseled the Smyrna church to be faithful unto death (verse 10). He also mentioned a tribulation that would last for ten days. It is interesting that in prophetic reckoning, using a "day for a year," this period of time represents ten years. History tells us that Diocletian and his co-emperors (a tetrarch) inflicted a severe persecution of Christians from AD 303 to AD 313, thus prophetically fulfilling this prophecy. Therefore, the church of Smyrna prophetically includes the second era of Jesus' universal church. Emperor Constantine ended this persecution in AD 313, by his Edict of Toleration, thus beginning the third era of the church.

In the interest of keeping this overview brief, we will omit Jesus' promises of rewards to those who overcome. However, these rewards are wonderful promises for our consideration, and you would do well to mine these letters in their entirety, again and again, for precious gems of truth.

PERGAMOS

In verse 12 of chapter 2, we come to the church at Pergamos. Remember, Pergamos means "exaltation" or "elevation." The city was 1,000 feet above the surrounding countryside, as already mentioned. Pergamos was not only a capital city, but it was also the center of Babylonian and other pagan religions.

One major problem in the church was allowing immoral influences to enter it. This occurred in the local church and also during the Pergamos era. Following the Edict of Toleration by Constantine, he made Christianity the state religion. Persecution then ceased, and Christianity became very popular. Standards became compromised, and the world naturally came into the church. Therefore, Jesus rebuked this church for its apostasy.

Notice that "Satan's seat" is mentioned in Revelation 2:13. This could be indicating the Roman governor's seat in this city. During the era of AD 313 to AD 538, emperor worship was a common practice in Pergamos. In addition, the worship of pagan gods, including Zeus who was considered the chief god, was prevalent there, which may more accurately explain "Satan's seat." Mention was made earlier of the altar to Zeus that was located here and the Babylonian priests that relocated in Pergamos after the fall of Babylon.

In verse 14, we notice that some in this church held to the doctrine of Balaam, who caused the children "to eat things sacrificed unto idols, and to commit fornication." While this may have been happening literally, the spiritual application may be seen in the growing church and state relationship. (See Revelation 17:2.)

In verse 15, there are others who "hold the doctrine of the Nicolaitanes." Two comments from the pen of Ellen G. White pertaining to the Nicolaitanes are especially interesting. These are found in *The SDA Bible Commentary*, volume 7, page 957: "Is it [our sin] the sin of the Nicolaitan[e]s, turning the grace of God into lasciviousness?"

In other words, the problem with the Nicolaitanes was immorality. Then in the next passage, we read, "The doctrine is now largely taught that the gospel of Christ has made the law of God of no effect; that by 'believing' we are released from the necessity of being doers of the Word. But this is the doctrine of the Nicolaitan[e]s, which Christ so unsparingly condemned" (Ibid.).

In the remaining verses to Pergamos, Jesus calls for repentance and offers a reward to those who overcome.

THYATIRA

In verse 18 we come to the church at Thyatira. Please notice that this church contained two distinct classes of people. In verse 24 we read, "But unto you I say, and unto the rest (i.e. remnant) in Thyatira, as many as have not this doctrine, and which have not known the depths of Satan."

This remnant is, most likely, the church in the wilderness, i.e., the Waldenses, Albigenses, etc., who refused to go along with the compromises of that era.

Going back to verse 20, we notice Jezebel is introduced in a symbolic role as a false prophetess who leads the church into idolatry and fornication. Apparently, the sins in the church of Pergamos were continued in Thyatira, but to a greater degree. We must acknowledge that the Christian Church of the middle ages strikingly resembled the church of Thyatira. As Jezebel used the power of the king (state) to persecute the prophets of God, so the Roman Catholic Church used the power of the state to persecute God's faithful followers. The state church grew exceedingly evil and idolatrous.

The Churches of Revelation

In verse 28, Jesus says, "And I will give him the morning star." John Wycliffe has been known for centuries as the "morning star of the reformation." He was one of the earliest of the reformers, paving the way for later reformers with his bold stand against abuses and his emphasis on the gospel.

SARDIS

Now, we come to the fifth church in Sardis. The message to Sardis is essentially a message to the Protestant churches. Sardis means "prince of joy." This truly characterizes the joy of the Protestant faith when the Bible became resurrected. For centuries there was a struggle between the papacy, which was the established Christian Church, and the Protestant churches. The Protestant faith was more pure in its beginning, however, similar to the literal city of Sardis, it had outlived its past glory. By the early 1700s, the Protestant reformation had nearly died, but in the later period of the reformation, the church of Sardis had a remnant who were faithful.

Notice what Jesus says about Sardis in Revelation 3:4: "Thou hast a few names even in Sardis which have not defiled their garments; and they shall walk with me in white: for they are worthy."

Prophetically, we now have Christ's supposed universal church and the Protestant churches all dead, or about to die. Thus, in the local church of Sardis, and during the Sardis era, Jesus has only a remnant that are "worthy."

PHILADELPHIA

Now, we come to the church of Philadelphia. It was a loving church. Like Smyrna, there is no rebuke or warning given. Jesus only mentions that they are weak.

Moving on to Revelation 3:8, we read, "I know thy works: behold, I have set before thee an open door." There is general agreement among Seventh-day Adventists, who looked for the soon coming of Jesus, that the Philadelphian era began in 1798 with the "deadly wound" of the papacy. Therefore, the "open door" probably applies to the worldwide availability of the gospel message of Christ's second coming. The "open door" for this message occurred after 1798.

Ellen G. White supports this view by aligning the Second Advent Awakening Movement with the Philadelphian church era. This application also correlates well with the "little book open" of Revelation 10:2, which refers back to the "sealed" book of Daniel 12:4, which was opened shortly after 1798. Other Bible students believe this "open door" for the Philadelphian church took place in 1844, which is the termination of the 2300-day prophecy. (Note: Using the year for a day principle, the 2300-day prophecy would be 2300 years.) In 1844 the door to the second apartment of the sanctuary was opened in heaven for the anti-typical Day of Atonement. Following 1844, Jesus revealed more truth to His followers.

Be that as it may, the church of Philadelphia appears to be involved in a worldwide conflict as revealed in verse 10, which says, "Because thou hast kept the word of my patience, I also will keep thee from the hour of temptation, which shall come upon all the world, to try them that dwell upon the earth."

LAODICEA

Now, we come to the seventh and final church of Laodicea. Laodicea means "judging of the people." This definition is appropriate in that it describes a people who are undergoing a pre-advent judgment before Jesus comes. This is an investigative judgment that precedes the executive judgment, similar to the investigative judgment in a court case where the judge and jury hear all the evidence before ruling for or against the defendant. This is the picture portrayed in Daniel and Revelation. For example, Daniel 7:10 says, "The judgment was set, and the books were opened." Then we see the executive judgment in verse 11: "I beheld then because of the voice of the great words which the horn spake: I beheld even till the beast was slain, and his body destroyed, and given to the burning flame."

As mentioned in an earlier chapter, this investigative judgment parallels the cleansing of the sanctuary, or the anti-typical Day of Atonement, when the life record of the saints comes up for review as the books are opened (Rev. 3:5, 20:12), after which Jesus returns to reward every man "according as his work shall be" (Rev. 22:12). We are not saved by our works, but our works testify whether or not we are truly converted and surrendered to Christ.

Unfortunately, Laodicea's condition is lukewarm. Thus, Jesus is telling us who are living today that we have lukewarm works. Lukewarm works are those works that have an important missing ingredient. In other words, we are attempting to do good works without the love of Jesus in our hearts. Therefore, without Jesus in our hearts, we cannot demonstrate any fruit of the Spirit in our lives.

Laodicea is a church lacking love, similar to the church of Ephesus when it had lost its first love. Perhaps you have noticed some parallels between Ephesus and Laodicea, the first and the last churches. There are also parallels between Smyrna and Philadelphia, the second and second to last churches. Finally, the third and third from last churches, Pergamos and Sardis, have parallels. Space prohibits a discussion on these parallels, but you are encouraged to study them for yourself.

In all of the letters to the churches, Jesus counsels the members to overcome. Thus, He repeats this counsel seven times, once to every church. Jesus also repeats the words found in Revelation 3:22 to every church, along with His counsel to overcome. Jesus says, "He that hath an ear, let him hear what the Spirit saith unto the churches."

In conclusion, I will quote a short passage from *The Lamb Among The Beasts* by Roy Naden. He says, "Looking at Laodicea, Jesus wrote: 'Despite the banks, you are poor. Despite the eye treatment, you are blind. Despite the tunics, you are naked. You don't need money from the bank; you need My gold purified in the fire of affliction. You don't need a black tunic; you need a white robe of My purest righteousness. You don't need Phrygian powder; you need the insight of My Spirit to see yourself as you really are, and Me as I really am. You need discipline, so repent."

Let's not keep our loving Savior on the outside of the door to our hearts. Right now, while the Holy Spirit is making an appeal to you, rededicate your heart and life in loving service to Him.

Chapter 11

An Overview of the Seals and The Trumpets

The purpose of this study will be to give a simple overview of the seals and the trumpets in the book of Revelation. Since these prophecies are two of the most challenging and difficult for biblical scholars, I need to begin with generalizations that are clear and easily understood. Many wild and fanciful speculations have been proposed by different theologians and Bible students on the timing and interpretations of the seven trumpets. Due to space constraints, these interpretations will not be included in my overview, except in rare occasions where popular misunderstandings may need to be addressed.

At the beginning of this study, there is an important truth that needs to be emphasized—the historicist method of interpreting Bible prophecy is the most sound. The historicist method embraces the entire history of the Christian Church, like an unrolling scroll, down through the ages. It does not zero in on one particular time period, but considers the conditions, circumstances, and developments of every era. This, we believe, is in harmony with the loving character of God, who knows what every one of His faithful followers has endured or will endure for the cross of Christ. I will, therefore, give a straightforward, historicist explanation of the events that are included in the seals and the trumpets.

Bear in mind, those of us with Western minds need to understand that John was a descendant of an Eastern culture, and he wrote Revelation using

An Overview of the Seals and The Trumpets

Hebrew parallelisms. In other words, Revelation was not written in a narrative story format. Instead, it was patterned in a similar manner to the book of Daniel, which has four parallel prophecies. Furthermore, the book of Revelation complements and expands the book of Daniel.

Here I would like to reiterate that in Revelation there are seven major prophecies, which are as follows:
1. The seven churches – chapters 1-3
2. The seven seals – chapters 4-8:1
3. The seven trumpets – chapters 8:2-11:18
4. The great controversy theme – chapters 11:19-14:20
5. The seven last plagues that accomplishes the fall of Babylon – chapters 15-18:24
6. Christ's second coming and Satan bound for 1,000 years – chapters 19-20:15
7. Establishment of New Jerusalem on earth – chapters 21-22:21

The first four major long-range prophecies in Revelation are somewhat parallel, similar, to the book of Daniel, as mentioned above, except the fourth prophecy in Revelation has a flashback to the war in heaven. Another exception includes the later starting dates of the first three prophecies, since the empires of Babylon, Medo-Persia, and Greece were past history. John began his prophecies with the empire of his day, the fourth empire of Daniel's visions, pagan Rome.

I believe it is necessary to begin this study with more background history before we discuss the seven seals and the seven trumpets. The seals and trumpets are intimately connected to the seven churches. In other words, all three of these prophecies span the entire Christian Church era and, consequently, run somewhat parallel with each other. Furthermore, they are interrelated, as already mentioned.

The seven seals operate on the principle of repetition and enlargement, in a similar manner as in the book of Daniel, i.e., the first seal expands on the first church, and the second seal expands on the second church, etc.

Recall that in the book of Daniel, the first prophecy in chapter 2 gives the basic prophecy, followed by another parallel prophecy in chapter 7, which repeats some of the basic details but enlarges the first prophecy with more details. Then, in chapters 8 and 9, another repetition and enlargement is provided. Finally in chapter 11, the fourth prophecy follows the same format of repetition and enlargement.

In a similar manner, the first five seals enlarge upon the first five churches. As noted in the previous chapter, the lessons in the letters to the seven churches not only applied to the local churches of Asia, but apply equally as well to the "seven eras" of the church, until Jesus' second coming. We cannot assign a strict time frame for each seal and church, for they at times overlap one another. In addition, the fifth and sixth seals reveal history as well as future events, spanning the time of both the sixth and seventh church ages, culminating in the second coming of Christ. The seventh seal, revealing silence in heaven, points forward to that time when heaven is emptied, as all the hosts of heaven accompany Jesus at His second coming.

Uriah Smith, in a lesson study titled "The Seven Seals," wrote these summary remarks about the seals: "Taken as a whole we may say that these seals represent the great apostasy in the church. The first seal represents the apostolic church in its purity. The succeeding seals, the church in its apostasy. But the true church occasionally appears this side the first seal. It is the oil and the wine of the third seal, the martyrs of the fourth and fifth seals; and those who will be saved at the coming of Christ to which the last seal brings us. While the apostate church will be among those who will call for the rocks and mountains to fall on them and hide them from his presence in the day of His wrath."

The seven trumpets are also connected to the seven churches, but in a different manner than the seven seals. In the trumpets, the judgments are executed upon the wicked, the enemies of God's people, during the entire history of the seven churches. In other words, while the seals reveal the internal workings of the church, the trumpets reveal the external environments such as political developments and war among the nations. In these trumpets we see how both heathen and religious powers are raised up by God to punish apostate Christianity, much the same way as Nebuchadnezzar was raised up to punish rebellious Israel.

Before we launch into some details of the seven seals, one more generalization should be noted. Although the first six seals began at different times, once a seal is opened, it remains open until the judgment of the seven last plagues. For example, the gospel can still go forth "conquering and to conquer" the hearts of men, subsequent to the opening of the first seal. When the balances of judgment are placed in the hands of men, as under the third seal, the results can be the same in every age. When too much power is placed in the hands of an apostate church, as under the fourth seal, persecution and martyrdom are sure to follow. In other words, the principles still hold true.

The sanctuary scene that introduces the seven seals is present in Revelation 4 and 5. In Revelation 4 John sees a worship scene in heaven with our heavenly Father sitting on a throne. Revelation 4:1 says, "After this I looked, and, behold, a door was opened in heaven." Many Christians, including theologians, presume John is indicating that all of the events from chapter 4 on through the rest of Revelation have nothing to do with the church but apply to literal Israel. They assume this open door represents the rapture of the church. This is incorrect. This open door into the sanctuary is an invitation for John to see "things which must be hereafter." Yes, John is in another vision, as indicated in verses 1 and 2, but this has nothing to do with the rapture. This vision and prophecy of the seven seals parallels the prophecy of the seven churches, as mentioned previously. This is an example of Hebrew parallelism. Therefore, John is witnessing the beginning of the apostolic church, on the day of Pentecost.

What evidence indicates that this sanctuary scene goes back to the beginning of the apostolic church? In Revelation 5:6, a continuation of this sanctuary scene, we read, "And I beheld, and, lo, in the midst of the throne, and of the four beasts, and in the midst of the elders, stood a Lamb as it had been slain, having seven horns and seven eyes, which are the seven Spirits of God sent forth into all the earth."

Jesus died on the evening of the Passover. After 40 days, He ascended to the heavenly sanctuary to attend His coronation as our High Priest, which was completed on the day of Pentecost. On Pentecost, the Holy Spirit was "sent forth into all the earth," known as the *early rain*. Jesus had promised the disciples that He would send the Comforter after He ascended to His Father, specifically instructing them to tarry in Jerusalem until this promised gift should be bestowed (Acts 1:2-4). I realize there is a lot of symbolism in Revelation 5 (as throughout Revelation), but it should be recognized by all that the "Lamb as it had been slain" represents Jesus. The setting indicates this was at the time His high priestly ministry began. The "seven Spirits of God" represent the Holy Spirit. Since this sanctuary scene introduces the high priestly ministry of Jesus, then the prophecy of the seven seals will likewise be a long-range one, covering the entire Christian era until Christ finishes His work in the heavenly sanctuary.

The two whole chapters of Revelation 4 and 5 include two worship scenes. In chapter 4, verses 10 and 11, we have the first worship scene where the twenty-four elders sing an abbreviated doxology: "The four and twenty elders fall down before him that sat on the throne, and worship him that liveth for ever and ever, and cast their crowns before the throne, saying, Thou art worthy, O Lord, to receive glory and honour and power: for thou hast created all things, and for thy pleasure they are and were created."

In chapter 5, we have another worship scene where the twenty-four elders sing "a new song" (verse 9), and in verse 12, we have a full seven-fold doxology: "Saying with a loud voice, Worthy is the Lamb that was slain to receive power, and riches, and wisdom, and strength, and honour, and glory, and blessing."

Then, in verses 13 and 14, we have the conclusion of this worship scene, which is separate and distinct from the worship scene in chapter 4, and follows the completion of Jesus' heavenly ministry, thus marking the consummation of the seventh seal.

The Seven Seals

Revelation 5:1-3 gives us the introduction of the seven seals: "And I saw in the right hand of him that sat on the throne a book written within and on the backside, sealed with seven seals. And I saw a strong angel proclaiming with a loud voice, Who is worthy to open the book, and to loose the seals thereof? And no man in heaven, nor in earth, neither under the earth, was able to open the book, neither to look thereon."

This book was in the right hand of the Father, and John even wept when he thought nobody could open it. However, Jesus took the book, and in Revelation 5:9 and 10 we read, "And they sung a new song, saying, Thou art worthy to take the book, and to open the seals thereof, for thou wast slain, and hast redeemed us to God by thy blood out of every kindred, and tongue, and people, and nation; And hast made us unto our God kings and priests: and we shall reign on the earth."

May we ever bear in mind that the only reason we even have the opportunity to study these seals is because Jesus was worthy to open them. May we also remember that it is only by His grace and presence in our hearts and minds that we can begin to understand these seals. With that in mind, let us turn to Revelation 6 and consider the seven seals, beginning with verses 1 through 8: "And I saw when the Lamb opened one of the seals, and I heard, as it were the noise of thunder, one of the four beasts saying, Come and see. And I saw, and behold a white horse: and he that sat on him had a bow; and a crown was given unto him: and he went forth conquering, and to conquer. And when he had opened the second seal, I heard the second beast say, Come and see.

"And there went out another horse that was red: and power was given to him that sat thereon to take peace from the earth, and that they should kill one another: and there was given unto him a great sword. And when he had opened the third seal, I heard the third beast say, Come and see. And I beheld, and lo a black horse; and he that sat on him had a pair of balances in his hand. And I heard a voice in the midst of the four beast's say, A measure of wheat for a penny, and three measures of barley for a penny; and see thou hurt not the oil and the wine.

"And when he had opened the fourth seal, I heard the voice of the fourth beast say, Come and see. And I looked, and behold a pale horse: and his name that sat on him was Death, and Hell followed with him. And power was given unto them over the fourth part of the earth, to kill with sword, and with hunger, and with death, and with the beasts of the earth."

Now, let us reconsider the book that Jesus took from God, our Father. In ancient times books were in the form of scrolls, which were sealed. Before one could read the scroll, all of the seals had to be opened, or removed. Therefore, once a seal is opened, it remains open until the scroll can be read. The same reasoning allows us to conclude that once a seal has been opened from this divine Book, it remains open and in effect until the last seal is removed.

We shall now consider some of the details in this passage. First, we cannot help but notice the colors of the horses. Also, the four horsemen and their accessories are quite notable. A more subtle feature is that there is no exit, or departure, of each horse. In other words, it is implied that each horse joins the previous one, until all four ride together into the sunset of our history. This is not to imply, however, that all the riders are in harmony with one another.

We notice the first horse was white, and its rider had a crown. "And he went forth conquering, and to conquer." This symbol fitly describes the beginning of the apostolic church, not only at Ephesus, but in all of the churches that were established in the first century. They were a pure people, who proclaimed a pure gospel. White represents purity, thus the white horse and rider represent Jesus' true followers who went forth in His name, "conquering, and to conquer" the hearts of men, turning people from sin to salvation through Christ. Furthermore, Jesus always has a minority of godly Christians in every era of His universal church. Even in our day, wherever His followers go forth in His Spirit and power, they may still be conquerors over sin and the sinful hearts of men.

The red horse and the actions of its rider strikingly represent bloodshed. When we compare this scene to the church of Smyrna, in Revelation 2:8-11, we notice the similarities. In the second era of Jesus' true church, there was a terrible tribulation, especially from AD 303 to AD 313 by Emperor Diocletian and his co-emperors.

A logical question might be why God would allow this to happen to a church for which He had nothing negative to say, for there was no rebuke given to Smyrna. Perhaps the answer is found in 2 Timothy 3:12 where Paul warned, "Yea, and all who will live godly in Christ Jesus shall suffer persecution." Christians, no matter how pure, are not given a free pass from trials and tribulations. Jesus warned that the world would hate His followers because it hated Him first.

In addition, Jesus said to Laodicea, "As many as I love, I rebuke and chasten: be zealous therefore, and repent" (Rev. 3:19). When we consider that Jesus said, even to the church of Ephesus, "Nevertheless I have somewhat against thee, because thou hast left thy first love" (Rev. 2:4), we can understand that it may have been necessary for God to allow this chastening of the Smyrna church in order to strengthen them. The color red not only symbolizes bloodshed but also sin. There may have been some residual sin from Ephesus that was carried over into Smyrna.

The third horse, under the third seal, was black. Black is the opposite of white, and therefore, suggests the opposite of purity, which is apostasy. This was precisely the case in the Pergamos era, as the church fell away, teaching the doctrines of the Nicolaitanes and introducing idolatry. The rider is holding a pair of balances in his hand, possibly representing the usurpation of the justice of God by the leaders of the church. It may also represent materialism or unholy commerce, dealing with unjust measures and weights. It became a common practice to sell offices and positions in the church, sometimes making the office of bishop open to the highest bidder.

The pale horse of the fourth seal has been described as a sickly amber. And remember, its rider was Death. Thus, this horse fitly represents both the martyrdom of the faithful and the spiritual death of "professed" Christians. Furthermore, these "professed" Christians were apportioned to "Hell" (*hades*, the grave), which followed "Death." This parallels the era of Thyatira, the Dark Ages of papal rule. Millions of faithful Christians were sent to their death for not submitting to papal authority, and wherever the Church of Rome reigned, the spiritual mortality rate was high. During this period of time, God's true church fled into the wilderness, as portrayed in Revelation 12:6: "And the woman fled into the wilderness, where she hath a place prepared of God, that they should feed her there a thousand two hundred and threescore days." Using the day for a year principle, this would be 1260 years, spanning from AD 538 to 1798, when the papacy received its deadly wound.

As we consider the curses that came upon the fallen church during this time, we should perhaps remember the "blessings" and "curses" that were offered to ancient Israel. They appear to apply equally well to the New Testament churches. The same judgment curses pronounced against ancient Israel are found within the fourth seal (verse 8). These curses include the sword, hunger or famine, death, and beasts of the earth.

In Leviticus 26:14-22, we find all four of these curses listed. Israel would suffer these judgments if she turned away from God and was disobedient. In Ezekiel 14:21 we see this concept repeated. Notice what the Lord said about sending judgments upon His people: "For thus saith the Lord GOD; How much more when I send my four sore judgments upon Jerusalem, the sword, and the famine, and the noisome beast, and the pestilence, to cut off from it man and beast?"

Therefore, the curses that came upon apostate believers in ancient Israel match the judgments that were inflicted upon apostate Christianity during the Dark Ages. No doubt, these four curses were experienced literally, but even more so spiritually. There was spiritual famine, as well as spiritual death and oppression from "beasts" or kingdoms that aligned themselves with Rome.

Let us move on now to the fifth seal, which was mentioned earlier. In Revelation 6:9-11, we read, "And when he had opened the fifth seal, I saw under the altar the souls of them that were slain for the word of God, and for the testimony, which they held: And they cried with a loud voice, saying, How long, O Lord, holy and true, dost thou not judge and avenge our blood on them that dwell on the earth? And white robes were given unto every one of them; and it was said unto them, that they should rest yet for a little season, until their fellowservants also and their brethren, that should be killed as they were, should be fulfilled."

This fifth seal reveals martyrs "that were slain," that is, in the past tense. Therefore, these martyrs had already died when the fifth seal was opened, though doubtless, there would be more martyrs added during the time of this seal. (By the way, this is not a passage supporting the immortality of the soul. This is clearly symbolic, in the same way that Abel's blood cried from out of the ground in Genesis 4:10.)

Furthermore, it suggests that their cry, which was heard at the opening of the seal, occurred sometime during the pre-advent judgment, for it says, "And white robes were given unto every one of them" (Rev. 6:11). The phraseology implies an action that goes beyond the imputed robe of Christ's righteousness, which every Christian receives at conversion. In other words, these saints have been investigated during the pre-advent judgment and have been sealed for God's kingdom while still in their graves.

Notice, though, that they were to "rest yet for a little season, until their fellowservants also and their brethren, that should be killed as they were, should be fulfilled." There were many martyrs during the Sardis era, and there will yet be martyrs in the Laodicean era. Remember, all of the four horsemen ride together until the end of probationary history. The true gospel will yet go for-

An Overview of the Seals and The Trumpets

ward (Rev. 14:6, 7), apostasy will continue (Rev. 18:2), martyrdom will take place, and the deadly wound of the papacy will be healed (Rev. 13:3). Soon after, probation will close, and the seven last plagues will begin.

Moving on to the sixth seal, let us read Revelation 6:12-14: "And I beheld when he had opened the sixth seal, and, lo, there was a great earthquake; and the sun became black as sackcloth of hair, and the moon became as blood; And the stars of heaven fell unto the earth, even as a fig tree casteth her untimely figs, when she is shaken of a mighty wind. And the heaven departed as a scroll when it is rolled together; and every mountain and island were moved out of their places."

Here we encounter some minor difficulties regarding when this seal is opened. Many Bible students believe it started with the Lisbon earthquake in 1755, shortly followed by the signs and wonders of the sun and moon in 1780, and then the falling of the stars, or the great meteor shower, in 1833. I believe this is true, placing us now between the symbolic casting of the figs and the heavens departing, which will take place at the second coming of Christ.

It should be noted that there is another "great earthquake" during the seventh plague (Rev. 16:17-21), which should not be confused with the earthquake in this seal. This second one takes place following the decree, "It is done," and is described as "a great earthquake, such as was not since men were upon the earth, so mighty an earthquake, and so great. . . . And every island fled away, and the mountains were not found." The seal earthquake is a sign to prepare for the Lord's return while probation is still open, whereas the plague earthquake, which is much more intense, signals that it is all over.

At this point, we need to skip over the seventh chapter of Revelation, which appears as a parenthetical discourse between the sixth and seventh seals. It includes the end-time sealing of the 144,000 saints. This period of time is very short, and occurs during the early part of the final tribulation, before probation closes. We will come back to this chapter later in this study.

The seventh seal is found in Revelation 8:1. It says, "And when he had opened the seventh seal, there was silence in heaven about the space of half an hour."

Although a number of explanations have been offered, it appears that the most satisfactory interpretation of the seventh seal is that the silence in heaven is brought on by the departure of Christ, with all His angelic hosts, at His second coming (Matt. 25:31 and 1 Thess. 3:13). If this one half hour is prophetic time, then it represents about seven days of literal time.

As mentioned earlier, the trumpets are judgments that target the enemies of God's people. These would also include "professed" Christians who have apostatized. Please keep this important fact in mind.

First, we begin with the sanctuary scene found in Revelation 8:2-5. Please recall what I mentioned earlier, that the seven trumpets parallel the seven seals, as well as the seven churches. In the sanctuary scene, the Angel, who represents Jesus, is performing a service at the altar of incense. This scene most likely portrays Jesus' ministry in both apartments, because this altar was used for both the first and second apartment ministries in the earthly sanctuary. Also, notice in verse 5 that the angel filled the censer with fire from the altar and cast it to the earth. I believe this act fitly portrays the close of probation. It could also refer to the *latter rain* of the Holy Spirit. Thus, the seven trumpets are a long-range prophecy, covering the entire Christian era, and probably the final judgment after the 1,000 years.

There is a lot of imagery and symbolism in this prophecy, but my purpose will be to give you just an overview. The first four trumpets are recorded from Revelation 8:2 to the end of the chapter. The historicist method interprets these first four trumpets as a series of attacks upon pagan Rome by four barbarian kingdoms, which divided the Western Roman Empire into ten kingdoms by the year AD 476. These barbarian kings and their kingdoms were as follows:

1. Alaric, the chieftain of the Goths who came from the North and ravaged the pagan Roman Empire.
2. Genseric, the barbarian king of the Vandals who came from Africa and continued the rampage of Rome.
3. Attila, the Hun who attacked Rome from the northeast, causing more destruction.
4. Odoacer, a barbarian of the Heruli who completed the disintegration of the Western Roman Empire.

We must understand that pagan Rome persecuted Christians for centuries. They put Christians into an amphitheater with lions and other beasts, for their

An Overview of the Seals and The Trumpets

amusement. Thus, God used the barbarian kingdoms to execute four trumpet judgments upon pagan Rome, certainly an enemy of God's people.

The remaining three trumpets are located in Revelation 9:1-11:18. They are announced in Revelation 8:13 by an angel who declares, "Woe, woe, woe, to the inhabiters of the earth by reason of the other voices of the trumpet of the three angels, which are yet to sound!" Hence, these are often referred to as the "woe trumpets."

As mentioned earlier, the first four trumpets were judgments against western pagan Rome, but eastern Imperial Rome was allowed to continue its sovereignty from the Grecian capital in Constantinople. However, the fifth and sixth trumpets were judgments inflicted upon eastern Rome, also known as the Byzantine Empire, and upon western papal Rome, as well. The sixth trumpet brought down eastern Imperial Rome in AD 1453 and finally delivered the deadly wound to papal Rome in 1798.

The seventh trumpet will be a judgment against modern Rome after the "deadly wound" is "healed" and Rome once again rules the world in partnership with modern Babylon (Rev. 13:3, 4, 11, 12; 17:16-18).

I realize this overview of the seven trumpets is very brief, but now we can consider some of the details of the last three trumpets, which the angel connected with three woes.

First, I want to mention the chapters and verses where these last three trumpets are found: fifth trumpet, Revelation 9:1-12; sixth trumpet, Revelation 9:13-11:14.; seventh trumpet, Revelation 11:15-18.

Second, I want to propose what I believe to be the time frames of these last three trumpets. I will give some support for these conclusions a little later: fifth trumpet, AD 622 until 1449; sixth trumpet, 1449 until 1844; seventh trumpet, 1844 until Jesus' second coming. (Note: the seventh trumpet may extend to include the post 1,000 year millennial judgment. See Revelation 20.)

Some important events and incidents connected to the three woe trumpets are as follows: the birth of Islam was in AD 622. This date also marks the beginning of the Muslim calendar. In this same year, Mohammed executed his "flight" (the Hegira) from Mecca to Medina because of heavy persecution from his fellow citizens of Mecca and an assassination plot on his life. He had been receiving "visions" since AD 610, and by 622, he was 52 years old. Mohammed died 11 years later (632), but the Islamic religion that he had founded multiplied exponentially, so that by AD 636 all of Arabia and most of Persia were Islamic. The irony of Persia's acceptance of Islam stems from an earlier letter written to the Persian emperor, inviting the nation to accept Islam. He disdained the offer and tore up the letter, but the sword of Islam prevailed.

Now, the question arises, what does Islam have to do with the last three trumpets? The answer is that the Islamic nations were used by God in a similar fashion as the barbarian tribes were used to inflict judgments against the pagan Roman Empire. In other words, the Saracens, and later the Turkish Muslims, inflicted judgments upon eastern Imperial Rome, and also upon western papal Rome, during the fifth trumpet.

During the sounding of the sixth trumpet, the Turkish Ottoman Empire brought down eastern Imperial Rome in 1453 and continued to inflict judgments against the western papal Roman Empire, until it's downfall in 1798. Thus, God used the Islamic people to inflict judgments against the enemies of His people during the fifth and sixth trumpets. It is logical that God will once again use Islam in the seventh trumpet (third woe), and we can certainly see evidence of that since September 11, 2001, as radical Islam has become a world threat and is at odds with the United States and the Vatican. Remember, papal Rome does not have its own army, but uses the military of the nations that she controls.

In the final crisis, modern Rome will be the head of modern Babylon, which is composed of three entities, namely:

1. The dragon – the governments of the whole world, which are controlled by Satan. See Revelation 16:13, 14 and 19:19, 20. These nations will be considerably influenced by spiritualistic elements.
2. The beast of Revelation 17 – modern Rome with its ecclesiastical structure in charge of Babylon.
3. The false prophet – apostate Protestantism, beginning in the United States and in the final remnant of time extending into all the world, which will be instrumental in setting up the image to the beast (Rev. 13:11-15).

Revelation 13:11-15, coupled with Revelation 16:13-19, describes this end-time final crisis. This final crisis is presented, or at least hinted at, in many

An Overview of the Seals and The Trumpets

of the first six parallel prophecies that John wrote in the book of Revelation, beginning with the seven churches, on through the sixth prophecy of Christ's second coming and Satan's confinement for 1,000 years in Revelation 18-20.

Now, let us look at some of the details of the last three trumpets, beginning in Revelation 9:1-4: "And the fifth angel sounded, and I saw a star fall from heaven unto the earth: and to him was given the key of the bottomless pit. And he opened the bottomless pit, and there arose a smoke out of the pit; as the smoke of a great furnace; and the sun and the air were darkened by reason of the smoke of the pit. And there came out of the smoke locusts upon the earth: and unto them was given power, as the scorpions of the earth have power. And it was commanded them that they should not hurt the grass of the earth, neither any green thing: neither any tree; but only those men which have not the seal of God in their foreheads."

First, we notice a "star" that is shortly afterward identified by the pronoun "him." The only beings that actually fell from heaven were Satan and his angels. In Revelation 12:9, we note that Satan is identified as a dragon in this passage, and his angels were all "cast out into the earth." In verse 4 of this same chapter, we read, "And his tail drew the third part of the stars of heaven, and did cast them to the earth." Thus, this "star" might possibly represent Satan, and not an earthly being.

On the other hand, a star might represent a prince or ruler. In the third trumpet, I identified Atilla the Hun as "a great star from heaven." Therefore, it is also possible that this fallen star could be Mohammed, believed by some to have known the gospel at one point but fell away from the truth. Adam Clarke, Uriah Smith, and many other commentators have identified Mohammed in this verse. So then, either Satan or Mohammed is given a "key," most likely from Christ, which was used to open the "bottomless pit" for the purpose of bringing judgment upon Rome.

Now, what is meant by the "bottomless pit"? This gets very interesting, as this bottomless pit is mentioned in two other chapters of Revelation. Turn with me to the sixth trumpet in Revelation 11:7, where we read, "And when they shall have finished their testimony, the beast that ascendeth out of the bottomless pit shall make war against them, and shall overcome them, and kill them."

This passage describes another power that arose from the "bottomless pit."

And in Revelation 17:8, we discover a third power that arose from this "bottomless pit." It says, "The beast that thou sawest was, and is not; and shall ascend out of the bottomless pit, and go into perdition: and they that dwell on the earth shall wonder, whose names were not written in the book of life from the foundation of the world, when they behold the beast that was, and is not, and yet is."

I believe these three powers that arose from the bottomless pit are in some way connected to the work of Satan, but this bottomless pit is not the physical abode of the underworld. It represents confusion and darkness, the perfect seedbed for all these aforementioned powers that ascend out of it, namely, the Muslim religion in chapter 9, atheism in chapter 11, and Catholicism in chapter 17.

Ellen G. White makes the following observation in *The Great Controversy*: "That the expression, 'bottomless pit,' represents the earth in a state of confusion and darkness, is evident from other scriptures. Concerning the condition of the earth 'in the beginning,' the Bible record says that it 'was without form, and void; and darkness was upon the face of the deep.' [The Hebrew word here translated 'deep' is rendered in the Septuagint (Greek) translation of the Hebrew Old Testament by the same word rendered 'bottomless pit' in Revelation 20:1-3.]" (p. 658).

It has been thought by many that the "smoke" from the bottomless pit refers to the errors and false doctrines of the Muslim faith. However, let us consider the use of the word smoke in the Scriptures. Stephen Dickie in his book *Islam, God's Forgotten Blessing* makes this observation:

"The word 'smoke' appears in forty verses throughout Scripture. Not one of these verses associates smoke with error, false doctrine, or deadly vapor. In fact, the word often denotes something quite different. Consider, for example, Psalms 74:1: 'O God, why hast thou cast [us] off for ever? [Why] doth thine anger smoke against the sheep of thy pasture?' Here smoke represents God's anger against sin in His people."

Several verses could be cited showing that smoke is associated with God's wrath and judgment, but one more will suffice: "Then the earth shook and trembled; the foundations also of the hills moved and were shaken, because he was wroth. There went up a smoke out of his nostrils, and fire out of his mouth devoured: coals were kindled by it. He bowed the heavens also, and came down: and darkness was under his feet" (Ps. 18:7-9).

The "locusts" that had the capacity to torment men for "five months," as mentioned in Revelation 9:5, represent the Arabian warriors who rapidly conquered the nations of the East and pushed even into northern Africa and southern Europe. It is interesting to note that the "children of the East," the ancestors of the Arabians, are described in Judges 7:12 as being like "grasshoppers for multitude." Bible commentator Adam Clark referred to these locusts as, "vast hordes of military troops: the description which follows certainly agrees better with the Saracens than with any other people or nation."

In Revelation 9:11 we note, "And they had a king over them, which is the angel of the bottomless pit, whose name in the Hebrew tongue is Abaddon, but in the Greek tongue hath his name Apollyon."

In the margin of many Bibles, we read: "that is, to say, A destroyer." Martin Luther, in the sixteenth century, identified this "king" as Mohammed. The historian J.A. Wylie, in his monumental work *History of Protestantism*, quotes Luther as saying, "It is God who has unloosed this army, whose king is Abaddon the destroyer. They have been sent to punish us for our sins, our ingratitude for the Gospel, our blasphemies, and above all, our shedding of the blood of the righteous."

He believed that God had raised up the Muslims to punish apostate Christianity. We must realize that the Muslim people, who originated from the peoples of the East, served God's purposes. They were both a "blessing" and a "curse." Going back to verse 4, which we read earlier, they were commanded to inflict judgments on "only those men which have not the seal of God in their foreheads." In other words, they spared true Christians, who were scattered in the "wilderness." They also provided a buffer against apostate Christianity, thus allowing the Protestant reformation of the sixteenth century time to get established, for although the Emperor, Charles V, was determined to stamp out Protestantism, he was forced to send his armies to fight the invading Turks.

There is a time prophecy mentioned in verse 5 of "five months," which I believe began when the Muslim people became an empire. Before AD 1299, the Muslim tribes had no centralized government, but by AD 1299, Othman became a strong leader, and he consolidated the disorganized bands of Muslims and defeated the eastern Roman commander near Nicomedia on July 27, 1299. Thus, this history begins the "five months" of the supremacy of the Ottoman Empire (using the day for a year principle, this would equal 150 years). Since Othman was rightfully a "king," some have interpreted the "king" in verse 11 as being this leader of the Ottoman Empire. At the termination of this time prophecy in AD 1449, we begin the period of the sixth trumpet as mentioned in Revelation 9:13. Notice verses 14 and 15: "Saying to the sixth angel which had the trumpet, Loose the four angels which are bound in the great river Euphrates. And the four angels were loosed, which were prepared for an hour, and a day, and a month, and a year, for to slay the third part of men."

Here we have another time prophecy, which totals 391 years and 15 days, using the day for a year principle. The starting point for this time period would naturally be at the close of the previous time prophecy, AD 1449. At this time the Muslims under the four Sultanies of the Turkish (Ottoman) Empire were "loosed," or released, to inflict even more serious judgments than those of the fifth trumpet. This time prophecy of the sixth trumpet ended on August 11, 1840, which was 391 years and 15 days later. On that very day, the sovereignty of Turkey was lost as the European powers intervened to save Turkey from Egypt. Turkey remained a nation, but it had surrendered much of its authority to the European powers and was from that time labeled "the Sick Man of the East."

Near the beginning of this period, in AD 1453, Constantinople, the capital of the Greek Byzantine Empire, was conquered by the Muslim Turks, thus marking the end of the eastern Imperial Roman Empire. With one of the enemies of God's people eliminated (eastern Rome), that left only the papal Roman Empire in the west to continue its persecutions. However, papal Rome was also apportioned a time prophecy, pointing to when its supremacy would end—the 1260 days (literal years) that ended in AD 1798. (This time prophecy is mentioned seven times in the Bible, but that is the subject of another study. See "Prophetic Principles of Interpretation" in the appendices.) Both the Turks and the Protestant reformation played a role in weakening the Papacy, but it was left to yet another power from the bottomless pit to inflict the "deadly wound." We will come to that shortly.

We now come to Revelation 10 and 11, which have a lot of history that I can only summarize in this brief study. Revelation 10 begins with the "little book open" in verse 2, which refers to when the book of Daniel, which was formerly sealed (Dan. 12:4, 9, 13), was "open" to the understanding of students of prophecy at "the time of the end," which began shortly before the termination of the time prophecy under the sixth trumpet. Interestingly, when the book of Daniel was opened, it helped prophecy students to better understand the book of Revelation and the day for a year principle. This made it possible to predict the fall of Turkish sovereignty before it actually happened. This remarkable interpretation, coming a year before the event took place, and being fulfilled on the very day, added great impetus to the message of Christ's soon return.

These truths were "sweet" in the mouths of the Lord's people who were expecting Jesus to return on October 22, 1844, but Revelation 10 also reveals that a "bitter" disappointment was to come to these end-time heralds—Christ did not come as they had hoped. They had correctly reckoned the time, but had misinterpreted the event. Rather than Jesus coming to the earth, He was to begin His ministry in the Most Holy Place of the heavenly sanctuary. Once this was understood, they had the commission to "prophesy again" in verse 11.

Revelation 11, which was previously mentioned in connection with another power from the bottomless pit, likely represents the Satanic power of atheism, which occurred during the French Revolution. The "two witnesses" represent the Old and New Testaments, the Word of God. In the year 1793, France attempted to remove God and His word entirely from its nation.

"The atheistical power that ruled in France during the Revolution and the reign of terror, did wage such a war against God and His holy word as the world had never witnessed. The worship of the Deity was abolished by the National Assembly. Bibles were collected and publicly burned with every possible manifestation of scorn" (*The Great Controversy,* p. 273).

True to the prophecy, three and one half days (years) later the prohibition of the Bible was reversed. It was this atheistic power, however, that God allowed to remove the pope from his throne in 1798. The third power that came from the "bottomless pit," found in Revelation 17, is identified with the resurgence of the Papacy, but that is also another subject which will be discussed in a subsequent chapter.

Students of history recognize that France, ironically, was known as the "eldest daughter of the church." Clovis, king of the Franks, was the first monarch of Europe who was converted to Catholicism in AD 496. When the Protestant reformation surged into Europe, France resisted it, cooperating with the Jesuits to the point of bloody persecution against the French Protestants, better known as Huguenots. This detestable action helped turn France to an abhorrence of religion. In the French Revolution, the Catholic Church ultimately reaped what she had sown. Revelation 11:3-14 tells this story.

As we come to the seventh trumpet, the key verse is Revelation 11:18: "And the nations were angry, and thy wrath is come, and the time of the dead, that they should be judged, and that thou shouldest give reward unto thy servants the prophets, and to the saints, and them that fear thy name, small and great; and shouldest destroy them which destroy the earth."

This verse is a very brief preview of the remainder of the book of Revelation. In other words, all of these events—"the nations were angry," God's "wrath," "the time of the dead, that they should be judged," and God's giving "reward" and the destruction of "them that destroy the earth"—are sequential events. These are more fleshed out in Revelation 12 through 22.

That the sounding of the seventh angel covers an extended time is seen in Revelation 10:7, which says, "But in the days of the voice of the seventh angel." The seventh trumpet begins with the pre-advent judgment and the marriage of Jesus to His kingdom, which both began in 1844. This is alluded to in Revelation 11:15, which says, "And the seventh angel sounded; and there were great voices in heaven, saying, The kingdoms of this world are become the kingdoms of our Lord, and of his Christ; and he shall reign for ever and ever."

Let us review what we learned in a previous chapter. In Daniel 7:9 we find some clues that unlock the truths of the pre-advent judgment. "I beheld till the thrones were cast down [or, set in place], and the Ancient of days did sit . . . the judgment was set, and the books were opened" (verses 9, 10).

In these verses we perceive that there is a judgment scene that has commenced in heaven. Notice that "books" were investigated during this judgment. Now, skipping down to verses 13 and 14, we read, "I saw in the night visions, and, behold, one like the Son of man came with the clouds of heaven, and came to the Ancient of days, and they brought him near before him. And there was given him dominion, and glory, and a kingdom."

In this passage we have clear evidence that not only is there a pre-advent judgment but also Jesus will be receiving His kingdom during this period of time. The New Jerusalem with the subjects of His kingdom, hopefully you and I, will be numbered with Jesus during His marriage, at this time. Most Christians do not realize that Jesus is now in His marriage, and when it is consummated, He will return to earth to take us home. Jesus taught this in His parable in Luke 12:36, which says, "And ye yourselves like unto men that wait for their lord, when he will return from the wedding; that when he cometh and knocketh, they may open unto him immediately." Therefore, Revelation 11:15 echoes Daniel's portrayal of Jesus receiving His kingdom (Dan. 7:9-14) and consummating the marriage during this pre-advent judgment.

In Revelation 14:6, three angels (messengers) are proclaiming three worldwide messages prior to Christ's return and the harvest of the earth. Part of the first angel's message is "the hour of His judgment *is* come." He does not say *will* come, or *is about to* come, but *is* come, indicating that this is a pre-advent judgment. I believe this judgment began in 1844, if we consider another time prophecy, found in Daniel 8:14, foretelling when the cleansing of the sanctuary would begin. I apologize for not including more information on this time prophecy, but it is beyond the scope of this overview. There is more information on this in my subsequent chapter titled "Movement of Destiny," and in the appendices of this book titled "Principles of Prophetic Interpretation."

Going back to Revelation 11:18, we see a sequence of events. We are now in the time of the first event, namely, the "nations were angry." This has been the case since 1844, but the winds of strife have been held in check by the four angels mentioned in Revelation 7:1-3. It is apparent that the four winds will not be let loose until the sealing of God's servants has been accomplished. When this sealing is finished, probation will be closed, and God will commence the seven last plagues, known as the "wrath of God." (See Revelation 15:1 through 16:21.) Thereafter, as provided in Revelation 11:18, there will be "the time of the dead, that they should be judged," followed by rewards for the righteous and the punishment of the wicked. I believe the mention of both reward and destruction in this verse indicates that John is speaking of the final judgment, which takes place after the millennium. (See Revelation 20:12-15.)

I recognize there was a lot of information included in this chapter, and much more could have been added. But the bottom line is to remember that the seals and trumpets are linked with judgments. The judgments of the seals targeted professed Christians who were in apostasy, while the judgments of the trumpets were inflicted upon the enemies of God's people.

We are nearing the final crisis. Let us get our priorities established. Now is the time to "make our calling and election sure." Dear reader, re-consecrate your life to Jesus today and every day, so you will be ready for His second coming.

Chapter 12

The Three Angels' Messages

Our Bible study in this chapter will be an overview of the three angels' messages found in Revelation 14:6-12. Included will be significant and generous background history during the time when these messages were brought to the forefront in post-reformation times. All Christians need more than a mere acquaintance with the content of these three angels' messages; therefore, I encourage you to study them diligently.

The three angels' messages are interrelated and form a complete unit. These three messages (sometimes referred to as a three-fold message) are designed to prepare a people to stand in the last great conflict between Christ and Satan, which will involve the entire world as it is divided into two classes—those who are followers of Christ and refuse the mark of the beast, and those who reject Christ by submitting to the authority of the beast.

As is often the case, we can miss the big picture, or the overall thrust of a passage of Scripture, by focusing entirely on the immediate context. For example, when the disciples were looking for a Messiah who would deliver them from the oppression of the Romans, they were missing the big picture of a Messiah who would deliver them from sin and from the power of Satan. Likewise, we can make the mistake of missing the greater message behind Revelation 14:6-12.

Near the end of the nineteenth century, two elders, E.J. Waggoner and A.T. Jones, were preaching the third angel's message. In 1895 Jones gave a series of sermons on the third angel's message. I have, in my study, a copy of sixteen of these sermons, which I have read. To my amazement, in all these sermons,

Jones did not quote even one verse from Revelation 14. I noticed that he primarily used the epistles of Paul and preached on justification by faith.

He apparently was not alone with his emphasis on justification by faith. In the *Review and Herald*, April 1, 1890, Ellen G. White said, "Several have written to me, inquiring if the message of justification by faith is the third angel's message, and I have answered, 'It is the third angel's message, in verity.'"

The greater message behind Revelation 14:6-12 is the message of righteousness by faith. It is no wonder that many have been weak in both their understanding of the message and their proclamation of it. We need to keep Jesus as the focal point of these three angels' messages for He is "our righteousness" (Jer. 23:6, 33:16; Isa. 54:17).

The three angels' messages not only declare Christ's righteousness but they also include a declaration for God's people to leave the fallen churches and get ready for Jesus' second coming. They reveal the close relationship of Christ to His people and His intercessory work for them in the heavenly sanctuary. They provide a criterion whereby the followers of God can determine if they are truly converted and surrendered to the Lordship of Christ. Furthermore, it provides us with identifying marks of the true remnant of the woman's seed (Rev. 12:17), Christ's church in the last days.

The "great Advent movement" (the worldwide proclamation of the soon coming of Christ) arose at God's appointed time and recovered many lost truths of the "faith which was once delivered unto the saints" (Jude 3). Therefore, I believe this movement is a continuation of the Protestant reformation. Unfortunately, most Christians of other Protestant churches fail to see that the reformation was never completed. In fact, Protestants are generally only Protestant in name only, knowing little or nothing of the history of the reformation. Consequently, it comes as no surprise that they question the validity of the Advent movement. They do not believe we have been given the last messages of warning to a doomed world. Intoxicated with the wine of Babylon, many fail to see that these warning messages of Revelation 14:6-12 apply to Christians. Having accepted the Jesuit interpretation of Daniel 9 (the seventy-week prophecy), they believe these messages are given to the unconverted and the Jews. They are resting dangerously in the false hope of a "secret rapture" before the appearance of the beast and his mark.

The Three Angels' Messages

In this study and the next chapter, we will explain in detail why these messages are considered "present truth," truth that is applicable for our time. The Bible is all truth, but there are times when particular truths are especially applicable. For example, the proclamation and warning of a worldwide flood was "present truth" in Noah's day, but not for our time. There are lessons to be drawn from that experience, but God has promised not to destroy the world again by flood.

Here we will quote a short passage from the pen of Ellen G. White found in the book *Early Writings*: "There are many precious truths contained in the Word of God, but it is *'present truth'* that the flock needs now. I have seen the danger of the messengers running off from the important points of present truth, to dwell upon subjects that are not calculated to unite the flock and sanctify the soul. Satan will here take every possible advantage to injure the cause. But such subjects as the sanctuary, in connection with the 2300 days, the commandments of God and the faith of Jesus, are perfectly calculated to explain the past Advent movement and show what our present position is, establish the faith of the doubting, and give certainty to the glorious future. These, I have frequently seen, were the principal subjects on which the messengers should dwell" (p. 63).

Notice the mentioning of "the commandments of God and the faith of Jesus." These are two characteristics of the people of God who will be alive to witness the second advent of Jesus, which is found in Revelation 14:13-20. Also, notice that these two characteristics are located in Revelation 14:12, the climax of the third angel's message. Furthermore, the phrase "the faith of Jesus," is the same as righteousness by faith, which is the essence of the "everlasting gospel" proclaimed in the first angel's message of Revelation 14:6. Therefore, the "everlasting gospel" of the first angel's message is the same message as the "faith of Jesus" in the third angel's message. Thus, we come full circle in the three angels' messages—they are interconnected.

Before going into the contents of the three angels' messages, I first want to briefly review the beginning of the Advent movement, which is intricately connected with the three angels' messages. In the eighteenth century (1720–1740) and early nineteenth century (1800–1840), there were two surges of religious awakenings, known

A Primer on Salvation and Bible Prophecy

as the First and Second Great Awakenings.

During these periods of time, Bible scholars were enlightened and revival took place as they began to understand the prophecies of Daniel and Revelation. Thus were fulfilled the words given to Daniel, which says, "But thou, O Daniel, shut up the words, and seal the book, even to the time of the end: many shall run to and fro, and knowledge shall be increased" (Dan. 12:4).

This "time of the end" was the end of the time prophecy "appointed" for papal Rome's supremacy, which ended in 1798. (Note: whenever the expression "time of the end" or "time appointed" is used in the book of Daniel or Revelation, it does not mean the end of time, but instead, it means the end of a prophecy.) In an earlier chapter, we mentioned the 1260 year prophecy of God's true church in the wilderness. This time prophecy began in AD 538 and ended in 1798. Also, see Daniel 7:25 and 12:7, which indicates the same 1260 years of papal Roman supremacy.

After 1798 knowledge increased in the understanding of the prophecies and culminated in the Second Great Awakening of 1840-1844. The year 1844 was another "time appointed" as it marked the end of the 2300-day time prophecy of Daniel 8:14 and 19. (For more information on the time appointed, the time of the end, and Bible prophecies, please see the appendices material titled "Principles of Prophetic Interpretation.")

Now, let's briefly review the beginning of the Advent movement, which was during the Second Great Awakening.

During the first half of the nineteenth century, Bible scholars made a gradual shift from their studies on Daniel 7 and the 1260 days, to the time prophecy of the 2300 days in Daniel 8:14. These students of prophecy, from various denominations and scattered throughout the world, began investigating the 2300-day prophecy and were arriving at similar dates for its conclusion. On August 11, 1840, the Ottoman Empire surrendered its power to the nations of Europe in fulfillment of the time prophecy of Revelation 9:14 and 15. (We discussed this prophecy in the previous chapter; however, for further study, it is well documented in Uriah Smith's *Daniel and the Revelation*.) Therefore, the "year for a day" principle became established by August 11, 1840, because it was predicted beforehand that the Ottoman Empire would be broken, in some fashion, on that very date. Josiah Litch made this remarkable prediction, and its wonderful fulfillment on the very day specified served as a powerful impetus in the proclamation of the 2300-day prophecy.

Using the "year for a day" principle, William Miller calculated that the 2300-day prophecy would end sometime in the year 1843. Assuming that the year commenced in the spring (as Israel's calendar reckoned years from spring to spring), the time was predicted to close by the spring of 1844. When Jesus did not come in the spring of 1844, they perceived His delay was consistent with the "tarrying time" in the parable of the ten virgins (Matt. 25:5). They also found encouragement from Habakkuk 2:3, which says, "For the vision is yet for an appointed time, but at the end it shall speak, and not lie: though it tarry, wait for it; because it will surely come, it will not tarry."

During this "tarrying time," the Millerites were proclaiming the first and second angels' messages according to the best light they had obtained up to that point. Upon discovering that the decree of Artaxerxes (Ezra 7:13) went forth in the fall of 457 BC, the predicted date for the Lord's return was adjusted to October 22, 1844. This decree "to restore and to build Jerusalem" (Dan. 9:25) was the starting point of both the 70-week prophecy and the 2300-day prophecy. However, Miller and his associates had made one major mistake—not in the date—but in the event to take place. They assumed that the sanctuary that was to be "cleansed" was the earth. In other words, they believed the earth was going to be cleansed with fire at Jesus' second advent. Well, October 22, 1844, came and went without the second advent of Jesus to our planet. One can only imagine their great disappointment.

Does the Bible give us any clue that there would be a disappointment for God's people after the time prophecy of Daniel 8:14? Yes, it does. In Revelation 10:1, we notice a "mighty angel," and in verse 2, he had a "little book open." Now, looking at verses 9 through 11, we read, "And I went unto the angel, and said unto him, Give me the little book. And he said unto me, Take it, and eat it up; and it shall make thy belly bitter, but it shall be in thy mouth sweet as honey. And I took the little book out of the angel's hand, and ate it up; and it was in my mouth sweet as honey: and as soon as I had eaten it, my belly was bitter. And he said unto me, Thou must prophesy again before many peoples, and nations, and tongues, and kings."

Here was a great disappointment similar to that experienced by the disciples when Jesus was crucified. They had expected a different event, namely, the overthrow of Roman power and Jesus ruling as king. So too, the Adventists had expected a different event than what God had planned. Now, if anyone may wonder if this passage really applies to God's people during 1840 to 1844 when they were proclaiming the first and second angels' messages, let us reflect upon the following points:

1. Revelation 10 portrays events near the end of the sixth and the beginning of the seventh trumpet that coincide with the Adventist movement. (See more on this in the next chapter, "Movement of Destiny—Adventist Heritage".)
2. The "angel" of Revelation 10:3, who "cried with a loud voice," parallels the "angel" of Revelation 14:6 and 7, who also proclaimed with a "loud voice" the first angel's message. Note: the first angel's message began to be proclaimed with power just after August 11, 1840.
3. Both of these angels mentioned the Creator in similar language. Read Revelation 10:6 and 14:7.
4. They both had a message based upon time, the one "that time should be no more," and the other that "the hour of His judgment is come." These references are also found in Revelation 10:6 and 14:7.

After October 22, 1844, the Advent believers recognized they were the people identified in the prophecy of Revelation 10. As mentioned, these were the same people proclaiming the first and second angels' messages from 1840 to 1844. Therefore, Revelation 10 tells the story of the Advent movement during the proclamation of the first and second angels' messages, from August 11, 1840, to October 22, 1844. Ellen G. White makes this comment on Revelation 10: "The first and second angels' messages were to be proclaimed, but no further light was to be revealed before these messages had done their specific work. This is represented by the angel standing with one foot on the sea, proclaiming with a most solemn oath that time should be no longer" (*The SDA Bible Commentary*, vol. 7, p. 971).

As mentioned earlier, the "time" referred to in this Bible verse (Rev. 10:6) and mentioned in the above quote, does not refer to the end of time but to the end of the time prophecies. Thus, Ellen G. White connects Revelation 10 to the first and second angels' messages of Revelation 14.

The Three Angels' Messages

In summary, those in the Advent movement expected Jesus to come sometime between 1843 and 1844. During this same period of time, no light was given them in regards to the third angel's message. After the passage of time, which they acknowledged was the "tarrying time," they suffered a great disappointment. The message of Jesus' second coming was indeed sweet in their mouths, but after October 22, 1844, their disappointment was a bitter experience.

A few believers, however, returned to a study of God's word to ascertain their mistake. Even their enemies could find no fault with their time calculations, so it was clear that something must have taken place at the time specified. Soon they discovered the truth that Daniel 8:14 was referring to the cleansing of the sanctuary in heaven. This truth about a heavenly sanctuary, with two different phases of ministry, had been buried for many centuries due almost entirely to the Roman Catholic Church's attempted usurpation of Christ's position as our great High Priest. Then followed the discovery of the Sabbath, which is the seal of the Ten Commandments and the test of loyalty to God. This truth had also been buried under the Roman apostasy, for it was her act to attempt to change God's law, transferring the solemnity of the Sabbath (the seventh day) to Sunday (the first day). Thereafter, these two newly revealed truths became unique characteristics of the Advent movement. This is clearly a continuation of the Protestant reformation, restoring to the church that which Rome had taken away.

The Adventists were not yet ready, however, to "prophecy again before many peoples, and nations, and tongues, and kings" (Rev. 10:11). Why were they not ready? First, they were a small fledgling movement; therefore, it would be years before they were fully organized to undertake this mission to the world. Second, many of the leaders at that time did not understand the message of justification by faith in the third angel's message. They were emphasizing sanctification by faith while de-emphasizing the role of justification, thereby obscuring the message of righteousness by faith. This is a sad chapter in the history of the movement.

To demonstrate the disagreement, around 1888, two prominent men in the Advent movement each wrote a book, both receiving a wide circulation. One wrote *The Law in the Book of Galatians*. He was among the number who was overemphasizing sanctification. The discovery of the true Sabbath had led him and others to dwell primarily on obedience by faith. Subsequently, they had lost sight of Jesus and His righteousness, or justification. Fortunately, this omission was later remedied, and both these aspects of righteousness by faith were incorporated into the third angel's message.

Waggoner published the second book on Galatians titled *The Gospel in the Book of Galatians*. In this work, Waggoner forcefully presented the good news of justification by faith. It was difficult for some of the leaders to embrace his teaching, for they incorrectly felt that he was weakening the obligation of keeping the Ten Commandments. Waggoner was to get a helping hand in the matter from Ellen G. White, who stated, "'The faith of Jesus.' It is talked of, but not understood. What constitutes the faith of Jesus, that belongs to the third angel's message? Jesus becoming our sin-bearer that he might become our sin-pardoning Saviour. He was treated as we deserve to be treated. He came to our world and took our sins that we might take his righteousness. And faith in the ability of Christ to save us amply and fully and entirely is the faith of Jesus" (*Selected Messages*, book 3, p. 172).

A careful analysis of this passage, especially the last two sentences, reveals that the "faith of Jesus" includes both justification and sanctification. With this background history, let us now go into the content of the three angels' messages. In Revelation 14:6 we read, "And I saw another angel fly in the midst of heaven, having the everlasting gospel to preach unto them that dwell on the earth, and to every nation, and kindred, and tongue, and people."

This passage, along with Revelation 10: 11, gives the remnant the same commission, to proclaim a message to the world. What was their message? The first angel's message was labeled the "everlasting gospel." Since the gospel is everlasting, it must be the same message of salvation in Christ that was preached to the ancient world of the Old Testament. Ancient people of the Old Testament were saved by grace, just as we are saved by grace during the New Testament dispensation. Everyone who is saved will be saved through the provisions of the everlasting covenant. No one was saved by the provisions of the old covenant. Why? Because there was no provision to remove sin in the old covenant. Yes, there were sanctuary services added, with animal sacrifices, but "it is not possible that the blood of bulls and of goats should take away sins"

(Heb. 10:4). Yes, people were saved during the Old Testament dispensation, but they were saved through the provisions of the everlasting covenant. All atonement came from the promise of God that Jesus would be the ultimate Sacrifice. Christ would ratify the everlasting covenant, which later became the new covenant.

The terms of the old covenant were to obey and live. In Exodus 19:8 and 24:7, the people said, "All that the LORD hath said will we do, and be obedient." In a sense, the old covenant was a prescription for salvation by works—an impossibility. Paul labeled the old covenant method of salvation "the works of the law," and he declared that "by the works of the law shall no flesh be justified" (Gal. 2:16). I believe that God used the old covenant as a teaching device for the ancient Hebrews. After the Israelites broke the covenant, God added the sanctuary and its services to point them to Jesus. It also teaches us that nobody can be saved without God's grace.

Now, let us examine Revelation 14:7. It says, "Fear God, and give glory to him." The word "fear" means respect, reverence, and to be in awe. This is essential, for "the fear of the LORD is the beginning of wisdom" (Prov. 9:10). How do we give glory to God? We give glory to God when our characters reflect His image. Notice in the rest of this sentence that the first angel makes an important statement, saying, "For the hour of his judgment is come" (Rev. 14:7). Therefore, a "judgment" has arrived in history. Furthermore, it precedes Jesus' second coming. This conclusion should be evident, for there are two more angels who follow this first angel, bearing messages of warning to the world.

Now, let us briefly discuss this pre-advent judgment. Attorney Lewis Walton comments on the function of a judgment. He said, "Any lawyer who stayed awake through his or her first year of law school can tell you that execution of judgment is merely carrying out a judgment that has already been rendered at an earlier time."

In summary, a judgment involves an investigation, prior to the execution of the judgment. In other words, there is an investigative judgment before the executive judgment. Unfortunately, many of our Protestant brothers and sisters do not see any need for God to conduct an open judgment. True, God does not need to openly investigate anyone, since He knows the thoughts and intents of the hearts of everyone. However, this judgment serves other purposes than keeping God abreast on what people are doing.

This judgment will disclose our characters to other intelligent beings in the universe. Every intelligent, created being must be genuinely interested in who will be their future neighbors. The angels have been engaged in combat with Satan and his hosts for millennia. They understand the consequences of sin. They may want to see if we have demonstrated, to their satisfaction, that we are truly converted in heart and mind, or if we are just pardoned criminals. Certainly, everyone could just trust God to do the right thing, but I believe God is making every provision for the inhabitants of the universe to be convinced that He is "just and true" (Rev. 15:3), while the "accuser of our brethren" (Rev. 12:10) is a liar. God wants intelligent beings to understand how He deals with sin and sinners. This is why God gave the ancient Hebrews an earthly sanctuary. It served as a type, or example, of the true sanctuary in heaven and the work of our great High Priest in dealing with the sin problem.

In a sense, God's character is being judged by the universe. What an awesome thought! This is Paul's suggestion in Romans 3:4 and Ephesians 3:10. Also compare Psalm 51:4. This is not to say that His created beings can pass sentence on their Creator but that His character, often maligned and falsely accused by Satan, is being examined. In His infinite wisdom, He has been able to demonstrate the love and righteousness of the Godhead while revealing the hate and depravity of His adversary.

Let us now move forward into the content of the second angel's message. Revelation 14:8 says, "And there followed another angel, saying, Babylon is fallen, is fallen, that great city, because she made all nations drink of the wine of the wrath of her fornication."

Who is this "Babylon . . . that great city?" She sounds like both a political and a religious power. This is clearly revealed in Revelation chapters 16 through 18. In these chapters, we discover that she is a worldwide apostate religious power. We also discover that she controls world governments, in addition to opposing and persecuting God's people. Do we see any religious groups today who are attempting to control civil governments worldwide? One day soon, these religious elements will control our world.

I want to present a biblical principle to help us understand more about

The Three Angels' Messages

Babylon. In an earlier chapter, we mentioned the law of the first and the last mention. To illustrate Babylon by this law, we need to go back to the Bible to when Babylon was first mentioned. With this information, it helps us to understand the latter mention of Babylon more clearly. So, going back to Genesis 11, we learn about the Babylonians building the tower of Babel. In effect, they were trying to save themselves from another flood, but God confused their language and scattered them. Babel, or Babylon, means confusion. In essence, it is a "do-it-yourself" religion based on man's power and wisdom rather than God's. Today, Babylon may be applied to many religious groups. These groups plan to pass civil laws in order to legislate morality. The final outcome will be a one world apostate religion.

Ellen G. White, in the summer of 1844, declared that the Protestant churches had already fallen. In *The Great Controversy* we read, "The message of Revelation 14, announcing the *fall* of Babylon must apply to religious bodies that were once pure and have become corrupt. Since this message follows the warning of the judgment, it must be given in the last days; therefore it cannot refer to the Roman Church alone, for that church has been in a fallen condition for many centuries" (p. 383).

In other words, since the Roman Church had fallen long before this point in history when the second angel's message was to be proclaimed, Babylon must include the Protestant churches that had fallen.

At this juncture, we have given a brief overview of the first and second angels' messages. It is important to recognize that these two messages were first proclaimed in the years 1840 through October 22, 1844. However, these two messages, along with the third angel's message, will be the last warning message before Jesus comes. HISTORY REPEATS ITSELF! Therefore, the three angels' messages will continue to be "present truth" for God's remnant people, subsequent to 1844. And their mission is to proclaim these messages to the world: "Thou must prophesy again" (Rev. 10:11).

All knowledgeable students of the Bible will recognize that both the first and the second angels' messages are repeated in Revelation 18. Remember, the "everlasting gospel" of the first angel's message also includes the message of righteousness by faith, which is the "faith of/in Jesus" found in the third angel's message. Also, in Revelation 1:1 and 3, it becomes clear that the "Revelation of Jesus Christ" includes "prophecy." Thus, prophecy is an intricate part of the everlasting gospel. The messages of Revelation will be proclaimed during the last segment of time, when every living person will be making a decision to be faithful to God or conform to the demands of the one-world religio-political government.

Now, let us give a brief introduction into the contents of the third angel's message. Anyone who casually reads Revelation 14:9-12, will notice some cryptic ideas and symbols. We notice a beast is mentioned, and it wants worship. Also, we have an image to this beast, and a mark that will be placed on each worshipers' "forehead" or "hand" who worship the beast and his image. We also find the infamous passage about "for ever and ever," which appears to support an everlasting hell. Let us begin the identification of these symbols.

Throughout the Old Testament, just like in our day, symbolic beasts were used to represent kingdoms. For example, today we identify Russia as a bear, while the United States is represented by an eagle. In order to identify this prophetic beast in Revelation, we need another prophetic book, namely, the book of Daniel, to help us identify it. Remember, we must allow the Bible to interpret itself.

Let's turn to Daniel 7; beginning with verse 3, we note four beasts coming up from the sea. Going to verse 17, we read, "These great beasts, which are four, are four kings, which shall arise out of the earth." Then in verse 23, it says, "Thus he said, The fourth beast shall be the fourth kingdom upon the earth." So, in Daniel 7 we have outlined for us, in symbolic language, four consecutive world empires. Historically, these kingdoms were 1) Babylon, 2) Medo-Persia, 3) Greece, and 4) Rome. History also informs us that pagan Rome eventually transformed into papal Rome.

Now, we need to go to Revelation 13, which sets the stage for our understanding of Revelation 14. In Revelation 13:1, a beast appears who becomes the principle character in the drama of these last days. In verse 2 we discover that this beast is a composite of four beasts. In other words, it has features of a "leopard," a "bear," a "lion," and "the dragon gave him his power, and his seat, and great authority." Did you notice that these beast-like features are the same beasts mentioned in Daniel 7? The difference is that John was seeing them in reverse order. He was looking backward in history and saw the leopard, the

The Three Angels' Messages

bear, and the lion, whereas Daniel was looking forward and saw the lion first, then the bear, and the leopard.

The dragon represents Satan (Rev. 12:9), but also his kingdom is represented with heads and horns (Rev. 12:3). That kingdom in John's day was pagan Rome. "The dragon here is a symbol, not of the Roman empire in general, but of the HEATHEN Roman empire" (Notes on chapter 12 from *Adam Clarke's Commentary*). The dragon was to give "his power, and his seat, and great authority" to this beast that now demands our attention. In the year AD 533, Emperor Justinian gave the pope of Rome with supreme power. In the year 538, the final obstacle was removed, allowing the Papacy to assume that power. Thus, this beast represents papal Rome, the religio-political kingdom that ruled over all the civil governments of the empire.

Let us continue the drama about this beast. In verse 3 we read, "And I saw one of his heads as it were wounded to death; and his deadly wound was healed." Then in verse 4, we read,

"And they worshiped the dragon which gave power unto the beast: and they worshipped the beast." Thus, both the dragon and the beast are the recipients of worship. In Revelation 12:9 we are told that the "dragon" is Satan. Then, in Revelation 13:14 and 15 we learn that an "image" to the first beast is to be formed. This "image" also demands worship (verse 15). Therefore, the image to the beast must also represent a religio-political power that arises in these last days. So, we have three major players in this drama of end-time events:

1. The beast – papal Rome, whose "deadly wound" will be "healed" and will return to power
2. The dragon – Satan, who works through the governments of our world
3. The image – the United States of America, represented as "another beast coming up out of the earth" (verse 11). However, it must be understood that it will be apostate Protestantism in the U.S., also known as the false prophet (Rev. 16:13) who will be instrumental in setting up this "image."

The Roman Catholic Church, particularly the pope, claims to have the authority to change God's law. In essence, this is placing the pope above God, thus fulfilling a number of prophecies. For example, Paul identified the "man of sin" as one "who opposeth and exalteth himself above all that is called God, or that is worshipped; so that he as God sitteth in the temple of God, shewing himself that he is God" (2 Thess. 2:4). Daniel described this same power that would "think to change times and laws" (Dan. 7:25).

Here are two quotes from official Catholic sources that will help you see the fulfillment of these prophecies:

- "We hold upon this earth the place of God Almighty" (Pope Leo XIII, quoted in *The Great Encyclical Letters of Pope Leo XIII*, p. 193).
- "The Pope is of so great authority and power that he can modify, explain, or interpret even divine laws. . . . The Pope can modify divine law, since his power is not of man, but of God, and he acts in the place of God upon earth, with the fullest power of binding and loosing his sheep" (Lucius Ferraris, "Papa," art. 2, in *Prompta Bibliotheca*).

The change of the Sabbath from the seventh day to the first day of the week is one of the Catholic Church's boldest modifications of God's law. Here are two more quotes:

- "Sunday is our mark of authority! . . . The Church is above the Bible, and this transference of Sabbath observance is proof of that fact" (*The Catholic Record*, London, Ontario, September 1, 1923).
- "Of course the Catholic Church claims that the change was her act . . . And the act is a mark of her ecclesiastical power and authority in religious matters" (Office of Cardinal Gibbons, through Chancellor C.F. Thomas, November 11, 1895).

In AD 321, Emperor Constantine, under the direction of the bishop of Rome, issued the first Sunday law, commanding all to cease from labor on Sundays. Our Protestant churches will likewise demand that Congress legislate Sunday laws in an effort to enhance morality in America. When this happens, Protestant America will have set up an image to the beast. Our beloved America will have another religio-political system of government, similar to papal Rome. And, like wildfire, religious laws will then be passed in all the other nations of the world as they follow our example and yield to the churches' demands. Then, spiritual Babylon, composed of the beast, the dragon, and the false prophet, will control the world.

All of this will occur in the last remnant of time, as portrayed in Revelation 16 and 17. The kings of the earth will "give their power and strength unto the beast" (Rev. 17:13). The civil governments of the world will be controlled by the religious powers and will enforce ecclesiastical laws. When these Sunday laws are passed, then the stage is set to test all mankind's loyalties.

After the Sunday law has passed, those who know the issues involved and still choose to worship on Sunday will then have chosen to receive the mark of the beast. When marked in the "forehead," it signifies they believe the concept of Sunday sacredness. In other words, they are self-deceived. Others are marked in the "hand," signifying that they might not believe in Sunday sacredness, but because of circumstances or expedience, they go along with Sunday worship.

Now, let's give a short summary, in order to make a deeper impression of the climax of this world's history:

1. The beast represents papal Rome, and her religion is Catholicism. Her power will be reestablished in the very near future.
2. The image represents a worldwide religio-political power, formed initially by U. S. Protestants, similar to the Roman papal regime, and it extends throughout the rest of the world into the three-fold union of modern Babylon. Both of these religio-political powers will demand worship in the manner prescribed by their religious laws.
3. The mark of the beast represents legislating Sunday laws in place of the Bible Sabbath as the day for worship. This mark will be implemented worldwide by all the apostate religions.
4. The Sabbath is the seal of God's Ten Commandment law. Thus the world is brought to choose between the seal of God or the mark of the beast.
5. The dragon primarily represents Satan. In a secondary sense, the dragon represents all the governments of the world through which Satan works.
6. Babylon represents a combination of all the apostate religions of the world, composed of Catholics, Protestants, Muslims, and pagan religions, all of whom will be in control of their governments. During the final crisis, all of these "do-it-yourself" religions will try to legislate morality.
7. The result is the final climax of the great controversy between Christ and Satan at the battle of Armageddon.

Now we need to consider the punishment of those who choose the "do-it-yourself" religion of Babylon. Will they be tormented "for ever and ever"? Are they going to "have no rest day nor night"? That is what Revelation 14:11 says, but just what does it mean? First, when reading our Bibles, we have to be guided by the Holy Spirit. Second, we must be careful not to read into a passage any of our preconceptions.

The concept of everlasting burning of the wicked is contrary to the Hebrew scriptures. It was also foreign to the Hebrew mind. Remember, John was Hebrew, even though the book of Revelation was written in Greek. Today, many Bible believers have the preconception of an immortal soul, but this idea comes from pagan Greek philosophy. Therefore, many people misunderstand the Hebrew thought in this passage. This text does not teach us that the soul is immortal. The Bible is clear that only God has immortality (1 Tim. 6:16). The soul is the whole being, not an entity that outlives the body. We need to go directly to the source to discover this fact. Let's examine the creation of man in Genesis: "And the LORD God formed man of the dust of the ground, and breathed into his nostrils the breath of life; and man became a living soul" (Gen. 2:7).

The combination of the body and the breath of life formed a living soul. At death, the opposite takes place: "His breath goeth forth, he returneth to his earth; in that very day his thoughts perish" (Ps. 146:4).

So, what did "for ever and ever" mean for the Hebrew? Simply stated, "for ever and ever" meant *as long as it takes to finish the job*. In other words, the fire will not be extinguished until the job is done. This is strange thinking for our Western modern minds, but not so for the Hebrew. The fire will be unquenchable, for our God is a "consuming fire." (See Hebrews 12:29.) His brightness consumes sinners and everything wicked, but the righteous can live in the full blaze of His glory.

Have you ever wondered why the righteous will not be consumed by God's glory? It will be because they have Jesus within their hearts! However, the wicked will be burned up, i.e., consumed and reduced to ashes. Malachi 4:1 and 3 says, "For, behold, the day cometh, that shall burn as an oven; and all the proud, yea, and all that do wickedly, shall be stubble: and the day that cometh shall burn them up, saith the LORD of hosts, that it shall leave them neither root nor branch. . . . And ye shall tread down the wicked; for they shall be ashes under the soles of your feet in the day that I shall do this, saith the LORD of hosts."

Hebrew writers believed that the result of the punishment is everlasting, but not the process of punishing. To illustrate Hebrew thought on "for ever and ever," let us compare Jude and Peter on the destruction of Sodom and Gomorrah. Jude stated that these cities were "suffering the vengeance of eternal fire" (Jude 7). (Remember, God is eternal fire.) Whereas, Peter said, "And turning the cities of Sodom and Gomorrah into ashes" (2 Peter 2:6).

The Hebrew mind acknowledged the truth that God is the source of all life. Therefore, all creatures have no inherent, natural life of their own. The life we receive is on loan to us, on the condition of obedience. Therefore, the "for ever and ever" ages of the righteous and the wicked will be different. Why? Because their natures will be different. The righteous will receive immortal bodies at Jesus' second coming. The wicked will be slain by the brightness of the second coming. (See 2 Thessalonians 2:8.) Only those given immortality can continue to live. The wicked will not receive this gift.

Also, the wicked will have "no rest day nor night" when they suffer during the seven last plagues. They have rejected Jesus, and their probation has closed, thus they cannot have rest that only comes with the presence of Jesus within us. (See Matthew 11:28, 29.) They will suffer torment while they are living, but not beyond death.

In conclusion, the three angels' messages provide God's remnant church with a message and a mission for evangelizing the world. All who are looking for the advent of Christ should know their content. Why? Because we are to be the messengers. It will not be long before the Lord's heralds of truth—present truth—will be under the scrutinizing eye of both Protestants and Catholics alike. We can witness to them by our godly example and by being prepared to answer their questions with the Word of God. Peter told us to "sanctify the Lord God in your hearts: and be ready always to give an answer to every man that asketh you a reason of the hope that is in you with meekness and fear" (1 Peter 3:15). Therefore, now is the time for preparation, with Bible study and prayer.

My appeal includes a personal invitation to you, dear reader, to join with me in a pledge to surrender all to Jesus.

Chapter 13

Movement of Destiny
Adventist Heritage

It is my privilege and responsibility to give an important message to God's people in whatever denomination they belong. This message is one that is not often heard from the pulpit, but it is a timely one, given the current events in the world and the increased interest in prophecy. As mentioned in the last chapter, Babylon is made up of Catholicism, apostate Protestantism, and other religions. It is crucial, therefore, to consider our own church affiliation and the message it bears. Perhaps at some point, you have wondered, "Am I in the right church?" After reading the preceding chapters of this book, you may wonder who these "Adventists" are and where they are to be found.

In this study, we will look at the characteristics of God's remnant church and identify the people who are proclaiming the three angels' messages. We will see that this is indeed a movement of destiny with a rich and significant heritage.

Perhaps you are also wondering, "Does it really matter?" It absolutely does matter! First, God is calling out a people from Babylon. Second, history repeats itself! This answer will make more sense as we progress through this presentation.

There is an axiom that says, "Those who fail to learn lessons from their past history are doomed to repeat that history." A corollary principle that I want to emphasize today, is that Adventist history, during 1840 to 1844, will be repeated just before probation closes. That is why I believe it is important to know that history.

Many Adventists have been pleasantly surprised to discover that our remnant movement has been revealed in numerous passages of Scripture. In other words, whenever the Bible is describing the "remnant" in an end-time context, it is describing the Adventist movement. Some people have even suggested that the Adventist movement is a continuation of the Protestant reformation. Is this spiritual arrogance? I don't believe so. It is simply an honest response to God's call. Our individual standing will depend on our future actions, after becoming enlightened, concerning our mission and message to the world.

Let us begin our story in Revelation 12. I have already given an overview of the book of Revelation in the chapter titled "Jesus, in the Book of Revelation." But, in this chapter, I want to emphasize three important points:

1. There are many symbols in the book of Revelation; however, these can be understood when we use the Bible as its own interpreter.
2. Revelation was not written in strict chronological order. In other words, it was not written like a modern novel, from the beginning to the end. Instead, John wrote using Hebrew parallelisms. He wrote the first prophecy (the seven churches) from its beginning to the end. Then, he wrote the second prophecy (the seven seals) as another parallel section from the beginning to the end. The third and fourth sections of Revelation are somewhat parallel, and three out of four of these prophecies end with Jesus' second coming. (Note: I believe the seven trumpets end after the millennium.)
3. The last three prophecies (chapters 15-22) begin with the seven last plagues, and move progressively into eternity. With this brief background information, let us first summarize Revelation 12.

In this chapter we will discover three phases of God's church, although the first phase is only implied. These three phases are as follows: 1) the early church, 2) the church in the wilderness, and 3) the remnant church. In Revelation 12:1 we read, "And there appeared a great wonder in heaven; a woman clothed with the sun, and the moon under her feet, and upon her head a crown of twelve stars."

A woman in prophecy symbolizes a church (Isa. 54 and Eze. 16). In Revelation 12:2 we notice she is "with child;" in other words, she is pregnant.

"Clothed with the sun, and the moon under her feet" demonstrates that this is God's church, clothed in the light of Christ and standing on the Old Testament, which was only a reflection of the New Testament (verse 1). Then, in verse 5 we are told this child "was to rule all nations." He also went "up unto God," making it clear that the child is Jesus. Then in verse 6 we are told that "the woman fled into the wilderness." This wilderness experience represents the second phase of God's true church. Certainly, many of God's people were members of the Roman Church, but the Roman Church members were led into darkness by its leadership, and no longer "clothed with the sun." God's "invisible" church was forced into the wilderness, or into seclusion.

Skipping further down in verse 6, we notice there is a time prophecy pertinent for the church in the wilderness. Using the year for the day principle, we recognize God's true church is in the wilderness for 1260 years. This period of time is the same 1260 years of papal Roman supremacy. In verse 14 we find this same time prophecy repeated but using a different formula. This second repetition of the prophecy is the same formula used by Daniel in Daniel 7:25 and 12:7.

Now, let us skip on down to verse 17. Here, we are introduced to the beginning of the third remnant church era. Verse 17 says, "And the dragon was wroth with the woman, and went to make war with the remnant of her seed, which keep the commandments of God, and have the testimony of Jesus Christ."

This verse is very important for all Christians living today: therefore, we need to clarify what it is saying. First, the dragon represents Satan, as brought out in verse 9. Satan makes "war" with the "remnant of her seed" (verse 17). Who are these people that constitute the seed of the woman? One thing should be apparent from this chapter: they come upon the scene of history after the 1260-year time prophecy. In other words they arrive in history after 1798, when the pope was removed from the Vatican and his empire collapsed.

Webster's Dictionary defines "remnant" as "a small remaining group of people." I believe this definition describes a remainder of people who continue the work of the Protestant reformation and would therefore constitute God's end-time denominated people. Furthermore, according to this verse, the "remnant" people have two characteristics:

1. They keep the "commandments of God." The issue is between Christ and Satan, thus the conflict will be between the commandments of God and the commandments of the usurper (Dan. 7:25). As we have noted earlier, the Sabbath of the fourth commandment has been set aside in favor of Sunday, a mere tradition. The remnant will obey God rather than men.
2. They have the "testimony of Jesus Christ." This "testimony" must be in some way related to the words of Christ. Thus, in a broader sense, this "testimony" would also include words from a prophet who speaks for Christ. In Revelation 19:10, we discover what the Bible says about the "testimony of Jesus": "And I fell at his feet to worship him. And he said unto me, See thou do it not: I am thy fellowservant, and of thy brethren that have the testimony of Jesus: worship God: for the testimony of Jesus is the spirit of prophecy."

Here we are told that John, along with his brethren, had the testimony of Jesus. However, another verse in Revelation is even more specific. In Revelation 22:9 we discover John, once again, attempting to worship this angel. Please notice what the angel says: "Then saith he unto me, See thou do it not: for I am thy fellowservant, and of thy brethren the prophets."

So, prophets, including this angel, are the "brethren" who have the "spirit of prophecy" or "the testimony of Jesus." True prophets have always spoken for Christ.

So far, we see that the remnant people of God will be keeping all of His commandments and they have the testimony of Jesus, which is the spirit of prophecy. Surely, we recognize that all of God's prophets were inspired by the Holy Spirit. There has been a chain of prophets, including Enoch, Noah, Abraham, Moses, and so forth, down through the ages and on into New Testament times with Paul, Peter, and John, etc. Furthermore, the Holy Spirit is the Author of prophecy. 2 Peter 1:21 says, "For the prophecy came not in old time by the will of man; but holy men of God spake as they were moved by the Holy Ghost."

Of course, not all of God's prophets prophesied, but they all spoke for God. Recall what was written by the prophet Amos in Amos 3:7: "Surely the Lord GOD will do nothing, but [or except] he revealeth his secret unto his servants the prophets."

It is the work of the Lord's prophets to convey the secrets of God to His people. Furthermore, God's people are blessed whenever they heed a prophet's counsel. Do you remember what King Jehoshaphat said in 2 Chronicles 20:20? "Believe in the LORD your GOD, so shall ye be established; believe his prophets, so shall ye prosper."

It is only logical that the remnant church will have a good understanding of Bible prophecy, especially those prophecies dealing with end-time events. In fact, the angel told Daniel that in the time of the end the "wise" will understand Daniel's prophecies (Dan. 12:9, 10). It is also logical that God would provide a prophet for His remnant people. Joel 2:28-32 alludes to this: "And it shall come to pass afterward, that I will pour out my spirit upon all flesh; and your sons and your daughters shall prophesy, your old men shall dream dreams, your young men shall see visions: And also upon the servants and upon the handmaids in those days will I pour out my spirit. And I will shew wonders in the heavens and in the earth, blood, and fire, and pillars of smoke.

"The sun shall be turned into darkness, and the moon into blood, before the great and the terrible day of the LORD come. And it shall come to pass, that whosoever shall call on the name of the LORD shall be delivered: for in mount Zion and in Jerusalem shall be deliverance, as the LORD hath said, and in the remnant whom the LORD shall call."

Peter used this passage in his sermon on the day of Pentecost (Acts 2:17-21), but that was only a partial fulfillment. Notice that Peter left out the significant conclusion of Joel 2:32, which specifies: "and in the remnant whom the Lord shall call." I believe the reason this phrase was omitted was because the "remnant" would not be called out until many centuries later. In other words, not until after the church had been in the wilderness for 1260 years. It only stands to reason that some time after 1798 there would be another fulfillment of Joel's prophecy. "Dreams" and "visions" should be present among God's people before the "great and the terrible day of the Lord come."

Of course, there are some other details of this prophecy we need to consider. Notice that Jerusalem is mentioned. It is well understood that Jerusalem, when mentioned in the Old Testament in an end-time context, does not apply to the literal city of Jerusalem today. After the cross the Hebrew nation lost

Movement of Destiny

their entitlement to God's promises. Therefore, whenever Jerusalem is mentioned in the Old Testament prophecies and in an end-time context, we understand it to represent God's church.

Joel also mentions "wonders" that will appear in the heavens and the earth; for example: the "sun shall be turned into darkness" and the "moon into blood." (We discussed these briefly in the chapter "Overview of the Seals and Trumpets.") These are the same "signs" mentioned by Jesus in Mathew 24:29 that would occur "after the tribulation of those days" (the 1260 years of papal rule when the true church was in the wilderness) and prior to His second coming. Joel also stated that all of this would occur before the "great and the terrible day of the Lord come." This "day of the Lord" includes Jesus' second coming to earth.

Now, let's take a closer look at the beginning of the Adventist movement. In the early 1800s, William Miller had a conversion experience. Formerly, Miller was an influential farmer and a Deist. A Deist is someone who denies supernatural events and doesn't believe that God is in control of His creation. Through a series of providences in his life, he accepted Jesus as His personal Savior. This is the first step everyone must take before becoming a member of God's church. This step encompasses all of the different denominations, including Baptist, Pentecostal, Methodist, Catholic, or whatever church one becomes a member of. God accepts everyone into His "invisible" church, regardless of what denomination they belong to, as long as they have Jesus as their personal Savior.

Upon his conversion, he began studying the Scriptures diligently. He would not read any further than his understanding allowed. In other words, he would not move on to another passage until he was satisfied of the meaning of the one before him. He would allow the Bible to be its own interpreter, searching out meanings of words, phrases and symbols in other portions of Scripture. Using his King James Version Bible and a *Cruden's Concordance*, he made a shocking prediction. He predicted Jesus would come to this earth and destroy it in 1843. Later, the date was re-calculated and changed to October 22, 1844. Miller and other pioneers arrived at this date by their interpretation of Daniel 8:14, which says, "Unto two thousand and three hundred days, then shall the sanctuary be cleansed."

His prediction naturally poses a couple of questions: 1) How could any Bible believing Christian, especially the Adventist pioneers, have made this incredible mistake in predicting the exact day of Christ's second coming? And 2) was October 22, 1844, a "non-event" as most of the Christians of the other Protestant churches believe?

Regarding the first question, Miller and the Adventists of his day had mistakenly believed the "cleansing of the sanctuary" to be the purging of the earth by fire at the second coming. The truth of the sanctuary in heaven and its cleansing—the anti-type of the earthly sanctuary with its cleansing on the Day of Atonement—was yet to be discovered. Therefore, they did not make a mistake in the final computation of the date, October 22, 1844, but in the event that was to occur on that date. Connecting the admonition in the parable of the ten virgins, "Behold, the bridegroom cometh; go ye out to meet him" (Matt. 25:6), with the first angel's message, "for the hour of his judgment is come" (Rev. 14:7), they concluded that Jesus was coming to judge the world.

Unfortunately, they failed to see that two more angels' messages were to follow this first angel's message, and the result was a bitter disappointment, similar to the one Jesus' disciples experienced when Jesus died on the cross, rather than establish His earthly kingdom as they had anticipated. However, just as the disciples had a mission and message to proclaim to the world after their disappointment, so the Adventists discovered they had a mission and message to proclaim worldwide. In spite of the clear teaching in the books of Daniel, Hebrews, and Revelation, no other church outside of the Seventh-day Adventist Church teaches the great truths of the sanctuary in heaven and Jesus' two-phase ministry in that sanctuary. And, to the best of my knowledge, no other church is proclaiming the three angels' messages of Revelation 14:6-12. Amazingly, both these truths are linked together, for the judgment hour message points to the work of Jesus in the heavenly sanctuary. There is ample evidence in the Bible to support a sanctuary in heaven, with two phases of ministry.

In Leviticus the earthly sanctuary is portrayed with two apartments. In Exodus 25:8, 9, and 40, Moses is told to make the earthly tabernacle "after their pattern." In other words, the heavenly sanctuary was the pattern. The writer of Hebrews clearly explains how the earthly sanctuary was patterned after the "true tabernacle, which the Lord pitched, and not man" (Heb. 8:2, 5). We also see in Hebrews and Revelation the various furnishings of the heavenly sanctuary, which belonged in one or the other of the two apartments. Specifically, what our pioneers failed to understand was that Jesus went into the second phase of His ministry on October 22, 1844, in fulfillment of the 2300-year prophecy.

At that time, Jesus, as our High Priest, began a new ministry of cleansing the record of sins that had accumulated therein since sin entered into our world. Both of these typical daily and yearly services were commanded by God and observed by the Hebrews. They were symbolic of the real ministry of Jesus, as they served "unto the example and shadow of heavenly things" (Heb. 8:5). Some may object that heavenly things need no cleansing, but in fact, Hebrews 9:22 and 23 tells us emphatically, "And almost all things are by the law purged with blood; and without shedding of blood is no remission. It was therefore necessary that the patterns of things in the heavens should be purified with these; but the heavenly things themselves with better sacrifices than these."

Our heavenly High Priest began His first apartment ministry on the day of Pentecost in AD 31. Then, at the commencement of the "time appointed," i.e., October 22, 1844 (Dan. 8:14, 19), Jesus began His second apartment ministry. The writer of Hebrews, in speaking of this second apartment ministry, wrote, "of which we cannot now speak particularly" (Heb. 9:5). It would not be until "the time of the end," when Daniel was unsealed, that this second phase ministry could be understood. Later in this presentation, we will clarify how Daniel 8:19 fits into "the end of the [God's] indignation," or "curses," and the beginning of Jesus' second apartment ministry.

The second apartment ministry of the high priest in the earthly sanctuary was well-known to the Hebrews as a day of judgment. Furthermore, the cleansing of the sanctuary during the Old Testament service coincides with an investigative judgment. This "judgment" was performed by God every year. In a similar manner, since Jesus lives forever, and He was sacrificed only once, He is both our sacrifice and our High Priest. This message is clearly explained in Hebrews 7:26-28: "For such an high priest became us, who is holy, harmless, undefiled, separate from sinners, and made higher than the heavens; Who needeth not daily, as those high priests, to offer up sacrifice, first for his own sins, and then for the people's: for this he did once, when he offered up himself. For the law maketh men high priests which have infirmity; but the word of the oath, which was since the law, maketh the Son, who is consecrated for evermore."

Therefore, what was symbolic for the Hebrews has become a reality for Jesus' ministry in the heavenly sanctuary. What was true in the typical (symbolic) services, namely, the cleansing of the sanctuary, which is coincident with an investigative judgment, is also true in its reality. Both of these activities of Jesus' ministry began on October 22, 1844. I will present proof for our position about the commencement of Jesus' activities on that date later on.

Despite Protestant denials of a pre-advent judgment, we have biblical evidence for this truth. In Daniel 7:9 we read, "I beheld till the thrones were cast down [i.e., set in place], and the Ancient of days did sit." Dropping down to the last sentence of verse 10, we read, "the judgment was set, and the books were opened." Thus, it is clearly apparent that a judgment has commenced in heaven. We also see that "books" were investigated during this judgment. Skipping down to verses 13 and 14, we read, "I saw in the night visions, and, behold, one like the Son of man came with the clouds of heaven, and came to the Ancient of days, and they brought him near before him. And there was given him dominion, and glory, and a kingdom."

Here we see Jesus coming to the Father (not to the earth) for a pre-advent judgment. This is especially clear when we include verses 22 through 27. Furthermore, Jesus will be receiving His kingdom during this judgment. More will be explained about this later when we discuss other events connected to October 22, 1844.

As mentioned in the previous chapter, this investigative judgment is not for God's benefit but for the benefit of all His created intelligent beings. When the time arrives for the executive judgment (the exoneration of the saints and the destruction of the wicked), there will be no lingering doubts about God's justice. Furthermore, with the proclamation of the three angels' messages in conjunction with the judgment, all the inhabitants of the earth will have been warned and given an opportunity to "give glory to God" and escape the "mark of the beast."

Since the Seventh-day Adventist Church is the only Protestant church proclaiming these three angels' messages, I believe this is pretty good evidence that this is God's remnant church. Our established mission statement is to proclaim these three messages. During the final harvest, others from the other churches will join our ranks as they respond to God's last warning message.

Most Christians have never heard of Jesus' ministry in the second apartment, or "holy of holies." Some who have looked into it consider the investigative judgment a mere "face-saving" invention, fabricated to cover up for the mistaken proclamation of Christ's second coming. They do not care to see the evidence of the investigative judgment often due to the fact that such a judgment would shatter their "once saved, always saved" doctrine. They also fail to recognize the "bitter" disappointment foretold in Revelation 10, which certainly fits the experience of the Advent believers in 1844.

Revelation 10 tells our story. It begins with a "mighty angel" coming down from heaven, having "a little book open" (verses 1 and 2). As we have already seen, this open book was the book of Daniel, which was formerly closed. Until 1798, to evangelical understanding, the book of Daniel was shrouded in mystery. However, when the Adventist movement began, especially from 1840 to 1844, this book was unsealed. We have already demonstrated how the day for a year principle was confirmed by the loss of Ottoman sovereignty on August 11, 1840, fulfilling Revelation 9:15. While earlier reformers may have understood this day for a year principle before the nineteenth century, Bible students were now in need of this confirmation. This predicted fall of the Ottoman Empire was under the sixth trumpet. It would not be until the seventh angel sounded that further light would come.

In Revelation 10:7 we read, "But in the days of the voice of the seventh angel, when he shall begin to sound, the mystery of God should be finished, as he hath declared to his servants the prophets."

Under the seventh trumpet, the door into the Most Holy Place was opened and the ark, containing the law of God, was seen (Rev. 11:19). This served to not only point the believers to the heavenly sanctuary, but also to the Ten Commandments. It was then discovered that the fourth commandment had been set aside by the beast power and Sunday put in its place. The third angel's message, which warns against the mark of the beast, ends with this key verse:

"Here is the patience of the saints: here are they that keep the commandments of God, and the faith of Jesus" (Rev. 14:12).

With these discoveries, the Adventists were convicted that they were given marching orders in Revelation 10:11, which says, "And he said unto me, Thou must prophesy again before many peoples, and nations, and tongues, and kings."

After the bitter disappointment of October 22, 1844, Hiram Edson, one of the leaders in the Advent movement, wrote, "I saw . . . that he [Christ] came to the marriage at that time [Oct. 1844]; in other words, to the Ancient of days, to receive a kingdom, dominion, and glory; and we must wait for His return from the wedding; and my mind was directed to the tenth chapter of Revelation where I could see the vision had spoken and did not lie; the seventh angel began to sound; we had eaten the little book; it had been sweet in our mouth, and it had now become bitter in our belly, embittering our whole being."

Here we have another truth mentioned, that of the wedding. The pioneers of the Advent movement rightly taught that Jesus would not return until after His wedding. This is taught by Jesus Himself in Luke 12:36, which says, "And ye yourselves like unto men that wait for their lord, when he will return from the wedding."

This wedding is between Christ and the church and is synonymous with Christ receiving His kingdom. As we have learned from Daniel 7, this happens during the investigative judgment (Dan. 7:14, 22, 27). That this takes place during the sounding of the seventh trumpet is evident from Revelation 11:15, which reads, "And the seventh angel sounded; and there were great voices in heaven, saying, The kingdoms of this world are become the kingdoms of our Lord, and of his Christ; and he shall reign for ever and ever."

Daniel 7:14 is a parallel verse: "And there was given him dominion, and glory, and a kingdom, that all people, nations, and languages, should serve him: his dominion is an everlasting dominion, which shall not pass away, and his kingdom that which shall not be destroyed."

Therefore, I believe Jesus' wedding, the reception of His kingdom, the cleansing of the sanctuary, and the sounding of the seventh trumpet all began on October 22, 1844. To firmly establish that October 22, 1844, was a genuine "time appointed" date, let us go back to Daniel 8:14. Some here may want to dispute my use of the KJV Bible, which employs the word "cleansed" in this verse. In Daniel 8:14, the KJV Bible says, "Unto two thousand and three hundred days; then shall the sanctuary be cleansed." The Hebrew word for "cleansed" in this verse is *tsadaq*, which literally means "justified, made righteous, or just." So, why did the KJV translators use "cleansed" in this verse? The reason they used "cleansed" was because they were familiar with the ancient Hebrew sanctuary services, and they recognized that a sanctuary becomes cleansed, whereas the people who were cleansed as well, became justified. Unfortunately, most of the popular modern versions use a different word than "cleansed" in this verse. The RSV uses "restored," the NASB uses "properly restored," and the NIV uses "re-consecrated."

Now, why would the modern translators translate *tsadaq* in the manner as described above? They did not recognize this verse having any connection to the Day of Atonement of the Hebrew sanctuary services. The modern translators believed the sanctuary, which was mentioned in this verse, had to be the earthly sanctuary, which needed to be "restored" or "re-consecrated." The Jewish sanctuary was desecrated by Antiochus Epiphanes for three years, between 168 BC and 165 BC, and finally, its temple services were restored in 165 BC. The modern translators believe the 2300 days apply to this period of time, because the Hebrew wording of days is "evening morning." Therefore, they thought the 2300 evening mornings should be divided in half, which is 1150 days. This presupposition is flawed for a number of reasons, but the evidence is conclusive that in their interpretation there is a discrepancy in the total time allotted for this prophecy.

Both the KJV Bible translators and the modern translators recognized there was no Jewish temple anymore, since it was destroyed in AD 70. A major difference between these two groups of translators was that the KJV translators, in addition to making a connection of this verse with the Day of Atonement, also must have recognized the "year for a day" principle and correctly translated the word *tsadaq* in its secondary sense as "cleansed," which also implies "justified."

At this point, we need to give a simplified explanation of how October 22, 1844, was determined. In Daniel 8:27, Daniel tells us he "fainted" before the angel gave an explanation of the "two thousand and three hundred days"

A Primer on Salvation and Bible Prophecy

of Daniel 8:14. The explanation was provided about twelve years later and is recorded in Daniel 9:23-27. In verse 24, we read, "Seventy weeks are determined upon thy people and upon thy holy city, to finish the transgression, and to make an end of sins, and to make reconciliation for iniquity, and to bring in everlasting righteousness, and to seal up the vision and prophecy, and to anoint the most Holy."

The Hebrew word for "determined" is *chatak,* which means "decreed, or cut off." Therefore, "seventy weeks" were "cut off" for the Hebrew nation. There is no doubt what these seventy weeks are cut off from, for the angel came to Daniel to explain the time prophecy of the former vision, the 2300 days of Daniel 8:14. Then, in Daniel 9:25, we are told the time prophecy would begin with the decree "to restore and to build Jerusalem." Finally, in Ezra 6:14 and 7:7, we discover this decree was issued in the seventh year of King Artaxerxes, which was 457 BC. Although Cyrus and Darius had issued earlier decrees, it was not until Artaxerxes' decree that permission was granted to actually set up a government in Jerusalem (Ezra 7:25).

Using the day for a year principle, by adding 490 years (70 weeks = 70 X 7 = 490 years) to 457 BC, we arrive at AD 34, at which time national Israel ceased to be the chosen people. (We had to add another year to this computation because we failed to account for the full year principle. Our pioneers had initially overlooked this fact, causing them to first arrive at 1843.) In AD 34, Peter had a vision of the unclean beasts coming down in a sheet, explaining that the Gentiles were no longer to be considered unclean. Also, in that year Saul was stopped on the road to Damascus and raised up to be an apostle to the Gentiles.

Subtracting the 490 years from the 2300, we are left with 1810 years. Simply add 1810 to AD 34 and we arrive at 1844. Artaxerxes' decree went forth in the fall of the year, thus the prophecy concluded in the fall. This is how our pioneers arrived at the date of October 22, 1844.

I kept this explanation simple, leaving out some of the details of the 70-week prophecy, but you are encouraged to study out the details, noting the accuracy of all the time divisions, including Christ's baptism and crucifixion.

With these explanations, it should be evident that 1844 was far from being a "non-event." Had William Miller been alone in this calculation, it might be considered a "private interpretation," but he was hardly alone. Unknown to one another, Bible students around the world were also interpreting the 2300-day prophecy and arriving at very similar conclusions. In England, in fact, a conference was convened to discuss the 2300-day prophecy. Scholars of good reputation were invited in to study and share ideas. It was not until the passing of the time in 1844, however, that the sanctuary truth unfolded before the eyes of the faithful, allowing them to see their mistake, not in the date, but the event.

So, in summarizing the events connected to October 22, 1844, we have the following:

1. The cleansing of the sanctuary (Dan. 8:14)
2. The beginning of the pre-advent judgment (Rev. 14:7)
3. Beginning of Jesus' wedding to New Jerusalem (Luke 12:36)
4. Christ begins receiving His kingdom (Dan. 7:13, 14; and Luke 19:12-15)
5. Beginning of the seventh trumpet (Rev. 10:7, 11:15-19)

Following is a passage from *The Great Controversy*, page 426, which I believe summarizes, at least in part, some of what we have discussed in this chapter: "The coming of Christ as our high priest to the most holy place, for the cleansing of the sanctuary, brought to view in Daniel 8:14; the coming of the Son of man to the Ancient of Days, as presented in Daniel 7:13; and the coming of the Lord to His temple, foretold by Malachi, are descriptions of the same event; and this is also represented by the coming of the bridegroom to the marriage, described by Christ in the parable of the ten virgins, of Matthew 25."

The year 1844 marked the end of time prophecies. (There is yet another time prophecy that ended in 1844, but it is not as well recognized today. It involved the "seven times" of Leviticus 26. You can read about this in one of my articles in the appendices, "Principles of Prophetic Interpretation.") Since 1844, the time prophecies have all expired, and further events are not based on time but rather on character development. Once the righteous have received the seal of God and the wicked have reached the limits of God's forbearance, the decree will go forth, "He that is unjust, let him be unjust still: and he which is filthy, let him be filthy still: and he that is righteous, let him be righteous still: and he that is holy, let him be holy still" (Rev. 22:11).

A Primer on Salvation and Bible Prophecy

God would not begin the gathering time of His remnant until the time prophecy of the "indignation" was fulfilled, i.e., 1844 (Dan. 8:19; 11:35, 36). Another way of expressing God's "indignation" is "curses" (Deut. 29:27, 28). As we noted in the chapter on the seals and trumpets, there were judgments and curses against both pagan and papal Rome, ultimately leading to the "deadly wound" of the papacy in 1798. So, repeating for emphasis, God would not gather His denominated, remnant people until all of the time prophecies were fulfilled. And remember, whenever the phrase "time of the end" or "time appointed" was used in Daniel's prophecies, he was referring to the end of a prophecy, not to the end of time.

So, in a short summary, the Seventh-day Adventist Church is the remnant church, for it meets the following criteria:

1. Our church was raised up after the 1260-year time prophecy of tribulation, when God's people were scattered in the "wilderness."
2. Our church encourages everyone to keep all of God's commandments, including the Sabbath.
3. Our church has the spirit of prophecy. This is manifest in the proclamation of end-time Bible prophecy and also in the writings of Ellen G. White.
4. Our church has a worldwide mission outreach and proclaims the three angels' messages before earth's final harvest. A fifth criterion that we should discuss is the parallel of the Adventist movement with the parable of the ten virgins. This parable is woven into the fabric of Adventism. In Matthew 25:6 we read, "And at midnight there was a cry made, Behold, the bridegroom cometh; go ye out to meet him."

Our pioneers proclaimed this message, but Jesus did not come to earth as they expected. Instead, He went into the second apartment (Most Holy Place) of the sanctuary. Henceforth, we are to participate in His wedding, by faith. When Jesus has been married to His kingdom, He will come back to earth to take us home. In this parable, we note a "cry" was made at "midnight." Shortly after 1844, this "midnight cry" became identified with our Adventist movement. During this "Midnight Cry" movement, there was a mighty manifestation of the Holy Spirit. It was also the time when our pioneers proclaimed the second angel's message, which was a call for God's other people, His "invisible church," to leave the churches of Babylon. That call is being repeated, consistent with the recurring theme that "history repeats itself." Therefore, as the "midnight cry" marked the beginning of our movement, likewise the "loud cry" of Revelation 18:1, 2 will finish it. There we find the last and final call to come out of Babylon.

The first call out of Babylon was when God confounded the languages at the tower of Babel. The second call was given to Abraham and his family to leave the land of Shinar (Babylon). The third call was given to Israel to come out of Babylon after their captivity. The fourth call was given in the "midnight cry" in response to the second angel's message (Rev. 14:8).

The final call out of Babylon is given in Revelation 18:1-4, which reads, "And after these things I saw another angel come down from heaven, having great power; and the earth was lightened with his glory. And he cried mightily with a strong voice, saying, Babylon the great is fallen, is fallen, and is become the habitation of devils, and the hold of every foul spirit, and a cage of every unclean and hateful bird. For all nations have drunk of the wine of the wrath of her fornication, and the kings of the earth have committed fornication with her, and the merchants of the earth are waxed rich through the abundance of her delicacies. And I heard another voice from heaven, saying, Come out of her, my people, that ye be not partakers of her sins, and that ye receive not of her plagues."

This "loud cry" message will be proclaimed by God's true remnant people who have heeded the call. There is no room for boasting on the part of any who join this movement. Instead, we are more accountable and bear a heavy responsibility to reflect the character of Jesus fully while sharing these three angels' messages to the world. With a love relationship with Jesus, we will naturally love others, and then we can tell them, in a winsome manner, about our wonderful Savior. Dear reader, will you be a part of God's remnant church? Will you "keep the commandments of God, and the faith of Jesus" (Rev. 14:12)? Will you come out of Babylon and participate in the loud cry of warning to the world?

Chapter 14

The Making of Modern Babylon

A Do-It-Yourself Religion

In this chapter I want to discuss the making of modern Babylon, which is a do-it-yourself religion. In earlier chapters I gave overviews on the biblical books of Daniel and Revelation. In order for me to give the essential features of modern Babylon, I need to include some information that has already been covered in those earlier chapters. The book of Daniel provides the background information that allows students of prophecy to have a better understanding of the book of Revelation. For that reason, I need to build upon Daniel's book, which complements Revelation. Furthermore, in order to understand modern Babylon, we need to begin our study with ancient Babylon.

The purpose of this study will be to trace the origin of Babylon and contrast its counterfeit worship system to the true worship of God. Our primary focus will be an overview of Revelation 12 through 19, although some comments will be made from the concluding chapters, 20 through 22.

Ancient Babylon was established soon after the Flood, as recorded in Genesis 7 and 8. In Genesis 10:8-10, we read, "And Cush begat Nimrod: he began to be a mighty one in the earth. He was a mighty hunter before the LORD: wherefore it is said, Even as Nimrod the mighty hunter before the LORD. And the beginning of his kingdom was Babel [margin, or Babylon], and Erech, and Accad, and Calneh, in the land of Shinar."

In these verses we learn that Nimrod was "the mighty hunter before the LORD." In Hebrew this means that Nimrod was the mighty hunter in the face of, or against the Lord. Furthermore, Nimrod and Cush (his father) established the first city on earth, which was Babylon "in the land of Shinar." Cush was the grandson of Noah, and the son of Ham.

Then, in Genesis 11:7-9, God said, "Go to, let us go down, and there confound their language, that they may not understand one another's speech. So the LORD scattered them abroad from thence upon the face of all the earth: and they left off to build the city. Therefore is the name of it called Babel; because the LORD did there confound the language of all the earth: and from thence did the LORD scatter them abroad upon the face of all the earth."

Here, in the early chapters of Scripture, we have the first mention of Babylon. What were they doing? Backing up to verse 4, we read, "And they said, Go to, let us build us a city and a tower, whose top may reach unto heaven; and let us make us a name, lest we be scattered abroad upon the face of the whole earth."

These foolish Babylonians were attempting to save themselves by building a tower "whose top may reach unto heaven." By building this tower, the inhabitants of Babylon were establishing a false religion. You see, the foundation of all false religion is the notion that we can save ourselves by our works. Furthermore, the Babylonians established a pagan worship system. How did Babylon do this? After the dispersion, Nimrod and Cush continued to build the ancient kingdom of Babylon, but later, Nimrod was violently killed. Thereafter, Semiramis (his widow queen), with the assistance of Cush, deified him. After Nimrod's death, Semiramis became pregnant. To save face and maintain power, she invented the story that Nimrod's spirit was alive and that he had become one with the sun, impregnating her with his rays. (Note the connection between Semiramis, apostate Israel, and modern Babylon in Isaiah 47:8 and Revelation 18:7.) Cush fully supported her in this deception. Thus, ancient Babylon was guilty of both a false worship system and the pagan worship of Nimrod, as well as the worship of a heavenly body—the origin of sun worship.

When her son was born, she named him Tammuz and claimed that he was the reincarnation of Nimrod. Furthermore, Cush became known as the god "Bel," who also received worship, and Nimrod became known by many different names, depending upon which nation perpetuated his deification. Semiramis would come to be known as the "queen of heaven," a goddess. Tammuz, her deified son, also died a violent death, as did Nimrod.

A Primer on Salvation and Bible Prophecy

The Bible speaks of these individuals. Notice a few selected verses from Jeremiah 44:11-30: "Therefore thus saith the LORD of hosts . . . For I will punish them that dwell in the land of Egypt, as I have punished Jerusalem, by the sword, by the famine, and by the pestilence . . . Then all the men that knew that their wives had burned incense unto other gods . . . answered Jeremiah, saying: As for the word that thou hast spoken unto us in the name of the LORD, we will not hearken unto thee. But we will certainly do whatsoever thing goeth forth out of our own mouth, to burn incense unto the queen of heaven."

This pagan worship system spread from ancient Babylon to Assyria, then eventually to Egypt and all of the surrounding nations. Pagan rituals were even practiced in the land of Palestine. Ezekiel was shown these "abominations" in Ezekiel 8:13 and 14: "He said also unto me, Turn thee yet again, and thou shalt see greater abominations that they do. Then he brought me to the door of the gate of the LORD's house which was toward the north; and, behold, there sat women weeping for Tammuz."

In the days of Hammurabi, circa 1728-1686 BC, he reunited the upper and lower kingdoms of Babylonia, known as Accad and Sumer, thus re-establishing the kingdom of Nimrod. During this time, Hammurabi fixed his capital in the city of Babylon, which later became known as the "holy city" of the god Marduk of Mesopotamia. Over the next twelve centuries, Babylon remained the capital of Babylonia, with minor interruptions, until the conquest of Babylonia by Persia in 538 BC.

The Neo-Babylonian kingdom was established by King Nabopolassar in 626 BC, and his son Nebuchadnezzar ascended the throne in 606 BC. King Nebuchadnezzar took a group of Hebrews, including the young prophet Daniel, to his capital city of Babylon in 606/605 BC. While in the pagan nation of Babylon, and later in the Persian empire, Daniel wrote his book, which included four parallel prophecies outlining the future history of the world, until the establishment of God's everlasting kingdom. In Daniel's second prophecy (chapter 7), he used word pictures to describe four pagan empires as beast-like creatures that would sequentially control the world until Jesus' second coming. These beast-like creatures were as follows:

1. A lion, representing Babylon
2. A bear, representing Medo-Persia

3. A leopard, representing Greece
4. A dragon, representing Rome

With this background history, we can now begin our study on "The Making of Modern Babylon." As mentioned previously, literal Babylon began as a singular pagan city on the plains of Shinar. However, after Jesus' death on the cross, it is essential that we recognize the transition that occurred. Just as that which was once applied to literal Israel now becomes reapplied to spiritual Israel, so too, that which applied to literal Babylon is now applied to spiritual Babylon. In 1 Peter 5:13 it says, "The church that is at Babylon, elected together with you, saluteth you." When Peter wrote his epistle, literal Babylon no longer existed. Peter was symbolically using Babylon to represent Rome. Spiritual Babylon, having its foundation in literal Babylon, continued through Medo-Persia, Greece, and pagan Rome.

Alexander Hislop, in his book *The Two Babylons*, demonstrates fully that ecclesiastical Rome is nothing more than baptized pagan Rome. Pagan Rome transformed into papal Rome, which is spiritual Babylon. In Revelation 13:2 we learn that the "dragon" (Satan in the primary sense, but using pagan Rome as his instrument) gave his "power," "seat," and "great authority" to the composite "beast," which has all the features of Daniel's four beasts of Daniel 7. In other words, this composite first beast of Revelation 13 has the features of a "leopard," a "bear," and a "lion," and the "dragon gave him his power, and his seat, and great authority." These are the same four beasts found in Daniel 7. Therefore, this composite "beast" must represent papal Rome, which is an amalgamation of all the preceding pagan empires, especially pagan Rome.

Finally, modern Babylon becomes a three-fold confederation when the "false prophet" is added to its makeup. In Revelation 16:13, 14, and 19, we read the following words: "And I saw three unclean spirits like frogs come out of the mouth of the dragon, and out the mouth of the beast, and out of the mouth of the false prophet. For they are the spirits of devils, working miracles, which go forth unto the kings of the earth and of the whole world, to gather them to the battle of that great day of God Almighty. . . . And the great city was divided into three parts, and the cities of the nations fell: and great Babylon came in remembrance before God, to give unto her the cup of the wine of the fierceness of his wrath."

Notice that all three of these entities work "miracles" and practice deception. In Revelation 13:13 and 14, we discover the same characteristics pertaining to the "false prophet." There we read that "he doeth great wonders, so that he maketh fire come down from heaven on the earth in the sight of men. And deceiveth them that dwell on the earth by the means of those miracles."

Thus, the three-fold makeup of modern Babylon is:
1. The dragon, who works through "the kings of the earth"
2. The beast, modern papal Rome, the end-time Papacy, i.e., the wounded head that becomes healed
3. The false prophet, apostate Protestantism, which begins in the United States of America

Now, having made these assertions, we need to provide the evidence. Revelation 12 through 14 are a complete unit. These three chapters introduce us to the great controversy between Christ and Satan. Chapter 12 deals with the controversy from its commencement in heaven until the final conflict with the "remnant" people of God in verse 17, which says, "And the dragon was wroth with the woman, and went to make war with the remnant of her seed, which keep the commandments of God, and have the testimony of Jesus Christ."

In a brief overview of chapter 12, verse 7 tells us there was a "war in heaven," and the "dragon," who is identified as "Satan" in verse 9, was "cast out into the earth, and his angels were cast out with him." After being expelled from heaven, "the dragon stood before the woman which was ready to be delivered, for to devour her child as soon as it was born" (Rev. 12:4). After Jesus was born, Satan attempted to have baby Jesus killed when King Herod ordered all the children, two years of age and younger, to be slaughtered in Bethlehem. Of course, Satan failed to achieve his purpose of overcoming Jesus and thwarting the plan of salvation. Therefore, in Revelation 12:13-17 Satan persecutes the woman, who represents Christ's church.

In addition, Revelation 12 outlines three eras of Christ's true church, which are as follows:
1. The early church era.
2. The church in the wilderness for 1260 years. Note that both verses 6 and 14 give the same time prophecy for this era.
3. The remnant church era.

The Making of Modern Babylon

Satan uses the kings of the earth and the governments of our world as his agents to destroy God's people. Thus, the "dragon" secondarily represents kings, rulers, and governors who execute Satan's malignity against God's church.

In Revelation 13, we are introduced to the other two partners in the threefold coalition of modern Babylon. We already mentioned that this composite beast (verse 2) had all the features of the four preceding beasts of Daniel 7. Thus, this empire had all the pagan features of Babylon (lion), Medo-Persia (bear), Greece (leopard), and Rome (dragon). Any student of history acknowledges that ecclesiastical (papal) Rome was a continuation of the Roman Empire under the leadership of the bishop of Rome, who ascended to the office of the pope. In Revelation 13:1 we read, "And I stood upon the sand of the sea, and saw a beast rise up out of the sea, having seven heads and ten horns, and upon his horns ten crowns, and upon his heads the name of blasphemy."

In verse 3 we learn that this beast had a "deadly wound," which later becomes "healed," and "all the world wondered after the beast." In verse 4 it says, "And they worshipped the dragon which gave power unto the beast: and they worshipped the beast, saying, Who is like unto the beast? who is able to make war with him?"

How can it be that the whole world will be involved in a false worship system? Please consider that it must have something to do with a counterfeit trinity being set up, who are all implicated in this false worship system, especially when we include the actions of the "false prophet," as previously mentioned in selected verses from Revelation 13:11-18.

Note the following points:
1. Satan, as the dragon, wants worship. (See Isaiah 14:13, 14.) In the last remnant of time, I believe Satan will even personate Jesus, as a counterfeit god.
2. The Pope, as the "holy father" and head of the beast system of worship, claims to be another god on earth, and he receives worship in the place of Jesus. Also, the beast becomes resurrected from death, thus counterfeiting Jesus' resurrection.
3. The false prophet represents apostate Protestants who claim to speak for God, and in the final crisis, there will be a false revival of the Holy

Spirit, with miraculous manifestations. Verses 12-15 read, "And he exerciseth all the power of the first beast before him, and causeth the earth and them that dwell therein to worship the first beast, whose deadly wound was healed. And he doeth great wonders, so that he maketh fire come down from heaven on the earth in the sight of men, And deceiveth them that dwell on the earth by the means of those miracles which he had power to do in the sight of the beast; saying to them that dwell on the earth, that they should make an image to the beast, which had the wound by a sword, and did live. And he had power to give life unto the image of the beast, that the image of the beast should both speak, and cause that as many as would not worship the image of the beast should be killed."

Then, in Revelation 14 the focus shifts from modern Babylon to the remnant people of God who have a mission and a message to proclaim before Jesus' second coming. In verses 14 through 20, John describes the final harvest and the second coming. In Revelation 15 and 16, John drops back in history and includes the wrath of God in the seven last plagues, which God inflicts upon the wicked just before Jesus comes.

We need to consider an important principle (mentioned in earlier chapters) regarding the construction of the book of Revelation: the book of Revelation was not written in strict chronological order. There is repetition and enlargement present in Revelation, similar to the Hebrew parallelisms of the book of Daniel. For example, Revelation 12 through 14 give us an overview of the great controversy, but following this overview, John repeats and enlarges upon this theme in the remainder of chapters 15 through 19. In other words, he gives us more details about the closing scenes of this controversy in chapters 15 through 19. Therefore, chapters 13 and 17 are parallel prophecies, with more details included in the latter that build upon chapter 13. Furthermore, chapters 17 and 18 include an expansion of the sixth and seventh plagues, as presented in chapter 16, verses 12 through 21. Then, chapter 19 gives a more detailed account of the battle of Armageddon and Jesus' second coming, which is an expansion of Revelation 14:14-20 and 16:12-21. Thus, chapters 16 through 19 all expand upon the fall of modern Babylon during the sixth and seventh plagues as first presented in Revelation 16:12-21.

The Making of Modern Babylon

Now, let us include more details that are found in Revelation 12 through 19. There are four creature-like monsters portrayed in chapters 12, 13, and 17, but in reality, there are only three players in this coalition, because the "scarlet colored beast" of chapter 17 is the same beast as the leopard-like beast of chapter 13. This is why I mentioned that chapters 13 and 17 are parallel prophecies.

In a brief summary, the three monsters in this coalition of modern Babylon are:

1. The "dragon" in chapter 12
2. The sea "beast" in the first half of chapter 13, which is later described as the "scarlet colored beast" of chapter 17
3. The earth beast with "two horns like a lamb" in the second half of chapter 13, who later becomes the "false prophet"

It is important to note the significance of the first beast arising "out of the sea," but the second beast comes up "out of the earth." We see that the four beasts of Daniel 7 also "came up from the sea" (Dan. 7:3). To understand what the sea represents, we need to allow the Bible to interpret itself. In Revelation 17:15 the interpretation is supplied: "The waters which thou sawest, where the whore sitteth, are peoples, and multitudes, and nations, and tongues." Backing up to Revelation 17:1, we read, "And there came one of the seven angels which had the seven vials, and talked with me, saying unto me, Come hither; I will shew unto thee the judgment of the great whore that sitteth upon many waters."

Therefore, chapter 17 resumes the story of the leopard-like beast of chapter 13, which arose out of the teeming multitudes of the old world. Chapter 17 presents the circumstances that lead up to the restoration of civil power to the beast, and her wound becomes healed. Furthermore, she will be in control of many "peoples, and multitudes, and nations, and tongues," a fact we realize today, but will become more evident in the future. In contrast, the beast "out of the earth" represents a government that came up in a formerly unpopulated land—the United States in the New World.

Now, returning to the sixth plague in chapter 16, verse 12, we read, "And the sixth angel poured out his vial upon the great river Euphrates; and the water thereof was dried up, that the way of the kings of the east might be prepared."

At this juncture, many of us with western eyeglasses need to change our mindset in order to comprehend the true meaning of this passage. Remember, John was a descendant of an eastern culture. When he writes about the "kings of the east," he was not referring to the kings of the orient, but the kings from the "sun-rising" (the literal meaning of "east").

Consider the following situation: Suppose we are living in China, and we are examining this passage in a literal sense, which essentially says, "the kings of the rising of the sun." We would conclude that these "kings" who come from the "sun-rising" would in fact be coming from the western hemisphere. Therefore, a literal interpretation from an eastern point of view would be the opposite of our western viewpoint, throwing the prophecy into confusion. When we make a spiritual application, the confusion is resolved. Celestial beings, when approaching the earth, first appear from the "sun-rising." John used the same Greek word in Revelation 7:2: "And I saw another angel ascending from the east, having the seal of the living God."

In other words, in Revelation 16:12 John was referring to the "kings" of heaven, who will be prepared to ascend from the sun-rising and come to our earth at Jesus' second coming. Furthermore, the "water" that "was dried up" should also be interpreted symbolically. Thus, during the sixth and seventh plague, the worldwide support for Babylon will be "dried up," or taken away. The multitudes will no longer support modern Babylon, just as the literal waters of literal Babylon were dried up, allowing Cyrus the king to conquer the city. Cyrus was a type of Christ, called the Lord's "anointed" in Isaiah 45:1.

We will now return again to chapter 17, where John gives us more information leading up to and including the sixth and seventh plagues. In verse 3 John writes, "So he carried me away in the spirit into the wilderness: and I saw a woman sit upon a scarlet colored beast, full of names of blasphemy, having seven heads and ten horns."

This verse is a parallel of Revelation 13:1, which says, "And I stood upon the sand of the sea, and saw a beast rise up out of the sea, having seven heads and ten horns, and upon his horns ten crowns, and upon his heads the name of blasphemy."

The minor differences reflect the added details that shed more light on the beast, especially after the healing of the deadly wound. In chapter 17 we also notice a harlot woman, representing an apostate church, sitting upon this beast.

Thus, in the near future there will be a union of church and state, wherein papal Rome will be the controlling force of the civil powers of this beast with seven heads.

What is represented by these heads? Simply put, they are the sequential empires beginning with Babylon that interacted with God's people, namely,

1. Babylon
2. Medo-Persia
3. Greece
4. Pagan Rome
5. Papal Rome
6. United States of America
7. United Nations, or a similar entity, which constitutes a one-world government

Furthermore, I believe the seven heads on the "great red dragon" in Revelation 12 represent the same empires that apply to the "beast" of Revelation 13 and 17. This is the most logical interpretation.

There are some riddles in Revelation 17. For example, in verse 8 we read, "The beast that thou sawest was, and is not; and shall ascend out of the bottomless pit, and go into perdition: and they that dwell on the earth shall wonder, whose names were not written in the book of life from the foundation of the world, when they behold the beast that was, and is not, and yet is."

At this juncture, we need to answer two questions:

1. How far ahead in time was John transported when he was carried "away in the spirit" in this vision (Rev. 17:3)?
2. Which of the seven empires was John addressing?

Since the beast is in the "was, and is not, and yet is" tense, John must be witnessing the beast sometime during the healing of the deadly wound. The beast with "horns like a lamb" was to follow papal Rome; therefore, John was transported beyond the fifth head to the time frame of the sixth head, which represents the United States of America. In other words, he was transported to our time. Then, going to verse 10, we read, "And there are seven kings: five are fallen, and one is, and the other is not yet come; and when he cometh, he must continue a short space."

Here again, the five fallen kingdoms are:

1. Babylon
2. Medo-Persia
3. Greece
4. Pagan Rome
5. Papal Rome

Thus, the one that "is" would be the United States of America. "The other is not yet come; and when he cometh; he must continue a short space." This seventh kingdom would be the one world government (or, new world order). Revelation 17:11 presents an enigma, as there are only seven heads. It says, "And the beast that was, and is not, even he is the eighth, and is of the seven, and goeth into perdition."

Therefore, the fifth head, which was wounded and resurrected, is said to be the "eighth," for in actuality, he will rule over the final confederation of kingdoms. In verses 12 and 13 we read, "And the ten horns which thou sawest are ten kings, which have received no kingdom as yet; but receive power as kings one hour with the beast. These have one mind, and shall give their power, and strength unto the beast."

In these verses we note that in the last remnant of time, the one world government will give up their seventh kingdom. In other words, the United Nations will have "one mind" and will give their kingdom to papal Rome. Thus "all the world wondered after the beast," as foretold in Revelation 13:3.

Now, please notice Revelation 17:17: "For God hath put in their hearts to fulfill his will, and to agree, and give their kingdom unto the beast, until the words of God shall be fulfilled."

At this point you may be wondering where the false prophet fits into this scenario? The false prophet is the United States of America, the sixth head, that makes "the image to the beast." It is the U.S. that is instrumental in bringing this end-time confederation of nations together. The U.S. will also be one of the ten kings of this new world order.

Furthermore, the false prophet was included earlier in verse 5, which says, "And upon her forehead was a name written, MYSTERY, BABYLON THE GREAT, THE MOTHER OF HARLOTS AND ABOMINATIONS OF THE EARTH."

The false prophet represents the collective daughter churches who first come into union with the mother church in the United States. This officially takes place when our country passes religious laws, thus setting up the "image" to the beast. This image to the beast is the union of church and state, similar to what existed during the "Dark Ages" when the Papacy ruled the world. Rome claims that Sunday sacredness, in place of the Bible Sabbath, is "her mark of ecclesiastical authority in the world." Therefore, when the U.S. passes a Sunday law, you will know that the "image" has been formed. The rest of the world will follow the example of the U.S.

So, how will all of this end? Revelation 17:14 gives us the comforting assurance: "These [Babylon] shall make war with the Lamb, and the Lamb shall overcome them: for he is Lord of lords, and King of kings: and they that are with him are called, and chosen, and faithful."

Jesus, as King of kings, will again defeat Satan and his coalition. And Jesus gives His church, those who are called, and chosen, and faithful, the privilege of being His ambassadors to warn the world about this false worship system being established in our world today. Revelation 18:1-4 says, "And after these things I saw another angel come down from heaven, having great power; and the earth was lightened with his glory. And he cried mightily with a strong voice, saying, Babylon the great is fallen, is fallen . . . For all nations have drunk of the wine of the wrath of her fornication, and the kings of the earth have committed fornication with her . . . And I heard another voice from heaven, saying, Come out of her, my people, that ye be not partakers of her sins, and ye receive not of her plagues."

As mentioned earlier, Revelation 18 is an enlargement on the fall of Babylon. The first part of the chapter focuses in on God's remnant people who proclaim the three-fold message of Revelation 14, only this time with the added power and enlightenment that is supplied by the "latter rain" of the Holy Spirit. Under this proclamation, the earth is "lightened with his glory." Consequently, this remnant is the object of Satan's wrath (Rev. 12:17).

The latter rain of the Holy Spirit is a biblical teaching that is little understood, or even recognized, by many Christians today. The early rain occurred collectively upon God's apostolic church on the day of Pentecost, but there will be a latter rain that will empower God's people just before Jesus comes to earth. Note these words from Isaiah 60:1-3: "Arise, shine; for thy light is come, and the glory of the LORD is risen upon thee. For, behold, the darkness shall cover the earth, and gross darkness the people: but the LORD shall arise upon thee, and his glory shall be seen upon thee. And the Gentiles shall come to thy light, and kings to the brightness of thy rising."

This is the occasion of which Revelation 18:1 is describing. Hosea 6:3 likens the experience of knowing the Lord, to the falling of the rains for the harvest: "Then shall we know, if we follow on to know the LORD: his going forth is prepared as the morning; and he shall come unto us as the rain, as the latter and former rain unto the earth."

The apostle James tells about the reception of the early and latter rain that results in the fruit of the earth, to be harvested at the "coming of the Lord." James 5:7 says, "Be patient therefore, brethren, unto the coming of the Lord. Behold, the husbandman waiteth for the precious fruit of the earth, and hath long patience for it, until he receive the early and latter rain."

Although the early rain fell on the day of Pentecost, this early experience of the Holy Spirit has been occurring all through the centuries upon individual Christians, even until the final showers of the latter rain. In fact, before any of us can receive the latter rain of the Holy Spirit, we must first be sanctified by the early rain. This process of getting ready for the latter rain is incorporated into the three angels' messages of Revelation 14:6-12, and likewise, the three angels' messages are incorporated into the loud cry message of Revelation 18:1-4.

In the chapter, "The Three Angels' Messages," we discussed the content of Revelation 14:6-12. For review, read verses 6 through 8, "And I saw another angel fly in the midst of heaven, having the everlasting gospel to preach unto them that dwell on the earth, and to every nation, and kindred, and tongue, and people. Saying with a loud voice, Fear God, and give glory to him; for the hour of his judgment is come: and worship him that made heaven, and earth, and the sea, and the fountains of waters. And there followed another angel, saying, Babylon is fallen, is fallen, that great city, because she made all nations drink of the wine of the wrath of her fornication."

An "angel" is a messenger. He represents, in this context, the "remnant" people of God who proclaim the "everlasting gospel" to the last living generation on this earth. Their mission will be to expose the false worship of Babylon and give the second angel's message—a call for God's people to come out of Babylon during the "judgment" in the heavenly sanctuary, prior to the falling of the seven last plagues and Christ's return. Given the extreme importance of these messages, God's remnant will need the power that attends the latter rain of the Holy Spirit, when people will be confronted with this choice to worship God or the false trinity (dragon, beast, false prophet).

Let us continue now with the third angel's message, found in Revelation 14:9-12: "And the third angel followed them, saying with a loud voice, If any man worship the beast and his image, and receive his mark in his forehead, or in his hand, The same shall drink of the wine of the wrath of God, which is poured out without mixture into the cup of his indignation; and he shall be tormented with fire and brimstone in the presence of the holy angels, and in the presence of the Lamb: And the smoke of their torment ascendeth up for ever and ever: and they have no rest day nor night, who worship the beast and his image, and whosoever receiveth the mark of his name. Here is the patience of the saints: here are they that keep the commandments of God, and the faith of Jesus."

The third angel's message has some cryptic words within it, but the bottom line in verse 12 is the fact that only those who "keep the commandments of God, and the faith of Jesus" will be able to stand through the final crisis and rejoice at Jesus' second coming. In the Greek, the "faith of Jesus" can also be translated as "faith in Jesus," which is the essence of the "everlasting gospel." Therefore, the "everlasting gospel" of the first angel's message is the same message as the "faith of Jesus" in the third angel's message. It is the true message of righteousness by faith that will separate the wheat from the tares at the passing of the counterfeit Sabbath, or Sunday law.

Revelation 19 expands upon the fall of Babylon during the battle of Armageddon. In the sanctuary scene of verses 1 through 10, however, we discover that the marriage of Jesus "is come" as "his wife hath made herself ready." The church has embraced the message of righteousness by faith, is keeping all of God's commandments, and has received the seal of God in their foreheads. Then, all of heaven's occupants return with Jesus as "KING OF KINGS, AND LORD OF LORDS" (verse 16).

Revelation 19:19-21 gives us another view of the battle of Armageddon, which begins during the sixth and seventh plagues. There we read, "And I saw the beast, and the kings of the earth, and their armies, gathered together to make war against him that sat on the horse; and against his army. And the beast was taken, and with him the false prophet that wrought miracles before him, with which he deceived them that had received the mark of the beast, and them that worshiped his image. These both were cast alive into a lake of fire burning with brimstone. And the remnant were slain with the sword of him that sat upon the horse."

The "remnant" in verse 21 are the remnant of the wicked, those who are still alive at the end of the seven last plagues. Even though all wicked humans are destroyed at the second coming of Jesus, Satan and his angels will remain alive during this conflagration. Why? The answer is provided in Revelation 20. God needs closure. The only way the justice of God's dealings with sin and rebellion can be disclosed will be through an investigative process that will be conducted during the 1,000 years (Rev. 20:2-4). This is what Paul was writing about in 1 Corinthians 6:2 and 3, when he said, "Do ye not know that the saints shall judge the world? and if the world shall be judged by you, are ye unworthy to judge the smallest matters? Know ye not that we shall judge angels?"

Revelation 20:4 gives the same testimony: "And I saw thrones, and they sat upon them, and judgment was given unto them: and I saw the souls of them that were beheaded for the witness of Jesus, and for the word of God, and which had not worshipped the beast, neither his image, neither had received his mark upon their foreheads, or in their hands; and they lived and reigned with Christ a thousand years."

God's methods and His government will be vindicated. His law will be seen to be "holy, just, and good." All the redeemed will say, "Great and marvellous are thy works, Lord God Almighty; just and true are thy ways, thou King of saints" (Rev. 15:3).

Finally, God will resurrect all of the wicked at the end of the 1,000 years to pronounce judgment against them. Then, whosoever is not found written in the book of life will be destroyed commensurate to their works: "For our God is a consuming fire" (Heb. 12:29). God's presence is "fire" to the wicked and consumes them. They will be reduced to ashes, never to rise again (Mal.

4:1, 3). God's people have Jesus' presence within, and therefore, they are not consumed by the fire.

Revelation 21 and 22 present the seventh and concluding prophecy of the book of Revelation. Herein, we get a word picture of Paradise: "And God shall wipe away all tears from their eyes; and there shall be no more death, neither sorrow, nor crying, neither shall there be any more pain: for the former things are passed away" (Rev. 21:4).

Even in our imagination, we cannot comprehend how wonderful it will be to live eternally with our Savior. In 1 Corinthians 2:9, Paul echoes the words of Isaiah the prophet (Isa. 64:4) as he ponders the future glory: "But as it is written, Eye hath not seen, nor ear heard, neither have entered into the heart of man, the things which God hath prepared for them that love him."

Dear reader, Jesus has revealed to us in Revelation the final events of this world's history. The decision is ours. Who will we worship? Will it be Jesus, who loves us and gave Himself for us? Or will we give worship to the dragon, the beast, and the false prophet, the gods of this world? I believe the final tribulation is imminent, which is one of the reasons I wrote this book. Soon our government will pass religious laws—a National Sunday Law—circumventing the U.S. Constitution for the "benefit" of our nation. Shortly thereafter, everyone will be restricted from worshiping our Creator on the Sabbath day, the fourth commandment of God's law. At that time, every inhabitant on earth will be tested in their loyalty to God. Will you worship God, or will you worship in the manner prescribed by the gods of this world?

Paul says, "Know ye not, that to whom ye yield yourselves servants to obey, his servants ye are to whom ye obey; whether of sin unto death, or of obedience unto righteousness?" (Rom. 6:16).

My hope is that you and I will reject the do-it-yourself religion of Babylon and fully surrender to the will of God, thus being found among the faithful described in Revelation 14:12, which says, "Here is the patience of the saints: here are they that keep the commandments of God, and the faith of Jesus."

Conclusion

In this book, I primarily gave an overview of salvation issues and Bible prophecies. In these closing remarks, I will give a simplified conclusion as presented in Revelation 21 and 22. In the letters to the seven churches (Rev. 1-3), Jesus gave promises to all those who overcome in every age until His second coming. Chapters 21 and 22 give us word pictures of the fulfillment of these promises. However, words alone cannot describe the full extent of our rewards for being a faithful child of God. In Revelation 21:1 we learn that God will create "a new heaven and a new earth."

Then, in verse 2 and 3, we read, "And I John saw the holy city, new Jerusalem, coming down from God out of heaven, prepared as a bride adorned for her husband. And I heard a great voice out of heaven saying, Behold, the tabernacle of God is with men, and he will dwell with them, and they shall be his people, and God himself shall be with them, and be their God."

These words tell me that when God restores paradise on earth, He will make our paradise the center of His universe. Our Father and beloved Savior will have completely reorganized things in a way that we cannot even imagine. Furthermore, in verse 4 we are told that "God shall wipe away all tears from their eyes; and there shall be no more death, neither sorrow, nor crying, neither shall there be any more pain: for the former things are passed away."

Can we imagine any place more wonderful than this? After John's description of the New Jerusalem in verse 22, he says, "And I saw no temple therein: for the Lord God Almighty and the Lamb are the temple of it."

If you consider the dimensions of this city, you get an idea of its huge size. Revelation 21:15 and 16 states that it measures twelve thousand furlongs, which is equal to 1500 miles in circumference. Each side is equal; therefore, the length of each side is 375 miles. The height of the city is also 375 miles. Thus, the New Jerusalem, with our Father and Jesus both dwelling within the city, makes it an ideal sanctuary. This antitypical sanctuary is a perfect cube fashioned like the Most Holy Place of the earthly sanctuary. However, I envision there will be a temple somewhere outside of the New Jerusalem, along with beautiful countryside where we can be property owners, enjoying country homes and gardens.

Chapter 22 continues the word picture of Paradise, and it repeats the information that there will be no night there (verse 5), which is also brought out in Revelation 21:25. However, since our planet is a sphere, there will be night on the opposite side of our world. Isaiah also adds more information that implicates there will be "one new moon to another" within our solar system, when God creates "the new heavens and the new earth." He makes these comments in Isaiah 66:22 and 23.

Dear reader, we have a wonderful inheritance waiting for us. There will be a reunion with our loved ones who have died in the Lord. And there will be happy fellowship with Christians of all ages throughout the endless years of eternity. The most enduring joy will be fellowship with our Savior, who loves us more than we can ever comprehend. May God's grace be with you all until we meet together in heaven.

–Larry Alavezos M.D.

Appendix A

General Principles of Prophetic Interpretation

Preparatory

1. "But the natural man receiveth not the things of the Spirit of god: for they are foolishness unto him: neither can he know them, because they are spiritually discerned" (1 Cor. 2:14
2. Begin with prayer for guidance and understanding.
3. Take into account the Hebrew thought patterns (i.e., remove our western "eyeglasses").
   a. Their thinking was often the reverse kind of thinking than ours (i.e., they thought from the effects back to the causes)
   b. They often wrote in thought parallels (e.g., writing the thought twice, the second time for emphasis).

General Interpreting Principles

1. The Bible is its own (best) expositor.
2. First, focus upon Jesus and His role as the Alpha and Omega, the Word of Scripture.
3. Next, focus upon the "big picture" (i.e., get a general idea what the passage is saying).
4. Then, study each verse within its context (i.e., the preceding and following verses).
5. The passage should be understood according to the plain, obvious, and literal meaning, unless a figure (symbol) is used.

General Principles of Prophetic Interpretation

6. Gather and use all Bible passages on a particular subject before formulating a conclusion.
7. It takes more than one witness (more than one Bible passage) to establish a Bible truth.
   a. See 2 Corinthians 13:1
   b. See Matthew 18:16
   c. See Hebrews 10:28
   d. See Deuteronomy 17:6
   e. See Genesis 41:31, 32
   f. See John 5:31, 32, and 39 – Jesus' testimony also required a second witness = John, and the entire Old Testament.
8. The book of Daniel is the basic foundation for apocalyptic prophecy.
9. Daniel's book has four parallel prophecies.
10. The book of Revelation unfolds Daniel's book.
11. Revelation has seven major prophecies (the seven churches, seven seals, seven trumpets, great controversy, seven last plagues and fall of Babylon, Christ's second coming and Satan bound, and the establishment of New Jerusalem on earth.)
12. The first four major long-range prophecies in Revelation are somewhat parallel. Note: the third prophecy has a delay in time, as each trumpet corresponds to its church and seal. Also, the fourth prophecy contains a flashback to the war in heaven, after which it continues the prophecy.
13. The latter three major prophecies in Revelation progress forward in time (each subsequent prophecy begins later in time).

Advanced Principles of Prophetic Interpretation

Writers/Prophets

Many of the Old Testament writers were prophets, and they included prophecies in their writings. (See 2 Peter 1:19-21.)

Old Testament

The Old Testament Hebrew canon is divided into three sections: 1) the law, 2) the prophets, and 3) the writings.

The law

A Primer on Salvation and Bible Prophecy

The first five books of the Bible (written by Moses, a prophet).

The prophets

- Former Prophets: Joshua, Judges (compiled by Samuel from previous documents), 1 and 2 Samuel, 1 and 2 Kings (compiled by Jeremiah from previous documents)
- Latter Prophets: Isaiah, Jeremiah, Ezekiel, "the twelve"= the "Minor Prophets"

The writings

These include all the other books of the Old Testament, many of which were written by prophets, e.g., Psalms, Job, Daniel, etc.

Literal and Future Prophecies

Most of the Old Testament prophets received information about future, end-time events, but they portrayed these events in the land of Palestine, and they involved literal Israel. Examples: they connected end-time events with the "day of the LORD" or "in that day" or " in those days." (See Revelation 15 and 16, especially Revelation 16:14, and compare 2 Peter 3:8, 10-12.)

- Isaiah 2:2-21 (compare Micah 4:1, 2 and Isaiah 2:19 with Revelation 6:15-17)
- Isaiah 4:1 ("seven women" represent the "harlot" woman and her daughters in Revelation 17)
- Isaiah 10-12 (Assyria prefigures Babylon)
- Jeremiah 4:23-31 (represents the desolation of the earth at Christ's second coming)
- Jeremiah 31:31-34, 32:40, 33:15-17, and 34:5, 6, 11-16 (represents the new/everlasting covenant inherited by the church)
- Jeremiah 50:4, 5, 17-20 (also see Ezekiel 37:15-28; these promises now apply to spiritual Israel, "in those days," is yet future)
- Ezekiel 36-39 (many of these prophecies are in the future)
- Hosea 2:14-23 ("in that day" Jesus says, "And I will betroth thee unto me for ever" [verse 19], which will include the Gentiles [verse 23])

General Principles of Prophetic Interpretation

- Hosea 3:5 ("the children of Israel return . . . in the latter days")
- Joel 2:28-32 ("in those days" the latter rain of the Spirit falls "before the great and the terrible day of the LORD come")
- Joel 3:12-21 ("the valley of Jehoshaphat"/"valley of decision" when judgment occurs during the "day of the LORD." See verse 14, including the margin, which equals "concision, or threshing.")
- Amos 9:11-15 ("In that day . . . And I will bring again the captivity of my people of Israel." This applies to spiritual Israel in the New Earth.)
- Zephaniah 2:1-3 (the "day of the LORD" will include His anger/wrath in the seven last plagues beginning in Revelation 15:1)
- Zechariah 2:11-13 ("in that day" the Lord "shall choose Jerusalem again . . . for he is raised up out of his holy habitation." Again, this applies to spiritual Israel, who will be chosen "again." Zechariah 12, 13, and 14 (especially 12:11 and 14:1). More on the "day of the LORD.")
- Malachi 4:1, 5 (final Old Testament prophecy on the "day of the LORD")

Literal Israel/Spiritual Israel

After the cross, those prophecies that applied to literal Israel in the land of Palestine became reapplied to spiritual Israel in a world-wide reapplication (i.e., God's church becomes worldwide) See the following examples:

- Genesis 49:10 – the "scepter," i.e., Judah receives the birthright, which includes the head of the kingdom, until Jesus came. But His own "received him not" (John 1:11).
- Matthew 21:43 – Jesus' pronouncement against the Jewish nation
- 1 Peter 2:9,10 – Spiritual Israel, including Gentiles, inherit the promises (See Hosea 1:10 and 2:23)
- Galatians 3:7, 28, 29
- Galatians 4:26, 28
- Romans 9:1-8, 25, 26 (See Hosea 1:10)
- Romans 11:20, 23, 25, 26, 30-32

Literal Babylon/Spiritual Babylon

After the cross, literal Babylon is replaced by spiritual Babylon, which is worldwide during the final crisis).

See 1 Peter 5:13. Note: At the time Peter wrote his epistle, literal Babylon was nonexistent. This church was in Rome.

See Revelation 16 through19.

Note: Babylon (Babel) began as a singular pagan city (Gen. 10:10), but later it transformed into spiritual Babylon, after pagan Rome, and, as an instrument of Satan, it gave its "power," "seat," and "great authority" to the first beast (Rev. 13:2).

Also see Alexander Hislop's book *The Two Babylons.*" He clearly documents that Rome was spiritual Babylon.

Finally, modern Babylon becomes a three-fold confederation, when the "false prophet" is added to its makeup. (See Revelation 16:13, 19.) Note that there are numerous instances wherein the Old Testament writers prefigured this three-fold confederation of modern Babylon. See four examples listed below:

1. 2 Chronicles 20:10-24 (Ammon, Moab, Mt. Seir = Edom)
2. Isaiah 10:26 (See Judges 6:33, 34 and 7:25 – Midianites, Amalekites, and the children of the east)
3. Isaiah 11:14 (Edom, Moab, Ammon)
4. Daniel 11:41 (Edom, Moab, Ammon)

"History Repeats Itself"

There are too many examples to list them, i.e., ancient Israel had multiple cycles of apostasy and revival.

Axiom: those who fail to learn lessons from their past history are doomed to repeat that history.

The Law of the First and the Last Mention

The law of the first and last mention is a corollary principle to "history repeats itself."

Note: the "last mention" of any historical episode is connected in some way to the "first mention" when it involves Israel. Since there are many other mentions in between the first and the last mention, we establish the principle that "history repeats itself."

The work of a student of prophecy is to gather all of these mentions in the Bible together before making a conclusion. Question: How can a knowledge of all of these mentions enhance our understanding of Bible prophecy?

Example #1

Armageddon in Revelation 16:16 is the Greek transliteration of the Hebrew "Har" and "Mageddon," which equals Megiddo. (Also see Revelation 16:14.) "Har" equals mountain, and "Megiddo" equals a valley below the Carmel ridge (where Mt. Carmel is located)

The conclusion is that something happened in this valley that is connected with a battle against God's ancient people, Israel. (See Judges 5:19, 20, and compare it to Judges 4:16.)

Since "history repeats itself," this battle in the valley of Megiddo also prefigures the last battle of Armageddon, when God intervenes on behalf of His people.

Other examples where Armageddon is illustrated include:

Judges 6:33 and 7:25 compared with Isaiah 10:26

Joel 3:2, 12 (the valley of Jehoshaphat is the valley of Jezreel, which also includes Megiddo)

Example #2

When we consider the three-fold makeup of modern Babylon, this helps explain and correlates well with the last three heads of the seven headed "scarlet coloured beast" in Revelation 17-19. In other words:

The beast equals the fifth head, which was wounded, but later becomes healed (the Papacy).

The false prophet equals the sixth head, which represents apostate Protestantism (primarily in the U.S.)

The dragon equals the seventh head as represented by the "ten kings" which have one kingdom.

See Revelation 17, especially verses 12 and 13. Note: In Revelation 17 "the eighth and is of the seven" represents the fifth head that was wounded, and becomes resurrected into power again, when the "ten kings" give their kingdom unto the "beast," i.e., unto the Papacy (Rev. 17:12, 13).

Remember: these heads represent sequentially the kingdoms of paganism, since the days of Daniel, who oppressed God's people, i.e., Babylon, Medo-Persia, Greece, and pagan Rome (four pagan kingdoms) followed by the last three heads we have already discussed.

Repetition and Enlargement

This principle is unique to the Hebrew writers. (This is also a technique used by John in Revelation.) Hebrew writers often wrote poetry using parallelisms (obscured in modern Bibles), which equals poetry of thoughts.

Examples:
- Synthetic parallelism – See Psalm 18:3
- Antithetical parallelism – See Psalm 20:7
- Synonymous parallelism – See Psalm 18:5

Note: the book of Daniel is a good example of synonymous parallelism, i.e., there are four parallel prophecies in his book.

Synonymous parallelism demonstrates the principle of repetition and enlargement.

Examples:
- Daniel 2 equals the basic skeleton of prophecy
- Daniel 7 equals the basic skeleton plus added details (repetition and enlargement)
- Daniel 8 equals eliminating the nation of Babylon and addingmore details to the remaining prophetic nations that follow
- (Daniel 9 explains some obscure parts of Daniel 8)
- Dan.11 equals finishing the parallel prophecies
- (Daniel 12 is the epilogue that corresponds to the introduction of Daniel 1)

The conclusion of these parallel prophecies is found in Daniel 11:40-45.

General Principles of Prophetic Interpretation

This portion of the prophecy demonstrates the principle that "history repeats itself," as it tells the story of the healing of the "deadly wound" on the fifth head of the Papacy. Note: Daniel 11:31-39 describes the medieval Papacy.

Daniel 11:40-45 parallels the history of papal Rome portrayed in verses 31-39. Thus, "history repeats itself."

Daniel 9-12 all build upon and refer back to the vision of chapter 8. All of these parallel prophecies end with Rome; thus, Rome establishes the vision. (See Daniel 11:14.)

Therefore, the U.S. is only a small portion of the prophecy in Daniel 11:40-45. It is found in verses 40 and 41, in figurative symbols ("chariots," "horsemen," "ships," and "the glorious land").

We need spiritual eyesight in order to see in these symbols the true interpretation of this prophecy. The "chariots" and "horsemen" represent military strength, and "ships" represent economic strength. The "glorious land" is the U.S. which gives its military and economic strength to the Papacy, in the last remnant of time.

Remember, papal Rome doesn't have an army of its own, but it uses the armies of other nations. The book of Revelation has more information about the U.S. and how it equals the "false prophet" in Revelation 13-19, but it has much more to say about the "beast," which represents papal Rome, otherwise known as the Papacy.

Triple Applications of Prophecy
Example 1 – the three Elijah's

Note that there are three participants in confrontation with each Elijah. Also the first two Elijah's prefigure (i.e., forecast) and typify added information about the third Elijah.

The first Elijah had a confrontation with three enemies, which came to a climax on Mt. Carmel. (Mt. Carmel overlooks Megiddo/Mageddon that lies in the plain of Jezreel.) His 3 enemies were 1) Ahab, 2) Jezebel, and 3) the prophets of Baal. Later, Elijah is translated.

The second (symbolic) Elijah was John the Baptist. John had a confrontation with Herod, Herodias (his brother's wife), and with the assistance of Herodias's daughter (Salome), he was put to death. We have been told by Jesus that a symbolic Elijah was provided to the Jews in the person of John the Baptist, who was a messenger sent to prepare the way of the Lord. (See Matthew 11:9-14, 17:10-12 and Mark 9:11-13.) Therefore, John the Baptist was the second Elijah.

The third Elijah can be discovered by carefully reading Malachi 4:5. This verse tells us that there will be another "Elijah" sent "before the great and dreadful day of the LORD." Since the day of the Lord is a future event connected with His second coming, we have another Elijah predicted who will be the messenger to prepare for our Lord's second coming. Please refer back to 2 Peter 3:8, 10-12.

Who might this person or persons be? Let me suggest that these will be the "remnant" who will proclaim the "loud cry" message of Revelation 18. This message will be a repetition of the three angels' messages of Revelation 14:6-12.

Note: If we go back to the history of the first Elijah, we discover Ahab was an accomplice controlled by Jezebel. Also, the priests did a dance of deception on Mt Carmel.

In the days of Christ, Herod was controlled by Herodias. Salome was the third participant, and she danced a dance of deception. (Salome's name is not mentioned in the Bible, but she was the daughter of Herodias and is disclosed to us by Josephus.)

Finally, the third Elijah will be the remnant Israel of God, i.e., spiritual Israel, who will be opposed by their three-fold enemies, namely:
1. The dragon – the kings of the earth (See Revelation 19:19, 20)
2. The beast – the papacy. (See Revelation 13:1-10)
3. The false prophet – apostate Protestantism primarily in the U.S. (See Revelation 13:14, "And deceiveth them that dwell on the earth." In other words, apostate Protestants will also be involved in deception.)

Remember, end-time Babylon is a three-fold confederation of the dragon, beast, and the false prophet. (See again Revelation 16:13, 19.)

Therefore, as demonstrated in the first and second Elijah's, there were three opponents, so likewise in the last days, there will be three opponents to spiritual Israel.

Furthermore, the first Elijah was translated, and the second Elijah was put

General Principles of Prophetic Interpretation

to death, but the end-time remnant of God have a mixed fate. In other words, some of them will be translated without dying, while others will be put to death, during the "little" time of trouble of the final crisis. (See Revelation 20:4.)

Example 2 – The 3 Woe's (The 5th, 6th, and 7th Trumpet)

Note: All three of these woe's are connected to Islam. The first woe represented the early history of Islam, which began in Arabia and rapidly expanded to engulf Persia, Macedonia, and Northern Africa. The Saracens of Arabia, and later the Turkish Muslims inflicted judgments upon eastern Imperial Rome and western papal Rome. These judgments occurred during the first woe (the fifth trumpet), but the damage was described as only hurting the armies of Rome.

In the second woe (the sixth trumpet), eastern Imperial Rome was conquered and became incorporated into the Turkish Empire. Furthermore, Islam continued to "kill," i.e., inflict judgments upon western papal Rome.

Even today, Muslims recognize these accomplishments were connected to the first and second jihads.

The third woe began when radical Islam attacked our United States of America on September 11, 2001. We must remember that modern Rome has no army of its own. Modern Rome considers the armies of the United Nations and Protestant America as its confederates. Thus, as radical Islam inflict judgments upon the armies of modern Rome, a confederacy will be formed between the fifth, sixth, and seventh heads of modern Babylon, in fulfillment of Revelation 17.

Time Prophecies

These prophecies connect with the scattering and the gathering of God's covenant people, a second time. The time prophecies are without a doubt some of the most difficult prophecies to understand in the Bible. We need spiritual eyesight in order to perceive the reapplication of the promises of God to literal Israel, as they now apply to spiritual Israel.

Furthermore, the promises are conditional, and when the conditions aren't fulfilled by God's covenant people, they suffer the penalties (curses) as outlined by Moses in Deuteronomy 28-32. These "curses" were connected to a time prophecy, which was repeated four times in Leviticus 26.

Since the Old Testament prophets wrote about Jerusalem, Mt. Zion, etc., which extends until the end of time, these promises and penalties must be reapplied after Christ's death to His church. Sad as it may be, we, as God's people have inherited these "curses."

Before introducing the time prophecies, we need to explain a few basic principles:

1. A "time" in Hebrew accounting represented a year, which in their calendar was 360 days. See Dan. 4: 16,23,25,32, and 34.
2. A "time", when used symbolically (as in a time Prophecy), represented a prophetic year. See Num. 14: 34; Eze. 4:6 (margin) Therefore, one "time" of 360 days, equals 360 years of prophetic time.
3. Also see Dan. 9: 24,25 wherein the "seventy weeks" or 490 days (1 ½ years) cannot represent literal days "unto the Messiah the Prince". the 70 weeks time prophecy began in 457 B.C. on the 3rd. decree of Cyrus, Darius, and Artaxerxes. See Ezra 6: 14 with Dan. 9: 24-27. The short period of 490 days cannot possibly account for this extended period of time. Therefore, the "seventy weeks" represents weeks of years.
4. The "time of the end", and the "time appointed", does not mean the end of time, but rather it means the end of a prophecy. See Dan. 8:17, 19 and Dan. 11: 40, with Dan. 12: 9.

Now, we can begin with the most familiar time prophecy in the Bible—the 1260 days.

This prophecy is mentioned seven times, but in three different formats:

1. Revelation 11: 3 – "1260 days"
2. Revelation 12: 6 – "1260 days"
3. Daniel 7:25 – "until a time and times and the dividing of time"
4. Daniel 12:7 – "for a time, times, and a half"
5. Revelation 12:14 – "for a time, and times, and half a time"
6. Revelation 11:2 – "forty and two months" (the Hebrew month was 30 days long, 30 times 42 = 1260 days)
7. Revelation 13:5 – "forty and two months"

This time prophecy applied to the period of time when the apostate "Christian" church oppressed other Christians, and even put millions of them to death as "heretics" for not accepting the doctrines of the Catholic Church.

The time prophecy began in AD 538, when the third horn was "plucked up by the roots." (See Daniel 7:8.) This was accomplished when the third Arian nation (the last of the three horns) was forced out of Rome and the Papacy ruled for 1260 years until 1798 when the pope was taken prisoner.

This prophecy is well recognized and has been accepted by Protestant churches for many centuries. However, this 1260 years only accounts for part of the prophesied penalty that would be inflicted upon the Israel of God for breaking the covenant. (See Isaiah 40:1-10.) And it should become apparent that this prophecy extends to Christ's second coming when His "reward is with him." (See verses 9 and 10.)

Note verse 2, which says, "Speak ye comfortably to Jerusalem, and cry unto her, that her warfare (margin, "time appointed") is accomplished, that her iniquity is pardoned: for she hath received of the LORD's hand double for all her sins."

Thus, the Israel of God, both ancient Israel and modern (spiritual) Israel's warfare, equals the time appointed, which has ended, and her iniquity is pardoned, meaning that it is blotted out during the pre-advent judgment, which began on October 22, 1844.

Note: I will say more about this "appointed time" later. Furthermore, a "double" penalty has been inflicted. This "double" penalty will be explained, shortly.

The Scattering and the Gathering

Now we can consider the time prophecy in Leviticus 26:14-28. In four different verses in this passage, Moses declared the duration of time that the children of Israel would suffer "curses." He said, "seven times . . . for your sins . . . according to your sins" (verses 18, 21, 24, & 28).

In Deuteronomy 31:16-21, God told Moses that the children of Israel would break the covenant. Also see Deuteronomy 28:45-53, which describes the nation of pagan Rome, which was another desolating power that would oppress the children of Israel, many centuries before the desolating power of papal Rome.

A Primer on Salvation and Bible Prophecy

Please note verses 27 and 28, in Deuteronomy 29. We notice that the "curses" are connected to God's "great indignation," and God would "cast them into another land."

Also, when we include Daniel 8:19, we notice the word "indignation" is used, and it is connected to the "time appointed." This verse says, "Behold, I will make thee know what shall be in the last end of the indignation: for at the time appointed the end shall be."(Remember, this "end" is referring to the end of a time prophecy, i.e., the end of the "curses.") Daniel 11:36 refers to this same indignation, and says, "The king . . . shall prosper till the indignation be accomplished: for that that is determined shall be done."

In summary, Israel would break the covenant, and after God's mercy is completely rejected, He finally has "indignation" upon His people and allows pagan nations to execute "curses" on them. In other words, these nations inflict "desolations."

Then, following the pagan "desolations" comes the 1260 years of papal "desolations." See Daniel 9:26, which refers to "desolations" in the plural. Thus, a "double" penalty has been inflicted upon God's people.

Now let's consider the duration of the prophecy of the "curses" pronounced upon Israel. When we multiply 7 times 360 days, we learn that the Israel of God will be under God's curses for 2,520 days, or years of prophetic time.

Therefore, all the "desolations," as referred to above, will be inflicted upon God's people for 2,520 years. There would be 1260 years of pagan "desolations," followed by 1260 years of papal "desolations" (1260 + 1260 = 2520 years).

Since this time prophecy extends many centuries beyond Christ's first advent, and since the Jewish nation rejected our Savior, their inheritance was awarded to spiritual Israel, who also inherited their penalties.

But the question that needs an answer is, When did the 2,520 years begin? The answer can be determined from history and a consideration of Deuteronomy 29:28, when they were "cast . . . into another land."

Recorded history tells us that the northern kingdom of Israel was taken into captivity and removed from their land in 723 BC by Assyria. (A pagan nation.)

When we add 2,520 years to 723 BC, we come to 1798 AD. This date ends

General Principles of Prophetic Interpretation

papal Rome supremacy. (Remember, there is no year zero in this computation.)

Also, if we add only 1260 years to 723 BC, we come to the year AD 538, the beginning of the rule of the Papacy.

Therefore, we have 1260 years of pagan "desolations" followed by 1260 years of papal "desolations" as mentioned above. But, we haven't told the whole story.

History tells us that the southern kingdom of Judah was also taken into partial captivity, just 46 years later, in 677 BC when King Manasseh was removed by Assyria and taken to Babylon. (See 2 Chronicles 33:11, and compare it to 2 Kings 23:26, 27.) This date is established by *Ussher's Chronology*.

If we likewise add 2,520 years to the scattering of the southern kingdom, as we did with the northern kingdom, we arrive at the date of 1844. I don't believe that this is an accident, or a coincidence, because 1844 happens to be the date that marks the end of another time prophecy in Daniel 8:14. In the KJV Bible, Daniel 8:14 says, "And he said unto me, Unto two thousand and three hundred days; then shall the sanctuary be cleansed." But, many perplexed Bible students may wonder, what is the meaning of this cryptic sentence? First, we need to recognize this text contains a time prophecy. Since this is a time prophecy, the 2300 "days" represent 2300 years.

Second, we need to investigate ancient Hebrew history in order to understand their earthly sanctuary services. Furthermore, these symbolic services were patterned after the heavenly sanctuary services. (See Exodus 25:8, 9 and Hebrews 9:23.)

Herein is a simple explanation of these services. In the daily services, the sins of the repentant Hebrews were transferred into the earthly sanctuary by the blood of the sacrificed animals. Then, once a year, on the Day of Atonement, these sins were removed/"cleansed" from the sanctuary. These services symbolized the real services that would be performed in the heavenly sanctuary by Jesus when He ministers as our High Priest after His death.

Now, the question remains, when did this time prophecy begin? In Daniel 8:27, we recall that Daniel "fainted" before he was given an explanation of the vision. At this juncture, we need to understand that there are two Hebrew words that are translated "vision" in the English language. *Mareh* in Hebrew means an apparition, appearance, or a snapshot, which is a specific part of the vision, i.e., the 2300-day time prophecy. Whereas, *hazon*, refers to the entire vision.

In Daniel 8:26, both words for vision are used. "And the vision (*mareh*) of the evening and the morning which was told is true: wherefore shut thou up the vision (*hazon*), for it shall be for many days."

Daniel didn't understand the *mareh*/vision, i.e. the 2300 days, which was only a part of the entire *hazon*/vision. Furthermore, this part of the vision was not explained to Daniel until about twelve years later. The explanation is provided in Daniel 9:23-27. In verse 24 we read, "Seventy weeks are determined" (Hebrew = *hatak* = decreed, or cut off) for the Hebrew nation, and it was cut off from the total time prophecy of 2300 days/years of Daniel 8:14.

Then, in Daniel 9:25, we are given the decree, from which both time prophecies were to begin. Finally, in Ezra 6:14 and Ezra 7, we discover this decree was issued in the seventh year of King Artaxerxes. That year was 457 BC. Adding 2300 years to 457 BC brings us to 1844. Remember, there is no year zero in this computation.

The timing of the beginning and the end of this prophecy is more precise, but I am trying to keep this explanation short and simple. Someone might question the validity of this 2300-day/year time prophecy, as it appears to be only mentioned once in the Bible. But, this is not true. In Daniel 8:16, 17, 26, and 27, with 9:23 and 10:1, it is referred to six more times as the *mareh*/vision that Daniel did not understand until later. (See Daniel 10:1)

Now, let us briefly consider two more time prophecies. They are found in Daniel 12:11 and 12. They are as follows: 1290 days and 1335 days. These two time prophecies are interconnected with the 1260 days/years of papal supremacy. This should become more apparent as we proceed.

Earlier in the study, in symbolic language, we learned that pagan Rome gave its "seat," "power," and "great authority" to papal Rome. (See Revelation 13:2.)

Since the book of Daniel is a complement to Revelation, we would also expect his book to mention this transition. And, so it does, in three different passages. (See Daniel 8:9-14; 11:31; and 12:11.)

Since the 1260-year time prophecy applies to papal Rome, these other two time prophecies (found in Daniel 12:11 and 12) must in some way be

General Principles of Prophetic Interpretation

connected with papal Rome as well. And they do. Both the 1260 and the 1290 time prophecies end in 1798. Therefore, the 1290-year time prophecy must begin 30 years earlier, when the seven nations of Europe became "Christianized" into the papal religion (AD 508). The history concerning the nations of Europe, during this period of time, confirms these facts. This process of "Christianizing" the nations of Europe began when Clovis, king of France, was baptized into the catholic faith. And it ended in AD 508 when the last nation, old Britain/Angle-land, became "Christianized."

This corresponds to the time when paganism, i.e., the "daily" (*tamiyd*, in the Hebrew) was taken away (Dan. 11:31 and 12:11) and Catholicism became the state religion of the nations of Europe.

The 1335-year time prophecy began in AD 508. By adding 1335 years to AD 508, we come to the year 1843. This year falls within the proclamation of the second angel's message of the three angels' messages (Rev. 14:6-12). At this time in history, a blessing (Dan. 12:12) is pronounced upon those who were involved with the proclamation of the first and second angel's messages.

In Revelation 14:13, just after John gives us these three messages, we read about the same blessing that attends those who die within the time frame of these three angels' messages. Note: this verse concludes as follows: "Write, Blessed are the dead which die in the Lord from henceforth: Yea, saith the Spirit, that they may rest from their labours; and their works (i.e.. what they have also written) do follow them."

Thus, those who were active in the proclamation of the three angels' messages during 1840 through 1844 would be accounted "blessed" in some manner. Since 1844, the time of the beginning of the third angel's message, there will be no more time prophecies for God's people.

In closing, Revelation 10:1-11 tells the story of the remnant, whom in verse 11 are told to "prophecy again." All of this will transpire during the sounding of the seventh trumpet. Verses 6 and 7 clearly indicate that there would be no more time prophecies during the time God gathers His people, when "the mystery of God should be finished, as he hath declared to his servants the prophets."

Appendix B

Supplement to Principles of Prophetic Interpretation

Following are select quotes from Ellen G. White regarding prophecy and end-time events:

"The mighty angel who instructed John was no less a personage than Jesus Christ. . . . But the mighty angel demands attention. He cries with a loud voice. . . . This time [given in Revelation 10:6], which the angel declares with a solemn oath, is not the end of this world's history, neither of probationary time, but of prophetic time, which should precede the advent of our Lord. That is, the people will not have another message upon definite time. After this period of time, reaching from 1842 to 1844, there can be no definite tracing of the prophetic time. The longest reckoning reaches to the autumn of 1844" (*The SDA Bible Commentary*, vol. 7, p. 971).

"I plainly stated at the Jackson camp meeting to these fanatical parties that they were doing the work of the adversary of souls; they were in darkness. They claimed to have great light that probation would close in October, 1884.

"I there stated in public that the Lord had been pleased to show me that there would be no definite time in the message given of God since 1844; and that I knew that this message, which four or five were engaged in advocating with great zeal, was heresy. The visions of this poor child were not of God. This light came not from heaven" (*Selected Messages*, book 2, p. 73).

"Jesus has told His disciples to 'watch,' but not for definite time. . . . We are not to know the definite time either for the outpouring of the Holy Spirit of for the coming of Christ" (*Evangelism*, p. 221).

"The world placed all time-proclamation of the same level and called it a delusion, fanaticism and heresy. Ever since 1844 I have borne my testimony that we were now in a period of time in which we are to take heed to ourselves lest our hearts be overcharged with surfeiting and drunkenness, and cares of this life, and so that day come upon us unawares. Our position has been one of waiting and watching, with no time-proclamation to intervene between the close of the prophetic periods in 1844 and the time of our Lord's coming. We do not know the day nor the hour, or when the definite time is, and yet the prophetic reckoning shows us that Christ is at the door" (*Manuscript Releases*, vol. 10, p. 270).

"Should we advance in spiritual knowledge, we would see the truth developing and expanding in lines of which we have little dreamed, but it will never develop in any line that will lead us to imagine that we may know the times and the seasons which the Father hath put in His own power. Again and again have I been warned in regard to time setting. There will never again be a message for the people of God that will be based on time. We are not to know the definite time either for the outpouring of the Holy Spirit or for the coming of Christ" (*Selected Messages*, book 1, p. 188).

"Brother Hewit from Dead River was there. He came with a message to the effect that the destruction of the wicked and the sleep of the dead was an abomination within a shut door that a woman, Jezebel, a prophetess had brought in and he believed that I was that woman Jezebel. We told him of some of his errors in the past, that the 1335 days were ended and numerous errors of his. It had but little effect. His darkness was felt upon the meeting and it dragged" (*Manuscript Releases*, vol. 6, p. 251).

"Let all our brethren and sisters beware of anyone who would set a time for the Lord to fulfill His word in regard to His coming, or in regard to any other promise He has made of special significance. 'It is not for you to know the times or the seasons, which the Father hath put in His own power'" (*Testi-*

monies to Ministers and Gospel Workers, p. 55).

"The Lord has shown me that the message of the third angel must go, and be proclaimed to the scattered children of the Lord, but it must not be hung on time. I saw that some were getting a false excitement, arising from preaching time; but the third angel's message is stronger than time can be. I saw that this message can stand on its own foundation and needs not time to strengthen it; and that it will go in mighty power, and do its work, and will be cut short in righteousness" (*Early Writings*, p. 75).

"The third angel is leading out and purifying a people, and they should move with him unitedly" (*Testimonies to Ministers and Gospel Workers*, p. 488).

"The third angel is leading up a people, step by step, higher and higher. At every step they will be tested" (*Spiritual Gifts*, vol. 2, p. 230).

"Time has not been a test since 1844, and it will never again be a test" (*Early Writings*, p. 75).

"It has been revealed to me that there is among our people a great lack of knowledge in regard to the rise and progress of the third angel's message. There is great need to search the book of Daniel and the book of Revelation, and learn the texts thoroughly, that we may know what is written" (*Selected Messages*, book 2, p. 392).

"The first and second messages were given in 1843 and 1844, and we are now under the proclamation of the third; but all three of the messages are still to be proclaimed. It is just as essential now as ever before that they shall be repeated to those who are seeking for the truth. By pen and voice we are to sound the proclamation, showing their order, and the application of the prophecies that bring us to the third angel's message. There cannot be a third without the first and second. These messages we are to give to the world in publications, in discourses, showing in the line of prophetic history the things that have been and the things that will be.

"The book that was sealed was not the book of Revelation, but that portion of the prophecy of Daniel which related to the last days. . . . By the increase of knowledge a people is to be prepared to stand in the latter days" (*Selected Messages*, book 2, pp. 104, 105).

"September 23, the Lord showed me that He had stretched out His hand the second time to recover the remnant of His people, and that efforts must be redoubled in this gathering time. In the scattering, Israel was smitten and torn, but now in the gathering time God will heal and bind up His people. In the scattering, efforts made to spread the truth had but little effect, accomplished but little or nothing; but in the gathering, when God has set His hand to gather His people, efforts to spread the truth will have their designed effect. All should be united and zealous in the work. I saw that it was wrong for any to refer to the scattering for examples to govern us now in the gathering; for if God should do no more for us now than He did then, Israel would never be gathered" (*Early Writings*, p. 74). (Note: God would not begin the gathering time, until the "curses" were fulfilled, i.e., 1844.)

"Kings and rulers and governors have placed upon themselves the brand of antichrist, and are represented as the dragon who goes to make war with the saints—with those who keep the commandments of God and who have the faith of Jesus" (*Testimonies to Ministers and Gospel Workers*, p. 38).

"As we approach the last crisis, it is of vital moment that harmony and unity exist among the Lord's instrumentalities. The world is filled with storm and war and variance. Yet under one head—the papal power—the people will unite to oppose God in the person of His witnesses" (*Testimonies for the Church*, vol. 7, p. 182).

Appendix C

A Study on Daniel Chapter 8

The purpose of this short essay will be to emphasize the importance of Daniel 8 for God's remnant people today, especially a correct understanding of verses 9-14.

Daniel 8 is the middle of three climactic chapters in his book. It is the third parallel prophecy. (Note: Chapters 2 and 7 are the first and second parallel prophecies, then chapter 8 provides the foundation for understanding the remainder of Daniel's book.)

There are interrelationships in Daniel 7, 8, and 9:

Daniel 7 – Judgment

Daniel 8 – Cleansing of the sanctuary (Note the relationship of judgment to the cleansing of the sanctuary, i.e., they both occur within the same time frame.)

Daniel 9 – Unfinished explanation of Daniel 8 vision, which includes Jesus becoming our supreme Sacrifice

Central Message of Daniel 8: Contrasting False and True Worship Systems

Point 1

Why would God use two sanctuary animals to represent two pagan nations? (A ram and a goat.) Answer: God wanted to direct Daniel and his readers to two contrasting sanctuary worship systems. (A false worship system in bold contrast to God's true worship system, portrayed by the defective ram and he-goat.)

A Study on Daniel Chapter 8

Point 2

What verses in Daniel 8 especially address these two worship systems? Answer: See Daniel 8:9-14. (See example of Hebrew parallelism on Daniel 8:9-12, Appendix D.) This parallelism isn't found in modern Bibles. Consequently, Daniel 8:11 and 13 are incorrectly interpreted by scholars today.

There are a few Hebrew words that are not adequately expressed by the English language in Daniel chapter 8:

Hazon and *mareh* are two different words for "vision"

Miqdash and *godesh* are two different words for "sanctuary"

Ruwm and *sur* are two different words that have different meanings. (*Ruwm* means "to lift up or exalt," and *sur* means to "take away.")

The correct understanding of the meaning of these words impacts the true meaning of the verse in question.

Daniel 8:1, 2 – the word "vision" in these two verses equals *hazon*, i.e., the entire/full vision (This includes the history that transpired during Medo-Persia, Greece, and Rome.)

Daniel 8:4 – the ram is described as "great"

Daniel 8:8 – the goat is described as "very great"

Daniel 8:9 – the "little horn" is described as "exceeding great." Note the escalating greatness in power. This "little horn" represents Rome in both pagan and papal phases. Note on the back page of this treatise in Appendix D, that Daniel's use of masculine and neuter/feminine pronouns to indicate which phase of Rome is being described.

Daniel 8:11 – this verse is incorrectly interpreted by theologians today. The subject of this verse is pagan Rome, not papal Rome. Thus, building a case against the Papacy from this verse is faulty exegesis.

Point 3

Why would Daniel use *miqdash* for "sanctuary" in verse 11, then use *godesh* for "sanctuary" verses 13 and 14? Answer: Because these are two different sanctuaries!

Note that *miqdash* can be used for an unholy or holy sanctuary, depending upon the context of the passage. Whereas, *godesh* always refers to a holy sanctuary. This holy sanctuary can be in heaven or on earth.

In Ezekiel 28:18 the word for sanctuaries in this verse is *miqdash*; therefore, Satan also has sanctuaries on earth. William Miller, with most of our pioneers, taught this "sanctuary" was the Pantheon, located in the city of Rome. When Rome conquered a nation, it brought their "gods" into this pagan sanctuary. Our pioneers recognized that the "place," i.e., Rome, not heaven, was "cast down" (Dan. 8:11) when the emperor Constantine moved the capital of the empire from Rome to Constantinople in AD 330. (Also see Daniel 11:24, a time prophecy.)

Daniel 8:12 unequivocally portrays papal Rome. In the KJV Bible notice that the word "him" is in italics, and therefore, not present in the Hebrew text. Remember, this verse is portraying papal Rome = feminine. Daniel uses the neuter/feminine gender for the subject/object of this verse = it. (This neuter gender is also considered feminine in the Hebrew language. Thus, Daniel is indicating a feminine form of Rome, i.e., a church/papal Rome.)

Daniel uses the same literary technique in Daniel 8:10. Therefore, Daniel oscillates from pagan to papal Rome in verses 9 and 10. Then, he repeats this sequence in verses 11 and 12. This is typical Hebrew parallelism. (Again, see Appendix D.)

Daniel 8:13, as interpreted by Adventism today, is diametrically opposite of what was taught by our pioneers. All the Protestant reformers acknowledged that papal Rome was a desolating power, but there are at least two desolating powers in this verse. (Also see Daniel 9:26.) The other desolating powers are grouped together in the word "daily" or continual. Daniel uses the Hebrew word *tamiyd*, which equals daily or continual, differently here in this prophecy than it is used elsewhere outside of the book of Daniel. Therefore, the "continual" desolating power should be considered "paganism." Paganism includes all the previous religions of the pagan nations, i.e., Babylon, Medo-Persia, Greece, and pagan Rome, all of whom oppressed God's people. (Assyria and even Egypt can also be included.) These pagan nations all had false religious worship systems and were responsible for trampling down "under foot" God's earthly sanctuary and His people.

Point 4

Why would God allow His people to be "trodden under foot" by at least

A Study on Daniel Chapter 8

two desolating powers? Answer: Because Israel had forsaken the covenant they had made with God. (See Daniel 9:1-20, Deuteronomy 28, and Leviticus 26.) Note that Daniel 9:26 mentions "desolations" in the plural.)

Point 5

Is there any evidence in Daniel 8:13 that God isn't exclusively focused upon the papal Roman desolating power? Answer: Yes, the word used for "vision" in Daniel 8:13 is *hazon*, which designates the entire vision, thus including the pagan nations of Medo-Persia, Greece, and pagan Rome.

Point 6

Does "sacrifice" belong to the Hebrew text? Answer: No, read what Ellen G. White wrote in *Early Writings*, page 74, where she addresses this issue in Daniel 8:12. She says, "the word 'sacrifice' was supplied by man's wisdom, and does not belong to the text." The word "sacrifice" was added to the text by the translators in all three of the verses in Daniel 8:11, 12, and 13. Thankfully, the KJV Bible placed the word "sacrifice" in italics. Our modern Bibles, by the use of "dynamic equivalence," have made about 30,000 changes from the authorized KJV. I wonder how many of these words don't belong to the text and are supplied by man's wisdom?

Point 7

Is the reason "sacrifice" doesn't belong to the text because Jesus' ministry includes much more than His sacrifice? Answer: No. As mentioned earlier, the word "daily" in the Hebrew is *tamiyd*. As used by Daniel as a noun in verses 11, 12, and 13, as well as Daniel 11:31 and 12:11, he is describing a "continual" entity/power that opposes and oppresses the true worship of God and His people. This word is used exclusively different here in these verses than elsewhere in the Bible. (Note: Elsewhere, the word *tamiyd* is used as an adverb or an adjective.)

Thus, the supportive verses used by scholars, outside the book of Daniel that connect to the "daily sacrifice," are inappropriate for assigning the "daily" as used by Daniel to any function of the daily ministry of the sanctuary.

In summary, the "daily" is paganism, i.e., pagan religions that are opposed to God's true worship system and not Christ's first apartment ministry in heaven. Paganism is the sum total of all the pagan false worship systems still present in our world today, and it is part of the three-fold makeup of modern Babylon. Paganism has existed at least since the tower of Babel was erected and the people were scattered thereafter when God confused their languages. Paganism preceded the false papal worship system, which introduced mass and other desecrations of true worship.

Daniel was considering all of these false worship systems and not just the papal worship system alone. In Daniel's prayer (Dan. 9:1-20), he is confessing Israel's sin of forsaking the covenant made with God through Moses, and for this reason, they were suffering the "curses" (Deut. 28-32) and "desolations" that were "determined" in Daniel 9:26. Furthermore, in the future from Daniel's time, Israel will continue to be under the curse until the "consummation." (See Daniel 9:27.)

Let's return to Daniel 8:11, and notice the words "taken away" as pertaining to the "daily." It is unfortunate that all Bible versions, including the KJV, translate *ruwm* in this fashion. The true meaning of *ruwm* is to "lift up" or "exalt." Therefore, pagan Rome, as the subject of this verse, exalted paganism. There is no controversy that pagan Rome exalted other pagan nation's religions by placing their gods within the Pantheon to be worshiped by the people.

However, there is a controversy when we consider the question, when did papal Rome ever exalt Christ's "daily" ministry? Of course, many scholars insist the papal worship system exalts a false worship system, thus usurping Christ's true "daily" ministry. But that is not the total substance of these verses. Daniel 8:11 is addressing pagan Rome, and although Daniel 8:12 is addressing papal Rome, look again at Daniel 8:13.

Let's rephrase the question asked in Daniel 8:13 using the prevailing interpretation proposed by those who insist that the "daily" represents the first apartment phase of Jesus' heavenly ministry. "How long [a question of duration, and not a point in time] shall be the vision [vision = *hazon* = the entire vision] concerning the daily sacrifice [exalting the false worship system of the Papacy], and [this word belongs in the text; thus, it is a conjunction connecting two entities] the transgression of desolation [a repetition of the false papal worship system], to give both the sanctuary [*godesh* = a holy sanctuary] and the host to be trodden under foot?"

Herein lies a problem. The papal system wasn't implemented until approximately 1,000 years after the beginning of the vision. The substance of this question asks how long will God's sanctuary (this includes the earthly and the anti-typical heavenly sanctuary) and His people be trodden under foot? Since the answer is 2300 years (Dan. 8:14), how can the papal system alone, which implemented the mass in AD 395, be a legitimate answer that would cover 2300 years? We can't stretch the usurping of Christ's heavenly ministry out to 2300 years!

In conclusion, Daniel 8:16 introduces a second Hebrew word for vision—*mareh*. This word generally indicates an apparition or a specific part (e.g., the time prophecy) of the whole vision. Daniel was "astonished" about the time prophecy, and he didn't fully understand it—2300 years! Daniel had studied Jeremiah's prophecy (Jer. 29:10-14), and he was anticipating Israel's return to Jerusalem as imminent. Therefore, Gabriel came to give him understanding of the *mareh*/vision, as verses 16-27 so indicate. The only time the *hazon*, entire vision, is mentioned again is in Daniel 8:26, which says, "And the vision [*mareh*] of the evening and the morning which was told is true: wherefore shut up the vision [*hazon*]; for it shall be for many days." In verse 27, Daniel "fainted" and "was astonished at the vision [*mareh*]."

Yes, the papal worship system usurps the true first apartment heavenly ministry of Jesus, but we must not use Daniel's prophecies out of context in faulty support of God's true worship system being replaced by the Papacy. In a careful study of Daniel 11:31 and 12:11, it becomes apparent that the "daily"/*tamiyd* cannot be a function of Christ's first apartment ministry. These two verses show the transition from pagan to papal Rome, with the latter prophecy connecting three time prophecies with the Papacy. (See Daniel 12:7-12.)

Appendix D

Daniel 8:9-12 Displays Hebrew Parallelism

Note: A horn can be masculine or feminine depending upon its context.

Verse	Gender	Pronoun/Verb	Horn's Phase
9	Masculine	(he) came (*yatza*)	Pagan
10	Feminine	it became great (*tigdal*)	Papal
11	Masculine	he exalted (*gadal*) from him (*mimmennu*)	Pagan
12	Feminine	it cast down (*shalak*) it worked (*asah*) it prospered (*tsalehach*)	Papal

Appendix E

History Repeats Itself - Supplement

The purpose of this supplement is to show parallels between the events connected with the beginning of Adventism (specifically between August 11, 1840, to October 22, 1844) and the triumph of God's end-time remnant during the "loud cry" of the third angel's message. (The "loud cry" is in Revelation 18:2.) There are at least six examples that demonstrate these parallels.

The angel of Revelation 18:2 and 3 repeats the second angel's message of Revelation 14:8.

The same angel (Rev. 18:2) who gives the "loud cry" parallels the "midnight cry" in the parable of the ten virgins (Matt. 25:6), which occurred in 1844. This "midnight cry" also gave power to the proclamation of the second angel's message.

The parable of the ten virgins (Matt. 25:1-13) was fulfilled in the history of Adventism during 1842 to 1844 and will be fulfilled again for Adventism in the parallel history of the "loud cry" of the angels of Revelation 18.

Jesus cleansed the Jewish temple at the beginning and near the close of His earthly ministry. These two cleansings prefigure (forecasts/foreshadows) the purification of Adventism at the beginning and near the close of Jesus' heavenly ministry.

Revelation 10 tells the story of Adventism. Our history begins between the end of the sixth and the beginning of the seventh trumpet (August 11, 1840, to October 22, 1844). This chapter describes our "bitter" disappointment. But, in verse 11 John, who symbolically represents the Adventist movement, is told to "prophesy again."

The "seven thunders," which were sealed at the beginning of Adventism (Rev. 10:4), become unsealed before the close of probation (Rev. 22:10, 11).

Now, let's include support from Ellen G. White on some of these parallels. Many Bible students have already recognized that the second angel's message (Rev. 14:8) is repeated by the angel of Revelation 18:2. In *Early Writings*, page 277, we read, "The message of the fall of Babylon, as given by the second angel, is repeated, with the additional mention of the corruptions which have been entering the churches since 1844. The work of this angel [the angel of Revelation 18] comes in at the right time to join in the last great work of the third angel's message [Revelation 14:9-12] as it swells to a loud cry. . . . This message [Revelation 18] seemed to be an addition to the third message, joining it as the midnight cry joined the second angel's message in 1844."

In this passage, Ellen White clearly states that the second angel's message "is repeated." Thus, history repeats itself. In summary:

First, the angel of Revelation 18 repeats the second angel's message, as already pointed out.

Second, the "loud cry" joins the third angel's message, in a similar manner as the "midnight cry" joined the second angel's message.

In these two examples alone, we have demonstrated that the history of the second angel's message, with the addition of the "midnight cry," is similar to, and I might also add, pre-figures the history that will transpire during the time when the "loud cry" of the angel of Revelation 18 repeats the second angel's message. Thus, history repeats itself.

Third, we need to examine the parable of the ten virgins. In the *Review and Herald*, August 19, 1890, Ellen White wrote, "When the third angel's message is preached as it should be, power attends its proclamation, and it becomes an abiding influence. It must be attended with divine power, or it will accomplished nothing. I am often referred to the parable of the ten virgins, five of whom were wise, and five foolish. This parable has been and will be fulfilled to the very letter, for it has a special application to this time, and, like the third angels message, has been fulfilled and will continue to be present truth till the close of time."

In *The Great Controversy*, page 393, she wrote, "The parable of the ten virgins of Matthew 25 also illustrates the experience of the Adventist people."

Thus, this parable teaches us that the beginning of Adventism illustrates the end of Adventism.

Fourth, Christ's cleansing of the earthly temple in Jerusalem, at the beginning and the close of His earthly ministry, prefigures a similar cleansing/purification of His people at the beginning and the end of the three angel's messages. The Spirit of Prophecy connects the two times that Christ cleansed the temple, in several different passages, to the second angel's message. "God's love for his church is infinite. His care over his heritage is unceasing. He suffers no affliction to come upon the church but such as is essential for her purification, her present and eternal good. He will purify His church even as He purified the temple at the beginning and close of His ministry on earth" (*Testimonies for the Church*, vol. 9, p. 228).

Question: Does this passage actually mean there will be two cleansings of His people? Let's look at another Spirit of Prophecy quote, from *Selected Messages*, book 2, page 118: "When Jesus began His public ministry, He cleansed the Temple from its sacrilegious profanation. Among the last acts of His ministry was the second cleansing of the Temple. So in the last work for the warning of the world, two distinct calls are made to the churches. The second angel's message is, 'Babylon is fallen, is fallen, that great city, because she made all nations drink of the wine of the wrath of her fornication' (Revelation 14:8). And in the loud cry of the third angel's message a voice is heard from heaven saying, 'Come out of her, my people, that ye be not partakers of her sins, and that ye receive not of her plagues. For her sins have reached unto heaven, and God hath remembered her iniquities' (Revelation 18:4, 5)."

Answer: Yes, there has already been one cleansing of the remnant, Israel of God, in 1844 when the Millerite movement went from fifty thousand to about fifty overnight. Furthermore, there will be another cleansing of His church near the close of our history in order to have a sanctified ministry prepared to finish His work.

Fifth, Revelation 10 portrays events occurring between the sixth and seventh trumpets (this must also include Revelation 11:1-13), and particularly begins on August 11, 1840, when the Ottoman Empire fell from power as predicted in the time prophecy of Revelation 9:15. Revelation 10 describes, in symbolic language, a "sweet" but later becoming a "bitter" experience for

John, who is representing God's end-time remnant. John portrays a group of people who have a "sweet" experience in expectation of Christ's return for them during the 1840 to 1844 period of time. But they experienced a "bitter" disappointment when Jesus didn't appear as they had expected on October 22, 1844. Ellen White informs us that the Angel who came down in Revelation 10 was Christ, and this Angel parallels the other Angel in Revelation 18, who was also Christ. In Revelation 10:11, we read, "Thou must prophesy again." So, history repeats itself.

Sixth, the seven thunders give us the strongest evidence that the history of 1840-1844 will be repeated. Revelation 10:4 says, "And when the seven thunders had uttered their voices, I was about to write: and I heard a voice from heaven saying unto me, Seal up those things which the seven thunders uttered, and write them not."

The Spirit of Prophecy gives us more insight into the content of what the seven thunders had spoken. Ellen White wrote, "The special light given to John which was expressed in the seven thunders was a delineation of events which would transpire under the first and second angels' messages. It was not best for the people to know these things, for their faith must necessarily be tested. In the order of God most wonderful and advanced truths would be proclaimed. The first and second angels' messages were to be proclaimed, but no further light was to be revealed before these messages had done their specific work. This is represented by the angel standing with one foot on the sea, proclaiming with a most solemn oath that time should be no longer" (*The SDA Bible Commentary,* vol. 7, p. 971).

Then, in another passage, Ellen White makes what some would mistake for a contradictory proclamation: "After these seven thunders uttered their voices, the injunction comes to John as to Daniel in regard to the little book: 'Seal up those things which the seven thunders uttered.' These relate to future events which will be disclosed in their order. Daniel shall stand in his lot at the end of the days. John sees the little book unsealed. Then Daniel's prophecies have their proper place in the first, second, and third angels' messages to be given to the world" (Ibid.).

In a brief summary of these two passages, we have the following:

The seven thunders were events that transpired during the first and second angel's messages. In other words, between the years 1840 to October 22, 1844.

The seven thunders will be future events, "which will be disclosed in their order."

What can be the most logical conclusion? I believe the future events will parallel, in some manner, those events that occurred between 1840 and October 22, 1844. Thus, history repeats itself. Furthermore, I believe John states the same conclusion when in Revelation 22:10 he said, "And he said unto me, Seal not the sayings of the prophecy of this book: for the time is at hand."

Question: What time is at hand? The answer is provided in the next verse, which proclaims the close of probation. "He that is unjust, let him be unjust still: and he which is filthy, let him be filthy still: and he that is righteous, let him be righteous still: and he that is holy, let him be holy still."

Therefore, those future events (paralleling the first and second angel's messages) will be unsealed to God's remnant before probation closes.

Appendix F

Sequel to Modern Bible Versions

After completion of my book A Primer on Salvation and Bible Prophecy, my brother brought to my attention that the chapter on modern Bible versions needed supportive evidence on the remarks made concerning Drs. Brooke Foss Wescott and Fenton John Anthony Hort. Therefore, I wrote this chapter to present the evidence by using printed comments gleaned from letters written by these two men. Both of these bishops had children who collected their letters and compiled them into biographies. Bishop Wescott's son wrote his biography Life and Letters of Brooke Foss Wescott. And Bishop Hort's son wrote Life and Letters of Fenton John Anthony Hort. Before quoting their printed words, I want to quote from Dr. William P. Grady's book Final Authority:

"Having carefully read both the Life and Letters of Brooke Foss Wescott by his son Arthur Wescott (1903) and the Life and Letters of Fenton John Anthony Hort by his son Arthur Fenton Hort (1896), this author is firmly convinced that the celebrated Cambridge professors were anything but what they professed to be. It is the central premise of this chapter that Drs. Wescott and Hort were a pair of unsaved liberals whose open Vatican sympathies cast them as the consummate Jesuit plants!" (p. 214).

Now, let's read some of these esteemed Cambridge University professors' comments. Dr. Hort wrote the following to Reverend John Ellerton: "Possibly you have not heard that I have become Harold Browne's Examining Chaplain. I have only seen him two or three times in my life, not at all intimately, and was amazed when he made the proposal, in the kindest terms. I wrote to warn him that I was not safe or traditional in my theology, and that I could not give up association with heretics and such like."

This remark might not raise any red flags, but there is more. In another letter to Reverend John Ellerton, Dr. Hort wrote, "We maintain 'Baptismal Regeneration' as the most important of doctrines . . . almost all Angelican statements are a mixture in various proportions of the true and the Romish view; 2nd, the pure Romish view seems to me nearer, and more likely to lead to, the truth than the Evangelical."

Dr. Hort continues with this bold remark in Life and Letters of Fenton John Anthony Hort: "I am very far from pretending to understand completely the ever renewed vitality of Mariolatry . . . I have been persuaded for many years that Mary-worship and 'Jesus'-worship have very much in common in their causes and their results."

Dr. Hort assured his eldest son Arthur that infant baptism was his salvation in another letter. I quote: "You were not only born into the world of men. You were also born of Christian parents in a Christian land. While yet an infant you were claimed for God by being made in Baptism an unconscious member of His Church."

These four letters clearly reveal that Dr. Hort's theological beliefs and sympathies were with Rome. But what about Dr. Westcott? Dr. Wescott wrote the following in his diary entry for May 8, 1846: "See Maurice's new lectures, with a preface on Development written apparently with marvelous candour and fairness, and free from all controversial bitterness. He makes a remark which I have often written and said, that the danger of our Church is from atheism, not Romanism."

Once, Dr. Wescott accidentally stumbled upon a shrine to the Virgin Mary after strolling through a Carmelite Monastery at Grace Dieu. He wrote, "After leaving the monastery we shaped our course to a little oratory (private chapel) which we discovered on the summit of a neighbouring hill, and, and by a little scrambling we reached it. Fortunately we found the door open. It is very small, with one kneeling-place; and behind a screen was a 'Pieta' the size of life [i.e., a Virgin and dead Christ] . . . Had I been alone I could have knelt there for hours."

I believe these few comments firmly establish that these two Cambridge professors, who were the leaders in the revision of the Bible, had Roman Catholic sentiments. But there are many more unbiblical remarks made by Drs. Westcott and Hort.

Dr. Hort wrote a letter to Reverend Rowland Williams dated October 21, 1858, which said, "Further, I agree with them [authors of Essays and Reviews] in condemning many leading specific doctrines of the popular theology . . . Evangelicals seem to me perverted rather than untrue. There are, I fear, still more serious differences between us on the subject of authority, and especially the authority of the Bible."

Can we trust this leading reviser of the authorized King James Version of the Bible? Dr. Hort didn't even believe in creation! He makes this comment recorded in Life and Letters of Fenton John Anthony Hort: "I am inclined to think that no such state as 'Eden' (I mean the popular notion) ever existed, and that Adam's fall in no degree differed from the fall of each of his descendants, as Coleridge justly argues."

Therefore, he believed in evolution. Both of these Cambridge professors believed in evolution. In the biography compiled by his son, Dr. Wescott wrote, "No one now, I suppose, holds that the first three chapters of Genesis, for example, gives a literal history—I could never understand how anyone reading them with open eyes could think they did—yet they disclose to us a Gospel."

When a student wrote to Dr. Hort for clarification on Article IX of the Church's Thirty-nine Articles, he received the following reply: "The authors of the Article doubtless assumed the strictly historical character of the account of the Fall in Genesis. This assumption is now, in my belief, no longer reasonable."

Dr. Hort wrote another supportive comment on evolution, which is found in his biography: "But the book that has engaged me most is Darwin. Whatever may be thought of it, it is a book that one is proud to be contemporary with . . . My feeling is strong that the theory is unanswerable."

I will conclude this chapter by quoting Dr. Hort: "I had no idea till the last few weeks of the importance of text, having read so little Greek Testament, and dragged on with the villainous Textus Receptus . . . Think of the vile Textus Receptus leaning entirely on late MSS; it is a blessing there are such early ones."

Given these comments made by the two leading revisers of the authorized King James Version, it is appalling that Christians don't recognize the subtle Roman Catholic doctrines and other unbiblical changes that have been introduced into our modern Bibles.

Selected Bibliography

Anderson, John T. *Investigating the Judgment.* Hagerstown, MD: Review and Herald Publishing Association, 2003.

Andrews, J.N. *History of the Sabbath.* Hagerstown, MD: Review and Herald Publishing Association.

Beale, David. *A Pictorial History of Our English Bible.* Greenville, SC: Bob Jones University Press, 1982.

Bacchiocchi, Samuele. *Divine Rest for Human Restlessness.* Rome: The Pontificial Gregorian University Press.

———. *From Sabbath to Sunday.* Berrien Springs, MI: Biblical Perspectives.

———. *The Advent Hope for Human Hopelessness.* Berrien Springs, MI: Biblical Perspectives.

———. *The Sabbath in the New Testament, Answers to Questions.* Berrien Springs, MI: Biblical Perspectives.

———. *The Sabbath Under Crossfire.* Berrien Springs, MI: Biblical Perspectives.

Burgon, John W. *Unholy Hands on the Bible.* Vols. 1 and 2. Edited by Jay P. Green Sr. Lafayette, IN: Sovereign Grace Publishers, 1990 and 1992.

———. *Causes of Corruption of the New Testament Text.* Lafayette, IN: Sovereign Grace Publishers, 1998.

Brownlee, W.C. *History of the Western Apostolic Churches.* Brushton, NY: TEACH Services, Inc.

Burnside, George. *The New International Version or the King James Version.* Payson, AZ: Leaves of Autumn Books, Inc.

Carter, Cecil J. *The Oldest and Best Manuscripts--How Good Are They?*

Selected Bibliography

Collingswood, NJ: The Bible for Today Press.

Cloud, David W. *Myths About the Modern Bible Versions*. Port Huron, MI: Way of Life Literature.

———. *Rome and the Bible*. Port Huron, MI: Way of Life Literature.

Daniels, David W. *Answers to Your Bible Version Questions*. Ontario, Canada: Chick Publications, 2003.

Damsteegt, P. Gerard. *Foundations of the Seventh-day Adventist Message and Mission*. Berrien Springs, MI: Andrews University Press.

Dickie, Stephen. *Islam God's Forgotten Blessing*. Kasson, MN: Strawberry Meadow Association.

Douglass, Herbert E., *Should We Ever Say, "I Am Saved?"* Nampa, ID: Pacific Press Publishing Association.

Down, Kendall K. *Daniel Hostage in Babylon*. Alma Park, Grantham, Lincolnshire: Stanborough Press Limited, 1991.

Emmerson, W.L. *The Reformation and the Advent Movement*. Ukiah, CA: Orion Publishing.

Fitch, Charles. *Sin Shall Not Have Dominion Over You (Guide to Christian Perfection)*. Brushton, NY: TEACH Services, Inc.

Froom, Leroy E. *Coming of the Comforter*. Hagerstown, MD: Review and Herald Publishing Association.

———. *Prophetic Faith of Our Fathers*. Vols. 3 and 4. Hagerstown, MD: Review and Herald Publishing Association.

Fuller, David Otis. *Which Bible?* Grand Rapids, MI: Grand Rapids International Publications, 1986.

Gane, E. Roy. *Altar Call*. Berrien Springs, MI: Diadem.

———. *Enlightened by the Spirit*. Nampa, ID: Pacific Press Publishing Association.

———. *You Ask, God Answers: Vital Questions on Salvation*. Wildersville, TN: Orion Publishing.

Garrett, Les. *Which Bible Can We Trust?* Gold Coast Mailing, Centre, Queensland: Christian Center Press, 1998.

Gibson, Ty Forrest. *The Path of the Just*. Malo, WA: Light Bearers Publishing Ministry.

Gipp, Samuel C., Th.D. *The Answer Book*. Northfield, OH: DayStar Publishing, 2003.

———. Gipp's Understandable History of the Bible. Northfield, OH: DayStar Publishing.

Goldstein, Clifford. *By His Stripes*. Nampa, ID: Pacific Press Publishing Association.

———. *One Nation Under God?: Bible Prophecy-When the American Experiment Fails*. Nampa, ID: Pacific Press Publishing Association.

———. *The Saving of America*. Nampa, ID: Pacific Press Publishing Association.

Grady, Dr. William P. *Final Authority: A Christian's Guide to the King James Bible*. Knoxville, TN: Grady Publications, Inc.

Gugliotto, Lee J., *Handbook for Bible Study*. Hagerstown, MD: Review and Herald Publishing Association.

Hardinge, Leslie, Ph.D. *His Name is Wonderful*. Brushton, NY: TEACH Services, Inc.

———. *Jesus is My Judge*. Harrisburg, PA: American Cassette Ministries, Book Division.

———. *The Lamb–God's Greatest Gift*. Harrisburg, PA: American Cassette Ministries, Book Division.

Hasel, Gerhard F. and Michael G. *The Promise–God's Everlasting Covenant*. Nampa, ID: Pacific Press Publishing Association.

Hayden, Keavin with David Merrill. *Saving Blood*. Edited by B. Russell Holt. Nampa: ID. Pacific Press Publishing Association.

Heschel, Abraham Joshua. *The Sabbath*. New York: NY. Farrar Straus Giroux, 2005.

Hislop, Alexander. *The Two Babylons*. Neptune, NJ: Loizeaux Brothers, Inc.

Holbrook, Frank B. *The Atoning Priesthood of Jesus Christ*. Berrien Springs, MI: Adventist Theological Society Publications.

Holbrook, Frank B. Editor and William H. Shea, M.D., Ph.D. *Daniel and Revelation Comm. Series*. Vols. 1-7. Hagerstown, MD: Review and Herald Publishing Association.

Hoskier, H. C. *Codex B and Its Allies-A Study and an Indictment*. Vols. I and II. Eugene, OR: Wipf and Stock Publishers.

Selected Bibliography

Jackson, Gregory L. *Surrender the Secret to Perfect Peace and Happiness.* Hagerstown, MD: Review and Herald Publishing Association.

Jones, Alonzo T. *The Empires of the Bible.* Washington, DC: Review and Herald Publishing Association.

Jones, Floyd Nolen, Th.D., Ph.D. *Chronology of the Old Testament.* 14th edition. Woodlands, TX: Kings Word Press.

———. *Which Version is the Bible?* Woodlands, TX: Kings Word Press.

Kang, David. *Behold the Lamb.* Rapidan, VA: Hartland Publications.

Knight, George R. *1844 and the Rise of Sabbatarian Adventism.* Hagerstown, MD: Review and Herald Publishing Association.

———. *A User Friendly Guide to the 1888 Message.* Hagerstown, MD: Review and Herald Publishing Association.

———. *A Brief History of Seventh-Day Adventists.* 2nd edition. Hagerstown, MD: Review and Herald Publishing Association.

———. *Exploring Hebrews.* Hagerstown, MD: Review and Herald Publishing Association.

———. *I Used To Be Perfect.* Boise, ID: Pacific Press Publishing Association.

———. *Millennial Fever.* Boise, ID: Pacific Press Publishing Association.

———. *The Pharisee's Guide To Perfect Holiness.* Boise, ID: Pacific Press Publishing Association.

Koranteng-Pipim, Samuel. *Receiving the Word.* Berrien Springs, MI: Berean Books.

Kubo, Sakae and Walter F. Specht. *So Many Versions?* Grand Rapids, MI: Zondervan Publishing House.

Larondelle, Hans. *How to Understand the End-time Prophecies of the Bible.* Sarasota, FL: First Impressions.

Maxwell, Mervyn C., Ph.D. *God Cares.* Vols. I and II. Boise, ID: Pacific Press Publishing Association.

———. *Magnificent Disappointment.* Boise, ID: Pacific Press Publishing Association.

Maynard, Michael, M.L.S. *A History of the Debate over I John 5:7, 8.* Tempe, AZ: Comma Publications.

Moore, A. Leroy. *The Theology Crisis-A Study in Righteousness by Faith.* Amarillo, TX: Life Seminars, Inc., 1980.

Moorman, Dr. Jack. *Early Manuscripts and the Authorized Version*. Ararat, VA: A.Y. Publications Corporation.

———. *Forever Settled*. Collingswood, NJ: The Dean Burgon Society Press, 1999.

———. *When the KJV Departs From the "So-Called" Majority Text*. Ararat, VA: A.Y. Publications Corporation.

Moskala, Jiri. *The Laws of Clean and Unclean Animals in Leviticus 11*. Berrien Springs, MI:
Adventist Theological Society Publications

Nadan, Roy C. *The Lamb Among the Beasts*. Hagerstown, MD: Review and Herald Publishing Association, 1996.

Odom, Robert L. *Sabbath and Sunday in Early Christianity*. Washington, DC: Review and Herald Publishing Association.

Ott, Helmut. *Perfect in Christ*. Hagerstown, MD: Review and Herald Publishing Association.

Owusu-Antwi, Brempong. *The Chronology of Daniel 9:24-27*. Berrien Springs, MI: Adventist Theological Society Publications.

Paulien, Jon. *Decoding Revelation's Trumpets*. Berrien Springs, MI: Andrews University Press.

Peters, John. *The Mystery of the Daily*. Berrien Springs, MI: Andrews University Press.

Pickering, Wilbur, Ph.D. *The Identity of the New Testament Text*. Nashville, TN: Thomas Nelson Publishers, 1980.

Reagan, Dr. David F. *The King James Version of 1611, the Myth of the Early Revisions*. Beebe Publications, 1995.

Riplinger, Dr. Gail A. *New Age Bible Versions*. Ararat, VA: A.Y. Publications Corporation, 2000.

———. *The History of the Bible-Erasmus and the Received Text*. Ararat, VA: A.Y. Publications Corporation.

——— with N.W. Hutchings. *Which Bible is God's Word?* Oklahoma City, OK: Hearthstone Publishing, Ltd.

Ruckman, Peter S., Ph.D. *The Christian's Handbook of Biblical Scholarship*. Pensacola, FL: Bible Baptist Bookstore.

Selected Bibliography

———. *The "Errors" in the King James Bible*. Pensacola, FL: Bible Baptist Bookstore.

Shuler, John L. *Your Best Helper the Holy Spirit*. Mountain View, CA: Pacific Press Publishing Association.

Smith, Uriah. *Daniel and the Revelation*. Washington, DC: Review and Herald Publishing Association.

Strand, Kenneth A., Ph.D., editor. *The Sabbath in Scripture and History*. Washington, DC: Review and Herald Publishing Association.

Waggoner, Ellet J. *The Everlasting Covenant: God's Promises to Us*. Berrien Springs, MI: Glad Tidings Publishers.

Waite, D.A., Th.D., Ph. D. *Defending the King James Bible*. Collingswood, NJ: The Bible for Today Press, 2002.

Waite, D.A., Jr., M.A., M.L.A. *The "Doctored" New Testament*. Collingswood, NJ: The Bible for Today Press.

Walker, Allen. *The Law and the Sabbath*. Rapidan, VA: Hartland Publications.

Wallenkampt, Arnold V. and Richard W. Lesher, editors. *The Sanctuary and the Atonement*. Washington, DC: Review and Herald Publishing Association.

Were, Louis F. *The Battle for the Kingship of the World*. Berrien Springs, MI: First Impressions.

———. *The Certainty of the Third Angel's Message*. Berrien Springs, MI: First Impressions.

———. *The King of the North at Jerusalem*. Berrien Springs, MI: First Impressions.

———. *The Kings that Come from the Sunrising*. Berrien Springs, MI: First Impressions.

———. *The Moral Purpose of Prophecy*. Berrien Springs, MI: First Impressions.

———. *The Woman and the Beast in the Book of Revelation*. Berrien Springs, MI: First Impressions, 1980.

———. *144,000 Sealed When? Why?* Maries, ID: LMN Publishing International, Inc.

White, Ellen G. *Early Writings*. Hagerstown, MD: Review and Herald Publishing Association.

———. *Faith and Works*. Hagerstown, MD: Review and Herald Publishing Association.

———. *Ministry of Healing*. Hagerstown, MD: Review and Herald Publishing Association.

———. *Patriarchs and Prophets*. . Nampa, ID: Pacific Press Publishing Association.

———. *Steps to Christ*. Hagerstown, MD: Review and Herald Publishing Association.

———. *Testimonies for the Church*. Vols. 1-9. Nampa, ID: Pacific Press Publishing Association.

———. *The Acts of the Apostles*. Nampa, ID: Pacific Press Publishing Association.

———. *The Desire of Ages*. Nampa, ID: Pacific Press Publishing Association.

———. *The Great Controversy*. Nampa, ID: Pacific Press Publishing Association.

———. *Thoughts from the Mount of Blessing*. Nampa, ID: Pacific Press Publishing Association.

Wilkinson, Benjamin G., Ph. D. *Our Authorized Bible: Answers to Objections*. Payson, AZ: Leaves of Autumn, Inc.

———. *Our Authorized Bible Vindicated*. Payson, AZ: Leaves of Autumn, Inc.

———. *Truth Triumphant: The Church in the Wilderness*. Payson, AZ: Leaves of Autumn, Inc.

Williams, Bradley R. *The Silencing of Satan*. Banning, CA.

Williams, Garrie F. *Give the Holy Spirit a Chance*. Hagerstown, MD: Review and Herald Publishing Association.

———. *How to be Filled with the Holy Spirit and Know It*. Hagerstown, MD: Review and Herald Publishing Association.

Wohlberg, Steve. *End Time Delusions*. Shippensburg, PA: Destiny Image Publishing.

———. *The Anti-Christ Chronicles*. Fort Worth, TX: Texas Media Center.

———. *Truth Left Behind*. Nampa, ID: Pacific Press Publishing Association.

Reference Materials

An Exhaustive Ellen G. White Commentary on Daniel and Revelation. Harrah, OK: Academy Enterprises, Inc.

Baker, Warren, D.R.E., and Eugene Carpenter, Ph.D. *The Complete Word Study Dictionary Old Testament.* Chattanooga, TN: AMG (Advancing the Ministries of the Gospel) Publishers.

Carpenter, Eugene, Ph.D., and Phillip w. Comfort. *Holman Treasury of Key Bible Words.* Nashville, TN: Broadman and Holman Publishers.

Green, Jay P., Sr., editor. *The Interlinear Bible Hebrew-Greek-English.* Peabody, MA: Hendrickson Publishers.

Handbook of Seventh-day Adventist Theology Commentary Reference Series. Vol. 12. Hagerstown, MD: Review and Herald Publishing Association.

Nichol, Francis D., editor. *Seventh-day Adventist Bible Commentary.* Hagerstown, MD: Review and Herald Publishing Association.

Perschbacher, Wesley J. *The New Analytical Greek Lexicon.* Peabody, MA: Hendrickson Publishers.

Strong, James, L.L.D., S.T.D. *The New Strong's Expanded Exhaustive Concordance of the Bible.* Nashville, TN: Thomas Nelson Publishers.

Wigram, George V. *The Englishman's Hebrew Concordance of the Old Testament.* Peabody, MA: Hendrickson Publishers.

We invite you to view the complete
selection of titles we publish at:
www.TEACHServices.com

We encourage you to write us
with your thoughts about this,
or any other book we publish at:
info@TEACHServices.com

TEACH Services' titles may be purchased in
bulk quantities for educational, fund-raising,
business, or promotional use.
bulksales@TEACHServices.com

Finally, if you are interested in seeing
your own book in print, please contact us at:
publishing@TEACHServices.com
We are happy to review your manuscript at no charge.

www.ingramcontent.com/pod-product-compliance
Lightning Source LLC
Chambersburg PA
CBHW070548160426
43199CB00014B/2413